HEARTS & MINDS II

AN ORIGINAL LOOK AT JEWISH FESTIVALS & SIGNIFICANT JEWISH DATES

אוצרות

RABBI PINI DUNNER

HEARTS & MINDS II

AN ORIGINAL LOOK
AT JEWISH FESTIVALS
& SIGNIFICANT JEWISH DATES

DEDICATED IN HONOR OF

JOSEPH "JOSL" ACKERMAN

ר' יוסף בן מרדכי מרקל נ"י עמו"ש

אוצרות

Beverly Hills, California

HEARTS & MINDS II

AN ORIGINAL LOOK
AT JEWISH FESTIVALS
& SIGNIFICANT JEWISH DATES

First Edition, 2023

Otzrot Books
Beverly Hills, California

9461 Charleville Blvd # 731
Beverly Hills, CA 90212
United States

www.otzrotbooks.com
© **Pini Dunner,** 2023

Cover Design, Layout and Printing by
Machon Sofrim 732.330.6653

ISBN 978-1-7361890-1-6, *hardcover*

A CIP catalogue record for this title is available from the Library of Congress

Printed and bound in the State of Israel

**THIS BOOK IS DEDICATED TO AN INSPIRATIONAL
FATHER, GRANDFATHER & GREAT-GRANDFATHER**

JOSEPH "JOSL" ACKERMAN נ"י

"Whoever is happy
will make others happy too."

~ Anne Frank

In memory of

Marvin Bernstein MD

an avid airplane pilot.

Because his relationship with Rabbi Dunner
gave him new confidence in God's ground crew.

לע"נ מנחם בן יחיאל ז"ל

Rabbi Pini's thoughts on so many issues
are the food for our souls we each need.

We are blessed to have his
kindness and wisdom
in our lives.

Barry & Laurelle Wolfe
Los Angeles, CA

לעילוי נשמת

אריאל יהודה בן פינחס צבי ז"ל

נפטר י"ז תמוז תשע"ח

In memory of

Ariel Klein z"l

In honor of our
incredibly wise and loving parents
Nina & Marty Rosenzweig

In memory of our
amazingly positive and inspiring parents
Dorothy & Sherman Broidy z"l

To our dear friend
and most trusted advisor
Rabbi Pini Dunner
Mazel tov and may you go
from strength to strength

Robin & Elliott Broidy
Boca Raton, FL

From London to LA,
Rabbi Pini and Sabine
lead and inspire wherever they are.

Distances don't separate our
admiration, friendship, and respect.
Proud to be their friends for decades,
and, God willing, for decades to come.

Maurice and Gabriella Golker
Jerusalem, Israel

IN MEMORY OF OUR DEAR FATHER

HERSHEL GOLKER

ר' שלמה צבי בן ר' משה מרדכי ז"ל

Who always taught us the importance of studying Torah
and to cherish Rabbis, Talmidei Chachomim, and Yirei Shomayim.
We feel his passing every day.

**His wife, children, grandchildren,
family and acquaintances in
Israel and England**

IN MEMORY OF A SPECIAL MOTHER
& GRANDMOTHER

PAMELA SPENCER

פעסא רחל בת ר' פייוול הכהן ע"ה

We miss her every day
and fondly cherish her memory.

Antony & Laurie Spencer
London, UK

Jerusalem, February 21, 2023

Rabbi Pini Dunner
Beverly Hills Synagogue
California, USA

Dear Rabbi Pini, my friend,

I write to thank you for sharing "Hearts & Minds", your fresh new look at our ancient, most sacred texts.

Although intended as a weekly companion for the *parasha,* I found myself fully engrossed in this rich, illuminating book. Your creative reasoning, coupled with your breadth of knowledge and rhetoric, invites discussion and introspection. I so enjoyed your perspective and your voice, always relevant and candid, and I am delighted "Hearts & Minds" will enable an even greater audience to be exposed to them.

Kind regards to Sabine, and Yishar Koach my friend to you and yours.

Warmly, and Shalom!

Isaac Herzog
President of the State of Israel

TABLE OF CONTENTS

FOREWORD

Jewish life and Jewish identity are inextricably bound up with the Jewish festivals cycle that runs through each calendar year. Every month of the Jewish year is connected to a holiday or a significant commemorative date—such as a fast day. These holidays and commemorative dates are the lifeblood of every Jew—the oxygen that gives being Jewish meaning and significance.

First and foremost is the religious connotation that accompanies each one of them, and the impact these connotations have on how we conduct ourselves on those days. For example, the *Yamim Nora'im* (usually translated as "Days of Awe", although my preferred translation is "awesome days") are intended to put us on a higher spiritual plane, to the extent that the entire preceding month of Ellul has evolved into a kind of *Yamim Nora'im* bootcamp, with customs and traditions that aim to put us in the right frame of mind for Rosh Hashana and Yom Kippur even before we get there.

Pesach is a festival of miraculous liberation and national identity, while Shavuot is the festival when we commemorate receiving the Torah from God at Mount Sinai. Sukkot is all about unbridled joy. Chanukah celebrates the unlikely victory of a small band of the faithful against the seemingly insurmountable power of a mighty army, as well as the incredible rededication of the Temple in Jerusalem that followed, while the theme of Purim is miracles that occur even as events seem to unfold via natural means.

We also have days set aside for sadness and reflection—such as the ninth of Av, a fast day when we recall the destruction of two Jerusalem Temples. The ninth of Av also comes with a preliminary bootcamp period—this one is three weeks long and begins with another day of fasting: the seventeenth of Tammuz. The customs and traditions over this three-week period reflect our collective sadness coupled with an overt acknowledgement of the relationship breakdown between God and His chosen nation that resulted in the Temples' destruction, and consequently, our resolute desire to right the wrongs of Jewish history.

But truthfully, there is far more to these festivals and fast days than just that. While Jewish life, in general terms, is governed by a preset calendar steeped in history and tradition, our personal lives as Jews are infused with an individual flavor that is far more subjective and idiosyncratic—and yet, this individual aspect is no less important, by any means. The foods, the prayers, the memories, the customs—all these elements of the festivals and the periods of the year when they occur form a powerful backdrop to our own experiences, no less powerful than the festival and fast-day associated laws mandated by the Talmud and Shulḥan Arukh.

My own upbringing brimmed with these atmospheric foundations. And as a result, each year, as the Jewish festivals approach, or as we anticipate Shiva Asar Be'Tammuz and Tisha B'Av, I find strength and meaning in recalling the foundations laid by the experiences of my youth and early adulthood.

Every Pesach, for example, I recall the Pesach seders with my grandparents—my mother's parents, survivors of the Holocaust who hid from the Nazis for two and a half years in a tiny room behind a false wall at the home of gentile friends in Rotterdam, Holland. I vividly remember walking with my Dutch grandfather to shul on yomtov—my grandparents always came to London from Holland for Pesach and Sukkot, and occasionally also for *Yamim Nora'im*.

I remember marveling at my grandfather's determined expression and at his deliberate pace; he was a rock of faith despite the many challenges he had faced in his life. And even today, many decades later, and long after their passing, I feel my grandparents with me at every Pesach seder, and my grandfather still walks with me to and from shul.

One particular memory stands out more vividly than the others. In 1976, my family moved from Stamford Hill, an area in North London, to Golders Green, in North West London. Each year thereafter, for many years, we returned to Stamford Hill for Yom Kippur, where my grandfather—my father's father—was the rabbi of a synagogue, and where he led the services for Kol Nidre, Mussaf and Ne'ilah. In 1983, my mother's father was with us for *Yamim Nora'im*, and he decided to join us in Stamford Hill for Yom Kippur rather than remain in Golders Green, and throughout Yom Kippur I stood beside him as he prayed.

That year, we reached the Ne'ilah prayer early, and my father's father—who was leading the services—decided to recite each *Avinu Malkeinu* out loud for it to then be repeated by the congregation, instead of just the limited selection of nine that are usually read out by the *ḥazzan* and then repeated. *Avinu Malkeinu* is a series of implorations, and their recitation is always highly charged even under normal conditions, but at the end of

Yom Kippur, and with each one being recited aloud in unison, *Avinu Malkeinu* took on a whole new dimension.

Close to the end of *Avinu Malkeinu* is a set of four that are connected to each other. They begin with אָבִינוּ מַלְכֵּנוּ עֲשֵׂה לְמַעַן הֲרוּגִים עַל שֵׁם קָדְשֶׁךָ – "Our father, our king, do it for the sake of those who were killed for Your holy name."

Suddenly, as he recited this first *Avinu Malkeinu* of the set, my mother's father began to sob uncontrollably. His whole body was shaking. Both his parents and most of his extended family had been murdered by the Nazis in the Holocaust, and in that moment, in those final minutes of Yom Kippur, their loss was so vivid to him, and so evocative, that he was overwhelmed with emotion, and this usually impassive man broke down and cried like a child.

We continued: אָבִינוּ מַלְכֵּנוּ עֲשֵׂה לְמַעַן טְבוּחִים עַל יִחוּדֶךָ – "Our father, our king, do it for the sake of those who were slaughtered for Your oneness." And then we all said out loud, in unison, אָבִינוּ מַלְכֵּנוּ עֲשֵׂה לְמַעַן בָּאֵי בָאֵשׁ וּבַמַּיִם עַל קִדּוּשׁ שְׁמֶךָ – "Our father, our king, do it for the sake of those who were burnt and drowned for the sanctification of your name." And as the congregation chanted these lines, my grandfather's emotional epiphany became even more pronounced, his voice broken by racking sobs.

Finally, we reached the fourth *Avinu Malkeinu* in the set: אָבִינוּ מַלְכֵּנוּ נְקֹם נִקְמַת דַּם עֲבָדֶיךָ הַשָּׁפוּךְ – "Our father, our king, avenge the spilt blood of your servants." For this, the last one in the series, my grandfather straightened up and responded with a full, strong voice – a piercing recitation. It almost seemed as if he was challenging God to give meaning to the death of his parents, whose only "crime" had been that they were Jews in the wrong place at the wrong time—resulting in their gruesome death at Sobibor death camp in May 1943.

Although it was more than 40 years after his parents' murder, the wound was still fresh and raw, and as painful as ever. And evidently, my grandfather wanted God to know how he felt— truly, it is a moment I will never forget for as long as I live. In fact, I think of it every year on Yom Kippur when I say the words נְקֹם נִקְמַת דַּם עֲבָדֶיךָ הַשָּׁפוּךְ. I think of my mother's father, shaking with emotion, alongside me, responding and repeating those words with all his might, not holding back. I also think of his parents, walking into the gas chambers, to be murdered in cold blood. And to top it all off, I think of my father's father, also a victim of Nazi persecution, who lost his parents in Auschwitz, and who led the prayers that fateful Yom Kippur.

For me, each year, at that particular moment in the service, Yom Kippur is not just a generic day of worship or a holy day in the Jewish calendar. Rather, it is a deeply personal experience that ties into the experiences of my forebears, and my memories of them on Yom Kippur.

In fact, my Yom Kippur experience as a whole is an amalgamation of all the many Yom Kippur experiences I have had throughout my life. It includes the many people I have prayed with and the many places I have prayed at. It includes the tunes I have sung; it includes the highs, and it includes the lows; and it even includes all the different post-Yom Kippur fast-breaking meals I have shared with so many people and in so many settings. And each Yom Kippur I continue to create new experiences that act as the setting and foundation for the years that follow.

It goes without saying that this phenomenon is not just limited to Yom Kippur. Every significant Jewish date is loaded with memories and past experiences, and all of them feed into the "mother ship," augmenting its efficacy and enhancing its meaningfulness.

I remember celebrating Chanukah and Purim in yeshivah – in Gateshead, Baltimore and Jerusalem – dancing with the rabbis and celebrating with my friends. I can remember a unique Tisha B'Av at the yeshiva in Montreux, Switzerland – presided over by the rosh yeshiva, Rabbi Moshe Botchko (1916-2010) – when I was only 8 years old. We happened to be vacationing in Verbier, just over 40 miles away, and my father brought us there to recite the traditional Tisha B'Av *kinot* ("lamentations"). And I can remember the many Shavuot night learning programs I've attended, with zany learning topics to keep me awake—the details of which I still recall in vivid detail decades later.

I also remember that one year, on the first night of Sukkot, it just would not stop raining. My father, ever the optimist, refused to give up hope of making the blessing of *leisheiv ba'sukkah* in the sukkah, and insisted that we wait until it stopped raining before we began eating. An hour or more went by, and we were all hungry, so, with my father's reluctant consent, we began the meal indoors—but he was still utterly determined. He was so sure it would stop raining. Every few minutes he went outside to check if the rain had stopped—it was simply unthinkable to him that we wouldn't make the blessing of *leisheiv ba'sukkah* in the sukkah on the first night of the festival.

Eventually—long after we had finished eating—he came running in, his eyes gleaming. "It's stopped raining," he announced excitedly, and we all traipsed into the sukkah to make the blessing and eat some cake. My father just couldn't stop smiling. He was like a child who'd received his favorite toy as a gift. And that's exactly how he felt: that God had given him a gift—the blessing of *leisheiv ba'sukkah* in the sukkah on the first night of Sukkot.

These memories and so many more turn each festival and each significant Jewish date into a combination of history, tradition, Jewish laws and customs, memories, nostalgia, and new experiences. And the result is so much greater than any one of those individual components. Every wine stain on the pages of the Haggadah we use. Every forgotten High Holidays schedule that we left tucked into the pages of the *maḥzor*. The special yomtov-connected drawings that our kids gave us when they were at pre-school that suddenly reappear at the relevant time of year. The smell of yomtov food cooking in the kitchen. Each one of these triggers and so many more – too many to mention – are the kaleidoscope of our Jewish experience which add color, context, and meaningfulness to the festival experience, augmenting the practical aspects of the festivals and notable Jewish dates that punctuate our lives.

My intention in having combined all the festivals into one book is to offer the full array of our Jewish experience in one volume – allowing you, the reader, to ride the roller coaster of Jewish experience without having to wait for each significant date to come around. The flavors and evocations of every date in the Jewish calendar are here for you to savor and ready for you to enjoy.

I would like to thank the many people who have had a hand in enabling this book to be published. Both Carly Einfeld and Madeline Kramer at the YINBH Beverly Hills Synagogue office are always on hand to make things easier, enabling my writing by taking care of the many other aspects of whatever needs to get done in terms of my role as rabbi of our wonderful community— while I'm closeted away behind my laptop screen. The members of the YINBH community also always encourage me, and act as a sounding board for my literary work, commenting positively on my articles, and showing their appreciation in so many different ways.

Thank you to Rabbi Eliezer Ralbag of Lakewood NJ for his patience with all my various publishing projects and countless ideas for these publications. I very much enjoy working together with him on the various book and publication projects – all scheduled to appear via our new publishing house, *Machon Otzrot*. The main purpose of *Machon Otzrot* is to publish English and Hebrew works relating to rabbinic scholarship and modern Jewish history, focusing principally on primary texts and reissuing previously published materials, with scholarly annotations, illustrations, and introductions composed and peer-reviewed by a range of contemporary experts.

In the next few months, we will be publishing a book that is the culmination of several years of painstaking work – Rabbi Shmuel Yitzhak Hillman's *Ohr Hayashar* on the Talmudic tractate Shabbat. Together with a team of scholars, I have composed footnotes that expand on Rabbi Hillman's cryptic annotations and references, which reflect the vast range of his incredible scholarship and knowledge. Aficionados of Talmudic studies will revel in the breadth and depth of this unusual publication, which will be utterly unique – a one-off exploration into a kaleidoscope of topics as seen through the eyes of one of the twentieth century's forgotten rabbinic heroes.

My heartfelt appreciation to all the generous sponsors who have made the publication of *Hearts & Minds II* possible. Without your support this book could never have been published. The book publishing world continues to decline and to face insurmountable challenges, and if it were not for the generosity of those who appreciate how important books are and remain, the publication of niche books such as this one would simply not be possible.

I also want to express my deepest gratitude to Sherri Henkin for the incredible job she did editing the book manuscript before publication. Her keen eye for detail, combined with exceptional writing skills, elevated the quality of my work to a whole new level. Sherri's suggestions and edits were insightful, and I was particularly impressed by the way she was able to maintain the voice and tone of the book while making it much more polished and cohesive. I am truly grateful for the time and effort Sherri put into making my book the best it could be. Her passion for the written word is evident in the high-quality work she produced, and I cannot thank her enough.

I am also so grateful to the many sources of inspiration that have fed into my writing – rabbinic colleagues who share their ideas on WhatsApp groups; websites and blogs which offer precious thoughts and wonderful source material; and the many people who email me with suggestions for articles, or just a good story they think I might find useful.

In particular, I want to mention the website "Sefaria" – which bills itself as "A Living Library of Torah." It is without question the ultimate game-changing resource for those, like me, who are in constant need of easy access to Tanakh, Talmud, Midrash, halakhic material, commentaries, and source sheets. And the most amazing part of this website is that it is a completely free resource – unbelievably, no part of the website is behind a paywall. I cannot overstate my appreciation for the simplicity and accessibility of this website, and truthfully, I am more than a little envious to its creators for their share in all the Torah that has been taught and studied as a result of their efforts.

As to the Torah-related ideas and so much else that I am able to share: via this book, my other books, my regular articles, my podcasts and my videos—all of this output has only been made possible because of the incredible support and remarkable forbearance of my wonderful wife, Sabine. No one could wish for a better life partner—and she is unequivocally an equal partner in all of my output: by being tolerant of the sound of my constant keyboard tapping, and of my endless reading, as well as the fact that she has to live surrounded by books and papers wherever she turns, and has to entertain a constant stream of rabbis and scholars who beat a path to our door for one reason or another.

It is exceptionally special that I can dedicate this book to Sabine's father, my father-in-law, the unfaltering Joseph "Josl" Ackerman, who turned ninety last year, and who continues to inspire us with his positive outlook and his boundless enthusiasm for life, ably supported by my mother-in-law Esther, and the extended Ackerman family. We pray for Josl's continued health, and for many more years of his youthful energy to keep us all on our toes.

I am also blessed with six wonderful children: Shoshana, Dalia, Shlomo, Eli, Meir and Uri. Each of them, in their own way, is able to get me to do better and to be better. My sons-in-law, Zion and Jonathan are the perfect counterpoints to my two beautiful daughters. And my three grandchildren (so far!) – Miri, Joseph and Esti – have created a new light in my life and a new glow in my heart that no words could ever sufficiently describe. May they all continue to be a pride and joy to their parents and grandparents, and I look forward to great things from all of them as the years ahead unfold.

Finally – a message to you, the reader. Without you, there would be no point in any of this. Why write, if there is no one to read? Why make your voice heard, if there is no one to listen? The fact that you, dear reader, are there to drink from the fountain of my literary output, is the greatest inspiration of all. I am more grateful to you than words can express.

But don't let it stop with the reading. Please – use my material and share it with others, as many others as you can. Every learner has the ability to be a teacher, which means that you, as a learner, have a duty to teach.

The late Rabbi Lord Jonathan Sacks z"l, chief rabbi of the UK and one of my most enduring inspirations, once shared a very powerful thought. "Not all of us have power," he wrote, "but we all have influence.... Always choose influence rather than power. It helps change people into people who can change the world."

When we teach others what we have learnt, we may not have any power over them, but we certainly have influence—and that influence can change them in ways that are often immeasurable, and in ways which last much longer than the exchange of words during that original teaching moment. Suddenly, just by teaching others, we have set off a chain reaction that may very well change the world.

So let me end with this blessing: may we all merit the privilege to teach others, and may we all have a part in changing the world into a much better place. And last, but not least, may we all merit to be part of the messianic redemption, and may that happen speedily, and in our days. Amen.

Pini Dunner

Beverly Hills CA

February 2023

ROSH HASHANA

THE RADOSHITZER'S SHOFAR

first published September 28, 2022

L et me begin by posing a question. Then, I want to tell you a story. And hopefully, the story will answer the question — and will also offer some inspiration.

Here's the question. The Talmud describes two types of sounds that you need to hear from the shofar. One of them is the tekiah — a long straight uninterrupted sound. The second one is the teruah — a series of sounds, which could either be three medium-length sounds, or nine or more staccato sounds.

The Talmud says that we must hear both kinds of sound from the shofar on Rosh Hashana — the tekiah and the teruah — and because there is a difference of opinion about the teruah sound, we need to hear various permutations and combinations of sounds so that we cover all the bases.

But here's the thing. Every combination always has a tekiah at the beginning, and then a tekiah at the end. That's the rule. Whatever sound or sounds are in the middle, whether it's a shevarim, or a teruah, or a shevarim-teruah — before them you must have a tekiah, and afterward you also must have a tekiah.

It seems strange. If you must hear a tekiah and a teruah, just do a tekiah and then a teruah. Or do the teruah first and then the tekiah. Why do you need the teruah sound to be preceded **and** followed by a tekiah? What's the message?

Let me park that question for a minute and tell you the story of the Radoshitzer's shofar. The story centers around a young prewar yeshiva bochur from the city of Piotrkow in Poland. His name was Moshe Weintreter, and he came from a family of Radoshitzer Ḥasidim. I'd be surprised if you've ever heard of the Radoshitzer Ḥasidic group. It's one of those Ḥasidic dynasties that thrived in prewar Poland, but which was utterly wiped out by the Holocaust.

The Rebbe of Radoshitz in the period just before and during the Holocaust was called Rabbi Yitzchak Shmuel Eliyahu Finkler (1892–1944). He was a relatively young man, in his late 40s, when the war broke out — but he'd been the rebbe since the age of 20, as his father died in 1912.

The Piotrkow Jewish community, where Rabbi Finkler led his followers, was a wonderful community. It was affluent and successful. There were thriving shuls, schools, yeshivas, and social welfare organizations — it was a model community, and life for Jews in Piotrkow was great. Then, the Second World War began — and everything changed overnight.

Life was cheap, poverty was everywhere, and danger lurked behind every door and on every street. But there was some money, and gentiles took bribes and hid Jews, or turned a blind eye to Jews in hiding in exchange for money and valuables. Still, the Nazis were resourceful and eventually, even the Jews in hiding were caught and sent to their deaths.

In 1943, after years of evading capture and doing everything they could to avoid being killed, both Moshe Weintreter and Rabbi Finkler were deported along with thousands of other Piotrkow Jews, many of them straight to extermination camps. But the Rebbe and young Moshe were spared certain death by being sent to the forced-labor camp in Skarzysko-Kamienna. Although, while it may not have been a death camp — thousands of Jews died there or were killed.

Rabbi Finkler was an inspirational figure, a lightning rod of faith and hope. He was undeterred by any danger and totally determined to stay as Jewishly observant as possible, even amid the dangers of Nazi tyranny and vicious brutality. He organized minyanim every day for shaḥarit, minḥa and maariv, and he inspired people with words of encouragement and optimism.

Then, as Rosh Hashana of 1943 approached, the Rebbe could speak about nothing else but blowing shofar. He desperately yearned for a shofar. He had managed to smuggle some diamonds into the camp, and he used them bribe a Polish guard to get him a horn that he would turn into a shofar. But the first horn the guard brought turned out to be an ox's horn — which is not kosher to be used as a shofar. The Rebbe didn't give up. He found another diamond or two, and eventually the Polish guard brought him a ram's horn.

The Rebbe now sought out his young protégé, Moshe Weintreter, who had secured a role as a metal worker, and was working in the metal workshop at the labor camp. The Radoshitzer Rebbe handed him the ram's horn — "Turn it into a shofar," he said. Weintreter was very taken aback. He'd never made a shofar in his life.

The Rebbe saw that he was surprised. "If you complete this task," he told Weintreter, "the merit of doing it will safeguard you — you will survive this hell and make it out alive."

Making a shofar isn't simple. First, the ram's horn has to be flattened and softened so that it has a long thin section to blow into. Then it needs to have a turned-up wide opening at the end, to amplify the noise. You have to heat the raw horn gently so that you can make a hole from the tip of the horn to the hollow part inside the horn, and you have to be sure you don't crack the horn while you're working on it.

Moshe Weintreter — who had never made a shofar in his life — secretly worked on the horn, for days, perhaps weeks, hiding it so that he wouldn't be spotted. Eventually, the shofar was ready, and he brought it to the Radoshitzer Rebbe just before Rosh Hashana.

As incredible as it seems, on Rosh Hashana in 1943, at the Skarzysko-Kamienna labor camp, in the fourteenth barrack building, the Radoshitzer Rebbe gathered together a group of the faithful and he blew shofar for them. It was a moment of pure spirituality and inspiration.

Within a couple of months, Weintreter was taken to do metal work at another camp, in Czestochowa. He insisted on taking his toolbox with him — and hidden in a secret compartment under the tools he stashed his precious shofar. He managed to keep it safe, until one day, towards the end of the war, he was randomly picked up and deported to Buchenwald. He didn't have a chance to take his shofar, and it remained hidden in the toolbox in Czestochowa.

Moshe Weintreter survived the war, just as the Radoshitzer Rebbe had promised him he would. His family was wiped out, but he survived. Sadly, the Radoshitzer Rebbe died of malnutrition, just three months before liberation.

After he was liberated, Weintreter went from Buchenwald to Italy, where he helped organize the illegal immigration of Jews by ship to Palestine. He changed his surname to Ben-Dov, and he got married to Ida, a fellow Holocaust survivor. They moved to Israel and settled in Bnei Brak. But Weintreter never forgot about his shofar — his constant dream was to honor the memory of Rabbi Finkler, the Radoshitzer Rebbe, by somehow bringing that shofar to Israel.

Over the years that followed, Weintreter wrote to anyone he could think of who might have found the shofar and described it to them. Unbelievably — after decades of searching — Weintreter received a letter from someone who knew where the shofar was. Apparently, almost immediately after the war the shofar was discovered in Czestochowa, in the exact hiding place where Moshe had left it, and it was given to the local Jewish community.

Later that year, a visitor came to Czestochowa from the United States. He was a prominent Yiddish author and journalist — and the community gave him the shofar as a gift. Weintreter tracked down the family of the Yiddish writer, and once they heard the story they were only too happy to reunite the shofar with the person who had made it. And so, in 1977, Moshe Weintreter got his shofar back and he gave it to Yad Vashem — where it is now part of the permanent exhibit.

Moshe Weintreter passed away some years ago, and so did Ida — but they left a wonderful family. Their son is Shmuel Ben-Dov, a retired banker who lives in Bnei Brak. And when Shmuel's youngest son went to Yad Vashem together with his IDF officers' training class, he showed his fellow trainee officers his grandfather's shofar, which was miraculously fabricated in the metal works of Skarzysko-Kamienna labor camp and used there in 1943.

What a story. But it is more than just a story about a random shofar, or about some Holocaust miracle. It is a story about a shofar that is emblematic of exactly the sounds we blow out of every shofar on Rosh Hashana.

Moshe Weintreter's life started out in Piotrkow with a tekiah — calm, straightforward, and uncomplicated.

But then his life when through every teruah possible. It was broken and shattered.

And finally, he came to Israel — and there was a tekiah again. The brokenness was gone, and the calm came back.

And that is exactly the message the shofar wants to convey. We go through hard times, as everyone does, and we think to ourselves, before things were tough, we had it so good!

The sounds of the shofar act to reassure us, "Don't worry, good times always follow bad times. Just like you had a tekiah before, there's going to be a tekiah afterward. The shevarim, the teruah, they are just for now. Listen to the shofar, pray for salvation and redemption, and the tekiah will surely follow."

THE TRUE VALUE OF LIFE

first published September 28, 2022

We all know that Rosh Hashana is meant to be a wake-up call. So much so, that it even comes with its own alarm clock: the shofar. In fact, the idea that on Rosh Hashana we are being shaken out of our slumber and being made conscious of something important is totally ingrained into the system.

Although — what exactly is that "something"? The answer is not so clear, and it desperately needs clarification if Rosh Hashana is going to have some enduring meaning, beyond just being another milestone in our lives and another check on the checklist of scheduled events that we repeat annually, without really understanding what that event should mean.

Rosh Hashana is the anniversary of the final day of creation — when human beings were created. I think it is very significant that we associate the beginning of the year with the birthday of humanity. The creation of humanity and teshuva are closely connected.

Animals — even intelligent animals — can't sin. But humans can because we were created with a sense of right and wrong. Although, it is worth exploring: What really makes us that different from an animal?

Have you ever heard the story of Gary Rosheisen? Actually, the story is really about Gary's cat — and it's a crazy story. Some years ago, Gary had a series of mini-strokes and, as if that wasn't enough, he also suffered from advanced osteoporosis. He was in very poor health, and to compound matters, he lived on his own with no support.

Not able to get out of his home, Gary decided to buy himself a cat. He named the cat Tommy, and Tommy was an absolute godsend. You might actually say that Tommy was a lifesaver — and you wouldn't be wrong.

As a result of Gary's significant health issues, which occasionally included seizures, he always kept a landline phone close at hand. But he was nervous that in the event of a seizure he wouldn't be able to dial 9-1-1, so in addition to the numbered buttons, he had a speed dial button on the phone that automatically dialed 9-1-1.

And just to be sure that in the event of an emergency he would be able to reach out to a first responder team, Gary tried to train Tommy to press the speed dial button on the landline phone. But as hard as Gary tried, Tommy didn't seem to understand what to do, and Gary eventually gave up trying to train him.

A few months later, Gary had a seizure and fell out of his wheelchair onto the floor. After a few moments Gary came to his senses, but he was unable to move. To make things worse, he didn't have his medical emergency necklace, and was too far from the emergency cord next to his bed. The nearest phone was out of reach, and it seemed as if all his plans for such an emergency had amounted to nothing.

But moments later the first responders arrived. Apparently, they had received a call from Gary's landline phone. Someone had dialed 9-1-1 — but when the emergency operator picked up no one said anything, the operator traced the call and the first responders rushed over to Gary's house as quickly as they could to see what was wrong. That's when they found Gary on the floor of his room. Meanwhile, Tommy the cat was in the living room, next to the phone on the floor. Obviously, Tommy's training had been far more successful than Gary had ever thought.

I love a good rescue story. Everyone does. Usually, rescue stories are about humans rescuing humans. But in this story Tommy the cat is the hero. And it's so heartwarming. A human life was saved. By a pet. What could be better? Although, of course, had we been there when Gary needed help, we would have called 9-1-1. We would have done everything we could. Right? Because humanity values human life above everything else.

And yet — is it really so true that human beings value human life to the utmost degree? Or, to put it slightly differently, is it really so true that human life matters to us more than anything else?

Consider this: wars and war crimes continue to plague the world — resulting in tens of thousands of deaths and millions of refugees every year. And closer to home? Mass shootings occur so often in the United States that the news reports about them barely last for one full 24-hour news cycle. And what's even worse — during those 24 hours, the news reports barely register in our consciousness. So, is human life really such a priority?

Let me share something even crazier. There's an academic called Dr. Richard Topolski — he is a professor of psychology at

Georgia Regents University. In 2015, as part of his research into human behavior, Topolski conducted a survey in which participants were given a hypothetical scenario: a bus is hurtling out of control, bearing down on a dog and a human — and you can only save one of the two. Which one would you save?

Over 500 people responded to the survey. Let me summarize their answers as follows: apparently, saving the human depends on what kind of human it is, and it also depends on what kind of dog is in danger of being crushed by the bus!

Of course, everyone said they would save a sibling, or a grandparent, or a close friend — if they didn't know the dog, that is. But if it was their dog about to be crushed by the bus, you'd be amazed at what people said they would do. I won't give you the grandparents and sibling statistics — but consider this: 40% of the respondents said they would be more likely to save their dog than a foreign tourist who they'd never met.

Topolski's question is similar to the one that has been asked dozens of times in sociology project surveys: if you saw your dog drowning in the river and at the same time a stranger drowning, would you first try to save your drowning dog or would you save the drowning stranger? For well over 40 years, the survey results have been fairly consistent: About a third would save their dog; the second third would save the stranger; and the other third don't know what they would do.

Now, you may be wondering where I'm going with all this. You may also be thinking, what's so bad about saving a dog, especially if a human being might be evil? I think the best way of understanding this concept, and making any sense of it, is to consider the emotions we feel when we hear that a child is terminally ill, or that a child has been killed in an accident, or by a murderer. Why do we feel so dreadful when we encounter such a scenario — much worse than when we hear about an adult in the same scenario?

I believe that what plagues us most of all about a child dying is the tragedy of lost potential. That dead or dying child will never have a chance to fulfill their potential in life — their life has been ripped away from them before they've had a chance to do anything meaningful.

And perhaps the reason we might save a dog instead of a human — or worse: why we don't do much more to save human lives — is because we are so cynical about human potential.

A few months ago, I debated Dennis Prager about whether or not human beings are inherently evil.[1] I argued that humans are not inherently evil. Dennis disagreed. But most shocking for me was that many people in the audience agreed with him. I found that both very depressing and very worrying. Because it's not a big leap from believing that humans are inherently evil to opting to save a dog instead of a human.

I would like to suggest that correlating Rosh Hashana and the creation of humanity is exactly because when we pray for life, we need to realize that we are not merely praying for living another year. We are praying for the opportunity to fulfill our potential. And the only way we can do that is by seeing the potential in humanity.

---

[1] A video of the debate is available here: https://rabbidunner.com/the-great-debate/

That is why the word for "life" in Hebrew is ḥayyim — in the plural — because there are so many opportunities and possibilities in the dynamic journey called human life, that speaking about "life" in the singular is simply inadequate.

Rosh Hashana is the birthday of humanity, which makes Rosh Hashana the perfect platform to promote the idea of human goodness. Every minute lived offers us another opportunity to do good. To serve God. To help others. To save lives. To value life. And to pray, not just for a life of breathing and existence — because that kind of life is just like the life of any other animal, an animal like Tommy the cat or a drowning dog.

On Rosh Hashana, when we pray for life, we pray for a life of potential, and of fulfilling our potential. May we all merit to be written in the "Book of Fulfilling Our Potential," and of helping others fulfil theirs.

THE MESSAGE OF THE HOLY HUNCHBACK

first published September 2, 2021

T here is no question that the primary focus of Rosh Hashana and Yom Kippur — as well as the days that lie between them — is teshuva.

Teshuva is usually translated into English as "repentance," but a better translation of this Hebrew word might be "return" — which is exactly what it means: When we do teshuva, we actively seek a return to our full relationship with God by going through a process of repentance.

But while the High Holidays period in the Jewish calendar is dominated by penitential prayers and a strong emphasis on ritual, Maimonides firmly reminds us in his seminal *Hilkhot Teshuva* (*Laws of Repentance*) that before seeking to refresh your relationship with God, you must first fix broken relationships with fellow humans.

Religious fervor and spiritual devotion have no meaning if you can't get on with the people around you, and it's pointless trying to reconcile with God if you have made no effort to reconcile with those you have offended, harmed, or mistreated during the previous year.

I would like to take this idea a little bit further, and to illustrate it via one of Rabbi Shlomo Carlebach's most inspiring stories. I heard the story from him many times, and with each retelling it made a deeper impression. Even now, decades after I first heard him tell it, I marvel at the simplicity of its message, and its profundity. Based on a random encounter that Rabbi Carlebach had with a student of Rabbi Kalonymus Kalman Shapira of Piaseczno (1889–1943), the story teaches us that it is never sufficient just to fix broken relationships, but rather one should always focus on doing kindness for others.

Rabbi Kalonymus Kalman Shapira of Piaseczno was a Polish Ḥasidic leader who found himself trapped in the Warsaw ghetto during the early years of the Holocaust. During his time there, despite the horrific and ever-worsening conditions, Rabbi Shapira regularly delivered inspiring homilies and sermons, boosting the faith of the faithful, and encouraging hope among the hopeless. All along he carefully recorded the homilies on scraps of paper, in the hope that one day he would be rescued, and they would be published.

Eventually it became evident that the end was nigh, so Rabbi Shapira gave the manuscript material to the Polish-Jewish historian, Emanuel Ringelblum (1900–1944), who had set about creating the Warsaw Ghetto "Oneg Shabbat" archives — a collection of tin canisters containing a comprehensive assortment of ghetto-related documents which were buried underground before the final deportations.

The canisters were eventually discovered in 1946 during Warsaw's reconstruction, long after all the ghetto inhabitants had been murdered by the Nazis. Among the countless documents in the archives was the Piaseczno Rebbe's manuscript, which somehow found its way into the hands of one of Israel's most dynamic Religious Zionist activists, Baruch Duvdevani (1916–1984), who published the homilies under the title *Eish Kodesh* (*Sacred Fire*) in 1956.

To this day, *Eish Kodesh* remains one of the most powerful religious documents to emerge from the darkest depths of the Holocaust, a testament to maintaining one's faith amid vicious cruelty and seemingly irredeemable crisis.

Before the Second World War, Rabbi Shapira was best known as a master educator. He had presided over a yeshiva of pre-bar mitzvah boys, and, as he would quip, with a twinkle in his eye: "I am unlike any other Rebbe in Poland — my Ḥasidim all eat on Yom Kippur, because they are not obligated to fast!"

Thousands of children attended his yeshiva over the years, but almost all remnants of his Ḥasidic sect and yeshiva students were swallowed up by the Holocaust, and very few survived.

After Rabbi Shlomo Carlebach read *Eish Kodesh* for the first time, he became utterly fixated with the idea of meeting one of the boys who had studied at the Piaseczno Rebbe's yeshiva — but despite his strenuous efforts to locate survivors, it seemed that they had all been killed, and eventually he abandoned any hope of a personal encounter.

Then, one day in the early 1970s, he was walking down Reḥov HaYarkon in Tel Aviv and he noticed a hunchbacked streetcleaner sweeping the sidewalk. Rabbi Carlebach was always drawn to people on the fringes as he wanted to lift their spirits, and he greeted the streetcleaner with a smile and a cheery "shalom aleichem!" The man looked up and answered him in a Polish-Yiddish accented Hebrew — "aleichem shoolem!"

Rabbi Carlebach stopped. "Hey brother, where are you from?" he asked the man.

"I'm from Piaseczno."

"Really? Piaseczno? Did you know the holy Rebbe, Reb Kalonymus Kalman?"

"Of course," said the man, "I studied at his yeshiva from the age of five until I was eleven."

The streetcleaner leaned on his broom, and he had a faraway look in his eyes.

"When I was eleven, the Nazis took me to Auschwitz. I was very tall for my age — they actually thought I was seventeen years old. I was very strong, so they used me for the hardest work. But I was feisty, and I didn't always follow orders, so I would get terrible beatings. That's why I look like this. During my time in the Nazi hell, I always recovered. Still, as you can see, the damage from Auschwitz is permanent. Look at me now, my body is a wreck. And who have I got in the world? I have nobody. Everyone in my family was killed. Because of how I look, no one would marry me and so I have no children. And" — he glanced back at Rabbi Carlebach — "that's the story of my life."

Rabbi Carlebach was stunned by what he'd heard, and he hugged the hunchback warmly. "I've always wanted to meet one of Reb Kalonymus Kalman's students," he said. "Please, I'm begging you, do me this kindness — can you tell me one of the teachings that the Rebbe taught you in his yeshiva?"

The hunched streetcleaner began sweeping again.

"Do you really think that after five years in Auschwitz I remember any teachings?" He gave a hollow laugh.

Rabbi Carlebach was undeterred. "Yes, I do think so. The words of such a holy man never disappear — they penetrate you forever."

The man stopped sweeping, and he looked at Rabbi Carlebach — a deep, penetrating gaze.

"Do you really want to know?" he asked.

"Yes," said Rabbi Carlebach, "and I promise you with all my heart that whatever you tell me — I will repeat it all over the world."

The streetcleaner nodded, stopped sweeping — and this is what he told Rabbi Carlebach in Tel Aviv that day.

"There will never be a Shabbes in the world like the ones we had with the Rebbe in Piaseczno. At the Kabbulas Shabbes prayers, hundreds — and sometimes thousands — of children were dancing around the Rebbe. He stood, beaming, like a king, at the center of all the circles.

"Then the Rebbe made kiddush — and we all hummed with him. The omeins were incredible.

"Then we ate. Throughout the meal he would teach us Torah, and he would always say: 'Kinderlech, taire kinderlech, my most precious children, always remember and never forget — the greatest thing in the world is to do someone else a favor.'

"By the time I arrived at Auschwitz, my whole family was dead, and I wanted to kill myself. But each time I was about to do it, I would hear the Rebbe's voice: 'Always remember and never forget — the greatest thing in the world is to do someone else a favor.'

"Do you know how many favors you can do in Auschwitz? With people dying all around you? People are crying, beyond despair… but most of the inmates who had any strength were just concerned for themselves. So, I stayed up all night, comforting people, finding scraps of food for the weakest, trying to cheer people up. And whenever I wanted to end it all, suddenly I would hear my Rebbe's voice again: 'always remember and never forget — the greatest thing in the world is to do someone else a favor.'

"Even here in Tel Aviv, I'm all alone — there are moments when I'm ready to finish myself off. One time I went into the sea up to my nose in the water. But there was the Rebbe's voice again: 'always remember and never forget — the greatest thing in the world is to do someone else a favor.'

"And do you know what? I can always find someone to help. And that's what I do. I'm still doing favors. I'm still alive. I'm still a student of my Rebbe. And I'm still a good Jew."

The streetcleaner patted Rabbi Carlebach on the shoulder: "My friend, that's the teaching: 'always remember and never forget — the greatest thing in the world is to do someone else a favor.'"

And with that, he picked up his broom and went back to his sweeping.

The encounter between Rabbi Carlebach and the streetcleaner took place just before Rosh Hashana. After Sukkot, Rabbi Carlebach came back to Reḥov HaYarkon to look for the streetcleaner, but he was gone. Rabbi Carlebach made inquiries —

apparently, the streetcleaner had died suddenly and unexpectedly on the second day of Sukkot.

Rabbi Carlebach stayed true to his word and repeated the teaching of the Piaseczno Rebbe at countless concerts and gatherings. The message of the "Holy Hunchback" — as Rabbi Carlebach called him — had to live on.

"Always remember and never forget — the greatest thing in the world is to do someone else a favor."

Or, to put it more bluntly, your relationship with God must always be preceded by kindness and consideration for others, otherwise life is simply not worth living.

WILL YOU PASS THE TEST?

first published September 17, 2020

In the midst of the holiest time in the Jewish year, on Rosh Hashana, we read a piece of scripture that relates the shocking story known as "The Akeida" — God's instructions for Abraham to bind and sacrifice his son Isaac, instructions which Abraham follows to the letter, until at the very last moment he is told by God, "Hey, I was only kidding — don't actually kill him!"

I'm not entirely sure how it's possible, but until a few years ago I was totally OK with this story. I think many of us are OK with it, possibly because we are lulled into believing that because the story has a happy ending — let's face it: Isaac didn't die, Abraham passed the test, and everyone lived happily ever after — that what happened before the happy ending was not actually so bad.

But truthfully, it is one of the most frightening stories in the whole Torah, raising countless challenging questions. Why did God give Abraham this gruesome test? Why would He put Abraham through such a shocking trial? More puzzlingly, why didn't Abraham resist? Did he have no feelings for his beloved child? Would it really have tainted his faith if he would have challenged God just a bit? It almost seems inhuman that he was willing to go along with what God had told him to do.

And what about Isaac? What was going through his mind as his father bound him to an altar and then raised a knife to cut his throat? How did he feel towards his father? How did he feel towards God?

And how did they all feel towards each other after it was all over? Did they look at what had happened as a fairytale happily-ever-after ending, like we do — or was there psychological trauma?

The Midrash informs us that Sarah's death is deliberately recorded immediately after the Akeida for the simple reason that when she was informed of what God had told Abraham to do, she was not told that Abraham hadn't gone through with it, and so she assumed Isaac had been killed — and consequently died from shock and grief. If that's the case, and if we accept that Abraham passed the test as a result of his willingness to go through with it unquestioningly, does that mean Sarah failed the test because she was not on board with it?

And finally, why do we read this story on Rosh Hashana? The traditional answer is that it ends with the sacrifice of a ram, and a ram's horn is used as a shofar. But to be perfectly frank, I find it hard to believe that the Torah reading for one of the holiest days of the year was chosen simply on the basis of such a tenuous associative connection.

Perhaps if we unpack the Akeida we can see things slightly differently and find an alternative perspective.

Abraham is undoubtedly one of the most admired heroes of the Torah — both for discovering God in the first place, and then for his willingness to stand up for his faith in God amid a hostile pagan world.

He is also celebrated for his incredible kindness. He was even willing to plead for Sodom and Gomorrah, bargaining with God to spare them from destruction.

But somehow, in the story of the Akeida, something goes awry — suddenly, in an episode that is seemingly out of character, Abraham was ready to offer up his son as a sacrifice on the altar, in behavior that is akin to the pagan culture he had rejected. What exactly went wrong?

There is an incredible passage in the Talmud (Berakhot 32a) that offers an insight into why we read this story on Rosh Hashana, but even more importantly — the passage can help us understand the significance of the Akeida story itself.

The Talmud recalls Moses's incredible efforts to convince God to spare the Jewish nation from annihilation after they committed the sin of the Golden Calf. Moses is relentless, using every possible form of persuasion. At one point, Moses even challenges God with a charge of dishonesty — "You promised Abraham, Isaac and Jacob that their descendants would proliferate like the stars in the heavens," he says, "and now you would destroy them? God, how can you lie?"

Moses's shocking challenge is characterized in a seemingly critical statement by Rabbi Abahu: "Were the verse not written in this manner, it would be impossible to utter it, in deference to God."

And yet, despite this veiled censure, Moses's efforts were completely successful — the Jewish people survived, and it was Moses's abrasive approach that ensured that they would.

It would appear that our biblical forefathers were great people with incredible characters and personality traits, but at the same time they lacked something which only Moses had. They may have been the patriarchs of our nation, but it was Moses who was the founder of Judaism and of the Jewish people that emerged from Egypt.

The reason for this is because Moses did not subscribe to the kind of blind faith which demanded self-destructive sacrifices. And although no one would have ever faulted him for allowing the entire nation to die for the sin of the Golden Calf, he was having none of it.

Moses knew that he held the key to their survival, and so he decided that he was not going to be a bystander and watch them perish. Precisely because of his spirited — if impudent — advocacy, the nation survived to live another day. Not just then, but time after time under his leadership.

Traditionally, the Akeida is believed to be a test that Abraham passed with flying colors. But perhaps that was not the case at all. Perhaps the reason it was his final test was because he didn't pass it at all, and God needed to step in — like a driving instructor with his foot on the brake — so that the horrific potential outcome could be averted.

Think about it. Abraham was presented with an incredible paradox: listen to what God is instructing you to do right now, or defy this instruction based on previous communications you have had with Him. But rather than try to contextualize it, Abraham passively accepted a new reality. And so did Isaac.

Had God not intervened at that crucial moment, none of us would be here today. In that situation, Abraham and Isaac's blind faith did not win the day, rather it let them both down. In fact, maybe it was Sarah's reaction that was most correct — shrinking in horror from an instruction that meant all promise for the future was over.

The Akeida is read for us on the most important faith day of the year to keep us all on our toes — to tell us that even as we aspire to faith perfection, we can still make mistakes. Evidently, even the greatest people make mistakes. And if great people like Abraham and Isaac can make mistakes by being on autopilot, we can certainly make mistakes.

During the period of the COVID pandemic, more than ever before in our lifetimes, our faith was challenged. The ordinary day-to-day existence of our faith lives was tested as never before. Crucially, there were those who blindly continued to follow the hallowed path, ignoring evolving realities, in the belief that the most important thing in the world is to just continue doing exactly the same things that they have always done — as if nothing has changed. That, to them, meant passing the test.

But, in reality, had we all stuck rigidly to how life was conducted until March of 2020, there would have been countless more unnecessary infections and deaths — and we would have failed the test miserably. Indeed, there are many in the Jewish community — and beyond, of course — who trod this path, with devastating consequences.

That is exactly why the Akeida is read on Rosh Hashana — to wake us up, so that we know how important it is to adapt to an ever-evolving situation and not fail the test, so that our faith can survive beyond our lifetimes, into the lives of our children and grandchildren, and so that all that we treasure and have fought for so hard will not disappear in senseless acts of whimsical folly and misplaced dedication.

THE VALUE OF ONE AND ALL

first published September 27, 2019

I n Rambam's foundational *Hilkhot Teshuva* (*Laws of Repentance*), he enumerates 24 types of people for whom the teshuva process will not be effective. He describes one of the types of people as follows (MT Laws of Repentance 4:2):

הַפּוֹרֵשׁ מִן הַצִּבּוּר לְפִי שֶׁבִּזְמַן שֶׁיַּעֲשׂוּ תְּשׁוּבָה לֹא יִהְיֶה עִמָּהֶן
וְאֵינוֹ זוֹכֶה עִמָּהֶן בִּזְכוּת שֶׁעוֹשִׂין

"Someone who keeps himself apart from the community is a person who cannot possibly repent effectively," says Maimonides, "because at the same time that the community is doing teshuva, he won't be there with them, and so he won't benefit from them in the merit of their actions."

On the face of it, this sentiment is wonderful — one needs to be part of a community to benefit from the group. In a sense, it's practical, like a sort of "economies of scale" idea — it is harder to get things done on your own, but for a group to get something done is easier, and the larger the group gets the easier it becomes to get whatever it is done. Teshuva, the Rambam seems to be saying, benefits from this group dynamic; it is more effective to do teshuva in a group than to do it on your own.

But I don't understand something — how does your personal teshuva actually benefit from being part of a group? Let me explain my question with an analogy. If you're hungry and you're in a room where lots of people are eating — just because they are eating doesn't mean you will stop being hungry. And if you eat, it doesn't matter if you eat by yourself or if you eat with lots of other people — once you've eaten enough you won't be hungry. Being part of a group has absolutely nothing to do with it.

Surely repentance is a very private, personal thing. **You** did something wrong, so **you** must repent. What use is it if you are in a room full of other people repenting? How will that make any difference? In fact, it might be better to do it on your own, so that you aren't distracted by others. And anyway, you are hardly going to be forthright with God in a group situation.

Parshat Nitzavim begins the final public address given by Moses before he died. In fact, it took place on the day he died — the 7th of Adar. For five weeks Moses had been lecturing and teaching, and this was his final talk to the Jewish people. Moses used the opportunity to forge a brand-new covenant between God and the Jewish nation, one that would connect the Torah with all future generations.

The new covenant was all-encompassing, and Moses wanted to ensure that everyone would feel included, so he began his address by listing every age group, men and women, every type of person imaginable (Deuteronomy 29:9-10):

> **You stand here today, all of you, before God —**
> **heads of tribes, elders, appointed officials, all the**
> **men of Israel, your children, your wives, even the**

stranger within your camp, from the woodchopper to the water drawer.

Even the lowest and least educated classes — woodchoppers and water drawers — are considered as important to the covenant as the most elevated leaders, elders, and officials — and they are all included on equal terms.

But what message was Moses conveying? Obviously if everyone is included — and the verse says "all" — then everyone is included. Why mention every individual diverse element and strand of society separately?

Since the dawn of history, human society has divided itself into many different classes, according to talent, profession, education, family, social status, and of course financial status. In this respect, Jewish society has not been any different from other societies. These distinctions existed as much within Jewish society as in any other — there were tribes, there were priests, there were kings, there were rabbis, there were judges, and of course there were the wealthy and there were the poor.

The easiest way to understand what Moses meant is the way most of the commentaries interpret his opener — the covenant would apply equally to all, notwithstanding their place in the pecking order.

The Torah does not buy into the idea of a classless society, where there is equality for all. On the contrary, this is an affront to reality. There are leaders and followers, successful people and less successful people, wellborn people, and not-so-wellborn people. It's just how it is. Nevertheless, says Moses, there is a covenant that binds one-and-all, no matter your station in life, and this is the covenant that forms the basis of the relationship between God and His Chosen People.

But I would like to take the solution to this problem in a slightly different direction than the commentaries.

In 1954, the social psychologist Leon Festinger (1919–1989) proposed what he called the "social comparison theory." He showed how all humans are driven to evaluate themselves as accurately as possible, and he suggested that people evaluate their own opinions and abilities by comparing themselves to others with whom they come into contact, so that they can make sure they are getting it right, and in that way they can properly understand themselves.

As the years progressed, Festinger and his students expanded the theory to focus on the idea of social comparison as a route to self-enhancement. Not only do we better understand ourselves by comparing ourselves to others, but we can use this approach as a platform to improve ourselves, or at the very least as a gauge to see how we might improve.

I think that Moses wanted to ensure that no Jew ever got so caught up in their own stratum that they became excluded from social comparison. The success of the covenant hinged on its equal application to all.

Everyone was in this together, notwithstanding where they stood by any measure of human existence — age, gender, social status, wealth, or intelligence. None of it makes any difference when it comes to upholding the covenant, and in fact the covenant needs a spread of everything if each person who is bound by it is going to successfully be a part of it.

And that is what Maimonides means when he says that those who exclude themselves from the community are never going to do teshuva properly. How can you truly repent if you have no yardstick to measure your behavior? And that yardstick is the range of people in your community — young and old, from all walks of life, and from every kind of background.

By engaging within that group, you will not only be able to accurately understand yourself, but you will find inspiration for self-improvement that will take you to the next level.

That, after all, is the purpose of teshuva, and that is why it is so important to be deeply embedded in a community — so that your teshuva can work.

THE LEGEND OF RABBI AMNON RECONSIDERED

first published September 6, 2018

Unlike all the other major and minor Jewish festivals, Rosh Hashana and Yom Kippur are not connected to a narrative counterpart. There is no exodus from Egypt or Sinai revelation, nor are there quaint wilderness dwellings. There are no villains to speak of — no Pharaoh, Haman or Antiochus; nor are there any heroes for us to celebrate, such as Moses, Esther, and Judah Maccabee.

It is a vacuum that leaves us with almost nothing to arouse historical meaning during this critical period in the Jewish calendar. I say "almost" because we do have the jarring story of Rabbi Amnon of Mainz, author of the prayer often cited as the one that truly captures the mood of High Holidays — Unetaneh Tokef.

Recited congregationally at a high point in the prayers, and then repeated by the cantor using one of the numerous haunting compositions that have emerged from various liturgical traditions, Unetaneh Tokef is an emotional supplication which encapsulates the urgency of Yamim Noraim (Days of Awe).

Rabbi Amnon's story was first recorded in the thirteenth century by Rabbi Isaac ben Moses of Vienna (1200–1270) in his influential book *Ohr Zarua* — a work that chronicles the rites and customs of German Jewry which went on to become a primary source of Ashkenazi customs.

Rabbi Isaac quotes Rabbi Ephraim of Bonn (1132–1196), an earlier rabbinic luminary who is most famous for his accounts of the Crusader persecutions against Jews in his own day, and he in turn named Rabbi Amnon as the author of this prayer.

Rabbi Amnon's story takes place in the early eleventh century, more than one hundred years before Rabbi Ephraim was born. At the time, Rabbi Amnon was apparently a leading Rhineland rabbi who maintained a warm relationship with the local archbishop.

The two religious leaders often met with each other, and among other things would engage in theological discussions and debates. At first these discussions were innocuous, but they eventually developed into attempts by the archbishop to convert

Rabbi Amnon to Christianity. Rabbi Amnon continuously resisted the conversion pressure, until, on one occasion, feeling more intimidated than usual, he asked to be given three days to think about it.

As soon as Rabbi Amnon arrived home, he regretted his response and decided not to return to the archbishop with an answer. A few days passed after the three-day deadline without any communication between the two, and the archbishop had Rabbi Amnon arrested and he was brought to him in chains, whereupon the Rabbi requested that his tongue be cut out for having misled the archbishop, as he was never going to convert.

The archbishop dismissed this suggestion, and instead offered Rabbi Amnon the choice of conversion or dismemberment. The pious Rabbi resolutely refused to convert, even as his limbs were removed one by one. Mutilated and in pieces, he was sent home to die.

It was Rosh Hashana morning, and Rabbi Amnon directed those transporting him to take him to the synagogue. A horrified hush gripped the community as Rabbi Amnon's brutalized body was brought inside the sanctuary. It was just before the kedusha prayer during the mussaf repetition, and Rabbi Amnon began to compose a Hebrew prayer that described the awe-inspiring atmosphere of High Holidays, when we endeavor to reestablish our commitment to the principal ideals of our faith.

Although Judaism maintains that God is omnipotent, He nonetheless has a personal relationship with each and every one of us. On these days, said the dying Rabbi Amnon, our fate is decided:

מִי יִחְיֶה? וּמִי יָמוּת? מִי בְקִצּוֹ? וּמִי לֹא בְקִצּוֹ?

Who will live and who will die?

Who will die at the proper time, and who will die before their time?

With his last breath, Rabbi Amnon proposed the only three things that can alter our fate:

תְּשׁוּבָה תְּפִלָּה צְדָקָה

Repentance, prayer, and acts of kindness.

And then he was gone.

The following year before Rosh Hashana, Rabbi Amnon appeared in a dream to his colleague, Rabbi Kalonymus ben Meshullam, and insisted that he insert Unetaneh Tokef into the liturgy, and that it should become a permanent fixture of the High Holidays prayers. Thereafter, Rabbi Amnon's tragic deathbed story became a staple narrative accompaniment to the High Holidays, heavily featured in sermons and festival prayer books.

The implied lesson of this jarring story was that Rabbi Amnon realized too late that his grisly fate had been decided on Rosh Hashana and Yom Kippur of the previous year, at a time when he had felt no threat from his friend the archbishop. The reason he composed the prayer and insisted on its permanent inclusion was to warn us against the hubris of complacency in the face of destiny, and to fire us up in anticipation of the unexpected.

But while this is both a wonderful lesson and appropriately timed, the legend of Rabbi Amnon is exactly that — a legend. Despite our detailed knowledge of rabbinic leadership in the

Rhineland during this era, there is absolutely no record of a Rabbi Amnon in Mainz, nor anywhere else for that matter.

Additionally, the torture and death of Rabbi Amnon bear remarkable similarities to the martyrdom story of the seventh-century Catholic saint, Emmeram of Regensburg. Indeed, traditional German folklore is full of stories which include shocking and gratuitous violence.

As recently as the nineteenth century, the German *Struwwelpeter* moral lessons short-story collection for children included the alarmingly violent *Die Geschichte vom Daumenlutscher*, in which a mother warns her son not to suck his thumbs, and after he disobeys her a roving tailor comes along and cuts off his thumbs with a giant pair of scissors. The rest of the stories in the collection are similarly grotesque.

Clearly the Rabbi Amnon story dovetails with a familiar Teutonic literary genre. It was also recorded for posterity at a time when German Jewry was reeling from Crusader atrocities against Jews. What is certain is that it has nothing whatsoever to do with the composition of Unetaneh Tokef, a fact that was proven beyond any doubt when the very same prayer was found in an eleventh century Middle Eastern Cairo Genizah fragment.

But while I will leave it to others to speculate on the origins of both the prayer and the strange legend of Rabbi Amnon, rather than finding this iconoclastic myth-busting revision disturbing, I actually find it quite liberating. Because as it turns out, the Yamim Noraim were never meant to be associated with stories and legends. Unlike other festivals where stories evoke the mood of the day, on Rosh Hashana and Yom Kippur they would be nothing but a distraction.

During these Days of Awe, we reflect on our lives and future unencumbered by literary gimmicks and narrative crutches. Rather we consider simple questions — "Are we connected to God?" "Will we live?" "Will we die?"

Hopefully, we will merit answers that bode well for us, for our families and for our communities, so that we may look forward to a wonderful year ahead.

PARTNERING WITH GOD

first published September 29, 2017

The saintly Apter Rav, Rabbi Abraham Joshua Heschel (1748–1825), was also known as the *Ohev Yisrael* after his book of that name. *Ohev Yisrael* means "Lover of Israel", and the Apter Rav was known for his enormous and unconditional love for every Jew.

In his signature book the Apter Rav poses the age-old question: Why did God need to create the world? Of course, he was hardly the first rabbi to ask this question — it crops up in the Talmud, in Kabbalah, in Jewish philosophy, and regularly within traditional works of theology. But the Apter Rav's answer is so beautiful and so meaningful. According to him, before God created the world, He could do everything except for one thing. He couldn't give.

It's simple if you think about it. Before the world was created, God had no one to receive anything, and so He was not able to give. Therefore, says the Apter Rav, the purpose of creation is giving. And when we give, we meet the highest goal — and possibly the only goal — of creation.

But there is something else that fits into the same paradigm. Before the creation of humanity, God could not partner with anyone. Partnership is another form of giving, because it allows two individuals to be greater than the sum of their parts. When I partner with God, what I do is not **for** God, but **of** God and together **with** God.

Being a good Jew is not just about doing what God demands. It's about God needing our cooperation to achieve His objectives for creation.

Before creation God permeated every aspect of existence. Everything was at one with everything else. There was no room for anything else. In order to create the world, God had to withdraw himself — tzimtzum, as it is known in Kabbalah — to create space for another. God made room for us to exist, thereby allowing us to be collaborators in His enterprise.

For example, God chose not to visit the sick, so that we could visit the sick; and God chose not to directly feed the poor, so that we could be His partners in feeding the poor. God left room in His world so that you and I could be His agents — so that we can give and be givers, just like Him. And what the *Ohev Yisrael* is really saying is that we are all predestined to be givers.

Interestingly, there is research that proves the Apter Rav's point. Lara Aknin, a Canadian social psychologist, has done studies that demonstrate the correlation between giving and happiness across ages, by looking at the relationship between happiness and pro-social behavior. She has looked at the relationship between money and happiness, and whether people are happier spending money on others than when they spend the same amount of money on themselves.

The results of Professor Aknin's research are remarkable. She has found that generous spending on others leads to higher levels of happiness than when you spend money on yourself. She also found that children as young as two years old experience greater happiness when sharing their own resources — such as candy or toys — with others than when receiving the same treats exclusively for themselves.

The way Professor Aknin proved her theory was by comparing scenarios in which very young children get a candy for themselves to situations where they give candy to a stuffed monkey that they are told loves getting candy. She then monitored their facial expressions for signs of happiness. The results overwhelmingly showed greater joy when they gave the candy to the stuffed monkey.

Aknin and her collaborators have also found that business teams and sports teams perform better when they engage in pro-social spending on each other. The data resulting from her research uniformly suggests that we enjoy giving much more than we enjoy taking.

My question, therefore, is this: As we enter the uncharted territory of the New Year, do we want to be happy? We were created to be givers, by God who created us so that He could give, and all the research points to the fact that when we give we will be happy.

In which case, if we want to be happy this year we need to find a way of giving more — more time, more love, more of ourselves, and more of our resources. And we need to make sure that even if we are the recipients of other people's giving, we must still also make sure to be givers ourselves.

That is why teshuva (repentance) and tefilla (prayer) are not enough to ensure that God will tear up the negative verdict for the upcoming year. We need to add the magic ingredient of tzedaka — which means charity and giving. Each of us must engage in tzedaka at our own level, and each of us in our own way — but we all need to do it. It is why we were created, and it is what God truly wants from us.

WHO WAS BEING TESTED AT THE AKEIDA?

first published September 20, 2017

The story of Abraham almost sacrificing Isaac, known in Hebrew as the Akeida, is read on the second day of Rosh Hashana. The story is neither very long, nor very detailed, but it ranks as one of the most controversial narratives in the Torah. While one could certainly examine it through the eyes of Isaac and Sarah, most of the commentaries see the Akeida as Abraham's story — a triumph of his faith in God, even when he was asked by God to commit filicide.

And yet, to many of us, this brand of blind faith is extremely disturbing. How could Abraham have agreed to kill his own child? Why didn't he challenge God, as he did when God told him He was about to destroy Sodom and Gomorrah?

The late Elie Wiesel offered a brilliant if somewhat jarring insight into this episode — an insight only a Holocaust survivor could conjure up and get away with. The Akeida may have started out as God testing Abraham, he suggests, but Abraham quickly turned the tables and turned it into a test of his own — a test aimed at God.

By fully and enthusiastically complying with God's command to sacrifice his son, it was as if Abraham was saying: "I defy You, God. Yes, I submit to Your will — but let us see whether You shall go through with what You are asking me to do in the end. Will You remain passive and remain silent when the life of my son — who is also Your son — is at stake?"

Wiesel goes on to offer a compelling scenario. In the final analysis, there were three victories for Abraham as a direct result of the Akeida. The first was that Abraham forced God to change His mind, as it were, and spare Isaac. The second was that Abraham forced God to involve Himself in the Akeida endgame, when he rejected the agency of the angel messenger. And the third result was that Abraham compelled God to allow this story to be invoked whenever His descendants erred before Him, as a reminder of what happened, and to ensure His mercy.

On Rosh Hashana we acknowledge God's control over every aspect of our lives, and we declare ourselves to be totally in His hands. By doing so, we deliberately emulate Abraham's calculated blind faith at the Akeida, reminding God that He doesn't really want us to suffer, just as He didn't want Isaac to die.

The paradox of Abraham's compliance with God's instruction to sacrifice Isaac, is that by leaving his son's fate in God's hands, he was challenging God to come to the rescue. As it turns out, it was precisely this blind faith that turned him from being a helpless victim into the hero of faith who was assured of God's help even in the darkest moment.

IT'S NOT ALL ABOUT YOU

first published September 19, 2017

There are very few groups of people about whom one can tell jokes these days. Although, I recently discovered a category of people that everyone doesn't mind making fun of or hearing jokes about: Narcissists.

Here's one for you: How many narcissists does it take to change a light bulb? One. The narcissist holds the bulb while the whole world revolves around him.

And here's another one: A woman came to see me a few months ago and she told me she was divorced. When I asked her why, she told me she divorced her husband for religious reasons — he thought he was God, and she didn't.

And now a story — and just to be clear, this one is not a joke; it's true. About fifteen years ago a guy came to see me, and he told me that he wanted me to help him find a wife. The guy was in his late 30s — you know what it's like, 39 is the longest year.

We sat in my office, and he took out a notepad, and began reading me a list of all the things he needed his prospective wife to be: "She needs to be tall, beautiful, college educated, a good job, but not too independent, from a nice family but not too involved with them…"

The list went on and on, and I sat there looking at this guy rattling off the checklist.

Eventually, he was done, and I was quiet. He said to me, "Well, what do you think?"

"What do I think? I think it's a very impressive list, and I think any woman with all those attributes and qualities would make a fantastic wife. But I have one question, and don't take this the wrong way. This girl you are describing is presumably out there somewhere, and I am pretty sure she also has a list of all the things she wants her husband to be. What do you think is on her list, and are you confident that you match up to all the things on that list?"

He stuttered something, but it became evident that he had never even considered this angle. It had never been about her, or about what she wanted, because it was always all about him. A true narcissist. Perhaps that's why he wasn't married at the age of 39!

In the Haftorah that we read on Rosh Hashana we recall the story of Hannah, the barren wife of Elkanah, and how she prayed for a child. As a result of her prayer that child was born, and he would go on to become the prophet Samuel, one of Jewish history's most influential leaders — a man who changed the course of our nation's destiny when he plucked a young unknown man called David from obscurity, made him king, and through him founded the Jewish royal family, the House of David.

Rabbi Ḥayyim of Volozhin, commenting on this Haftorah, points out that the verse describing Hannah's prayer does not use the expression we would expect "vatitpallel **el** Hashem" (and she prayed **to** God). Instead, the verse says "vatitpallel **al** Hashem," which translates as, "she prayed **over** God" or "**on** God" (I Sam 1:10). Why the strange phrasing?

Rabbi Ḥayyim of Volozhin answers that the minor word change is there to teach us something incredibly important. Hannah's prayer is the scriptural source for the Amidah, the most important of all our prayers, recited three times every day. It is a prayer that contains nineteen separate blessings, thirteen of which are requests for things that we need in our lives — knowledge, health, success, good leaders, a good system of justice, and other similarly important requirements.

But how exactly are we meant to pray? We are asking God for stuff. It seems like we have a long list of things we need — "I need this! I need that!" And we instinctively know that this is not the way we should be praying. The Zohar says that anyone who comes to God with a list of requests is acting like a dog that barks at its master — "Give! Give! Give!"

And even though on Rosh Hashana we don't submit any overt requests, we know that one of the functions of the shofar is that each note of the shofar is a means of request, a hint, as it were, of the things we need. In fact, the twelve shofar blasts — Tekiyah - Shevarim – Teruah - Tekiyah; Tekiyah – Shevarim - Tekiyah; Tekiyah – Teruah - Tekiyah — correspond to the twelve middle blessings of the daily Amidah (the thirteenth blessing, ve'lamalshinim, was added at a later stage of Jewish history). How is that appropriate for Rosh Hashana?

Moreover, how could Hannah devote an entire prayer to pleading for a son? Isn't that just very selfish? How can any of us base our prayers on such a faulty foundation? How can we devote so much of the Amidah to making requests?

The answer is that none of us should be praying "**el** Hashem," **to** God, bringing to Him a long laundry list of our personal needs and wants. Rather we need to pray "**al** Hashem," thinking about God's wants, and thinking about God's needs.

Hannah knew that the world needed a special person like her son Samuel who could lead the nation, be a spiritual inspiration, and shape their future. She knew that this was what God wanted. His people, the Jewish people, were floundering — and they needed Samuel. So, she prayed to God to give her the child that would benefit God, and in fact she later went and delivered Samuel into a life of public service, incubated by Eli Hacohen, so that Samuel could become the great leader he was meant to be.

Had Samuel never been born, the Godliness he brought to the world would have been absent. Hannah prayed "**al** Hashem", not "**el** Hashem" — she didn't come to God with a narcissistic request, she came to Him wanting to fulfill God's purpose through her.

We have the custom on Rosh Hashana evenings to eat a range of symbolic foods with accompanying prayers. Apple dipped in honey — so that we have a sweet year; a fish head — so that we are leaders, not followers; a pomegranate — so that we be plentiful, like the seeds of a pomegranate; and other similarly themed items.

Everyone thinks that the reason we eat these symbolic foods is because it is not enough to just ask for the list of things that we want, but we have to go a step further and translate those requests into symbolic actions to make them more real, and to give them more weight.

The truth is exactly the opposite. A symbol is just a hint. Our main concern on Rosh Hashana must be simple — for the world to be filled with the glory of God. But, while we are in the zone, as an aside, we sneak in a little hint about some of our own personal needs and wants as well. Not openly, but with symbolic foods and the use of puns — symbols and hints, because this is all secondary to our real focus, namely God's glory. We are saying — without actually saying it — that to make sure our primary directive is fulfilled, we need some help with other stuff to make it happen.

After Hannah finished praying, the text tells us (I Sam. 1:18):

וַתֵּלֶךְ הָאִשָּׁה לְדַרְכָּהּ וַתֹּאכַל וּפָנֶיהָ לֹא הָיוּ לָהּ עוֹד

**The woman went on her way, she ate,
and she wasn't sad anymore.**

In the first instance, this appears to be a great verse for all those who think that the best way to treat depression is to feed people. "Aww, you're sad? Come let me give you some lokshen kugel and brisket with fried onions. You'll feel much better." After all, who needs anti-depressants if you've got the recipe for latkes?

But in reality, that's not what the verse means. Hannah prayed, and she felt much better. So much better that she started eating again, and she cheered up. She went back to being her old self.

What had changed for her? Nothing! She had no guarantee that her prayers would be answered, or that her dire situation would improve. So why did she cheer up?

The answer is clear. It was not that Hannah was confident that her prayers would be answered. We know feeling that way is foolish hubris — there are no guarantees, no matter how hard we pray. What changed was that now that she had prayed properly — and she knew she had done it properly, for all the right reasons — she was willing to accept her situation even if it did not turn out exactly as she had hoped it would.

We have to do what we have to do, to pray that we are given the chance to fulfill God's mission for us, but once that effort is done, a person has to accept whatever it is that God chooses to do. Our duty on Rosh Hashana is not to close the circle. We need to do our piece, make sure it's not just about ourselves, but only about God.

Hopefully, if this is our mind frame, God will give us all the help we need to fulfill that mission. And when you're done praying, you should go and eat, and be happy — and whatever happens will happen.

YOUR THOUGHTS CREATE YOUR FUTURE

first published September 16, 2017

A couple of weeks ago, self-help supremo and bestselling author Louise Hay died in her sleep at the age of 90.

Born into poverty in Los Angeles in 1926, as a young child Hay was both physically abused by her stepfather and sexually abused by a neighbor. A school dropout at the age of fifteen, she gave birth to a daughter on her sixteenth birthday.

Unmarried and without the means to support the baby, Hay was forced to give her daughter up for adoption, and never saw her again. She eventually got married at the age of twenty-eight, but the marriage ended in divorce fourteen years later. Hay never remarried, nor did she have any more children.

Just that biography is enough to dampen anyone's day. What possible hope could someone have after such a horrible start to life? And it only got worse. In her early 50s, Hay was diagnosed with cervical cancer. But by that point Hay had stumbled across the teachings of Ernest Holmes (1887–1960) — the "New Thought" guru and founder of the Religious Science movement — and she adopted his metaphysical theories about a positive mindset affecting one's physical wellbeing.

Hay later claimed it was this approach that helped beat off her cancer, allowing her to live a healthy productive life long after the doctors had predicted her demise.

After beating cancer, Hay became a leading advocate of using positive thinking as a way of fighting off disease, and in 1984 published her bestselling self-help bible, *You Can Heal Your Life*, which has since sold more than 40 million copies in over 30 different languages.

According to the *New York Times*, "Louise Hay is one of the best-selling authors in history, and none of the women who have sold more [books] — like J. K. Rowling, Danielle Steel, and Barbara Cartland — owned a publishing empire, [nor did they] change the spiritual landscape of America and several of its Western allies."

It goes without saying that Louise Hay had her critics — people who accused her of being overly simplistic, or of giving desperate people unrealistic hope, based on quackery and New Age flimflam.

And although such accusations are not entirely without foundation, they kind of miss the point. While it would be foolish to refuse medical attention at the onset of a fatal disease, in favor of thinking positive thoughts as the curative remedy, every doctor will tell you that patients who have been diagnosed with a potentially fatal illness who choose to adopt a positive approach, are far more likely to pull through than those who regard their fate as signed and sealed. In the end, we are only ever able to make our dreams come true if we don't see them as dreams, but as credible possibilities.

If anything, the most inspiring aspect of Louise Hay's life is not actually her upbeat theories about self-belief as the key to health and happiness, but the fact that in middle age, after enduring a miserable life that for most people would have meant a descent into bitter old age, she rose to the greatest heights of success at no one else's expense and acted as an inspiration for others to do the same. Her life story is the living embodiment of making the impossible happen, against all the odds.

Most of us undoubtedly believe New Age optimism and Religious Science metaphysics to be the domain of the gullible and the desperate, but that is not the view of Judaism. In one of his final speeches to the nation he had led for forty years, Moses dismissed anyone who entertained the idea that the commandments of the Torah are ethereal concepts, beyond the reach of mere mortals (Deuteronomy 30:12):

לֹא בַשָּׁמַיִם הִוא לֵאמֹר מִי יַעֲלֶה לָּנוּ הַשָּׁמַיְמָה וְיִקָּחֶהָ לָּנוּ

It is not in the Heavens, so you say who can lift us up to the Heavens so that we can acquire it.

The medieval commentator, Rashi (1040–1105), makes an astounding assertion based on this verse. If the Torah had been in Heaven, he says, we would have been expected to go there and acquire it. Later rabbis struggled with Rashi's suggestion, particularly as it seems to undermine the impact of Moses's declaration.

Of all the suggested solutions to Rashi's puzzling assertion, I particularly like the one offered by Rabbi Abraham Bornsztain (1855–1926), author of the seminal work *Shem MiShmuel*.

Rashi is telling us that had we needed the means to get to Heaven to acquire the Torah, God would have given those to us, because the Torah and all its accompanying obligations must be attainable. This means that if any part of the Torah seems impossible to us, we should know that we have all been equipped to accomplish and achieve whatever God expects of us.

This idea is a phenomenally liberating concept. Even when Torah obligations seem to be asking us to ascend the Heavens, we need to know that this simply cannot be the case. For some of us it might be daily prayers at the synagogue. For others it might be certain aspects of Sabbath observance. Yet others might find setting aside regular time to study Torah a remote fantasy.

Moses was not suggesting we should see any of these as easy. Instead, he was telling us that there is no spiritual aspiration that is impossible if we set our sights on getting there.

And fundamentally, that is the core message of the High Holidays. As we consider our many limitations, and reflect on all our lofty aspirations, we might imagine that any change for the better over the coming year is as remote for us as a journey to Heaven.

Moses's message echoes through the ages telling us that nothing God wants us to achieve should ever be considered impossible. And while it may sound like New Age jargon, this idea is deeply embedded in our theology as the bedrock of our faith.

IT'S NOT THAT COMPLICATED

first published October 2, 2016

We all like to feel that we live very sophisticated lives in an increasingly sophisticated world. Everything around us is full of complexity. Getting the balance right is complicated. We need to keep our eyes on so many balls. Everything is in motion.

I remember watching the TV show *Star Trek* as a kid, and although I was never an obsessive "Trekkie," there was one aspect of the show that fascinated me — although I do feel that it was never adequately explained. I'm talking about three-dimensional chess. It seemed so much more exciting than plain old two-dimensional chess. Multiple boards on multiple levels, with pieces moving from one board to another — it was so compelling.

Until recently I was sure that 3D chess was an invention of *Star Trek* scriptwriters, but after some recent downtime Google research, I discovered that it predates *Star Trek* by many decades. Believe it or not, 3D chess is a real game, invented in 1907 by a German occultist called Dr. Ferdinand Maack (1861–1930). In fact, there are no less than 50 variations of the game.

As I read through the complex rules of 3D chess, with all of its multiple boards and multiple variations, it struck me that life is much more like 3D chess than it is like the 2D version.

Don't we all operate on multiple platforms? Family. Community. Country. Relationships with family. Relationships with friends. Relationships with work colleagues. The economy. The environment. God. Nature. Science. Income. Expenses. Emotions. Logic. Risk. Ethics. Time. Health. Weather. Distance. Intelligence. Politics. It's a really long list, and there's so much that goes into the mix and that we feed into every decision we make, or that affects everything that happens to us.

Sometimes, when we reflect on Rosh Hashana and Yom Kippur, it all seems so simple. Maimonides writes, in *Hilkhot Teshuva* (*Laws of Repentance*), that life is made up of binary options — good vs. evil, life vs. death — and on Rosh Hashana and Yom Kippur we face God and examine ourselves on that basis. We hear the primitive sound of the shofar blasts. We talk about God as a father, as a king, as a shepherd. There's no complex theology in the liturgy, and very little by way of sophistication.

But life isn't actually so simple. It's not all black and white. Although we know that there is good in the world, and people whose entire lives are devoted to good — we also know that we are not that. And in the same vein, although we know that there is evil in the world — Hitler, ISIS, urban terrorism — we know for certain that we are not that either.

Of course, we know that there is life and death. But connecting these things conceptually to stark definitions of good and evil seems like an oversimplification, and so unrelatable to the reality of our lives. Why waste High Holidays on this kind of two-dimensional simplicity? Why don't we use these special days as an opportunity to explore the meaning of an omnipotent creator

God? Surely that would be more useful and so much more meaningful.

I have always felt that this problem affects the way we relate to Rosh Hashana and Yom Kippur. How can we possibly treat our life as if it is a game of 2D chess, when in reality our lives are much more like 3D chess? Wouldn't it be better if Rosh Hashana and Yom Kippur were more 3D? Wouldn't it be better if they somehow reflected all the grey area in between black and white?

Those who study Talmud for the first time are often surprised by the very extreme ideas or scenarios suggested by the Talmud in an attempt to establish Jewish law. One famous piece in Tractate Pesaḥim (10b) involves a long discussion about a house that has been cleared of ḥametz before Passover.

The Gemara poses the following question: "What is the law if a mouse enters the house with a piece of bread in its mouth, and then a mouse leaves the house with a piece of bread in its mouth? Do we say that the same mouse that entered the house left the house, or do we assume that it is a different mouse and that the house now contains ḥametz?" The discussion continues, and the mouse scenarios become ever more obscure and unlikely.

Clearly, the point of these questions is not mouse anthropology, nor is it vermin control — rather the Gemara wishes to convey the extent to which we must take precautions to protect our homes from ḥametz on Passover.

The real lesson of the Gemara in Pesaḥim is this — don't get distracted by the improbability of the situation; look for the underlying message. We always need to be thinking — what is the subtext of a discussion? Because that subtext may be more important than any legal principle that could be gleaned from thinking through the problem to its most extreme destination.

I want to share two stories with you, both of which exemplify this idea. And I hope both of these stories will offer us an insight into the seeming superficiality and oversimplification of the objectives of Rosh Hashana and Yom Kippur.

A short time ago a rabbi in Baltimore tragically lost his son to cancer. He was a young married man, with three children. A friend of mine from New York who is a close friend of the rabbi drove to Baltimore during the period of Shiva (traditional week of mourning).

Apparently, there is a group of about a dozen young disillusioned ex-yeshiva students in Baltimore who have recently started meeting regularly. This group has decided to walk away from Torah-observant Orthodox Judaism. No Shabbat. No festivals. No kosher. No Torah study. No prayer. I am not sure why this has happened, but in Baltimore the group is quite well-known.

Some of the guys in this group grew up and went to school with the young man who died. Unlike them, their friend was a rock of faith. He died in August. Just two months earlier, in June, he wrote a public letter that was published online in which he asked for help from anyone who knew him. He didn't ask for money. Nor did he ask for a huge life-changing commitment. He simply requested that people turn off their cellphones before going into synagogue to pray, so that they can pray better, and as a result of that undistracted prayer perhaps he would merit a recovery. Although, sadly, that outcome was not to be.

In any event, while my friend from New York was at the Shiva house in Baltimore he overheard a discussion among the visitors about this group of former yeshiva students. One person said that he had heard the group was so shocked by the death of their friend, they had decided to fully observe one Shabbat, and to put on tefillin (phylacteries) and pray properly on one weekday, to honor his memory.

It's not unusual at a Shiva for a discussion to descend into banalities, and this one was no exception. Was this memorial commitment really such a good thing, someone asked, or was it actually pointless? Should the group be praised, criticized, or ignored for deciding to memorialize their friend in this way?

The conversation became quite heated. One person was particularly agitated: "What's the point of keeping one Shabbat," he blurted out, "if they didn't observe it the week before, and next week they won't do it either? It's as if they are mocking Judaism! How does that honor the memory of the person who died?"

The room went quiet, and everyone looked at the father of the young man who had been sitting there, so far without saying a word. He was quiet for a moment. Then he said: "How can you say one Shabbat is pointless? What wouldn't I do to spend just one more Shabbat with my son?"

Boom! You see, for the person who lost his son there was no complexity. His yardstick was very different to everyone else's. He wasn't hearing a discussion about the relative merits of former yeshiva students observing one Shabbat. This discussion was not about a mouse with ḥametz. He had crystal clarity. Every day is precious. Every positive experience is priceless.

The Talmud says (Shabbat 153a) one should treat each day as if it is our last. But in the real world, who does that? Except for our last day, every other day is not our last! Which is why when we are confronted by a Rosh Hashana or a Yom Kippur, the black-and-white aspect seems so overstated. Didn't we do exactly the same last year? And the year before? And the year before that? And here we are again!

Moreover — and this is the point the guy at the Shiva was trying to make — why keep one Shabbat if you are never going to keep Shabbat again? Why bother with anything Jewish if you don't buy into everything?

Let me add one more story. It takes this idea one step further. It's a painful story with a painful lesson.

There is a fellow who owns a jewelry store in Israel. A few weeks ago, a little girl — maybe eight or nine years old — walked into the store and said to him, "I am here to buy a bracelet."

She looked through the glass cases and pointed to a bracelet that was priced at $3,000.

The shop owner was surprised. "You really want to buy that bracelet?"

"Yes," she replied.

"Wow, you have very good taste. Who do you want to buy it for?"

"For my older sister."

"Oh, that is so nice!" the storekeeper replied, "Why do you want to buy your older sister this bracelet?"

"Because I don't have a mother or father," the little girl said, "they both died, and my older sister takes care of us — me and my siblings. So, we want to buy her a gift, and I have the money to pay for it."

She took a bag of coins out of her pocket and poured them out onto the counter. The storeowner counted them up; the total was just under eight shekels — a little less than two dollars.

The shop owner looked at the coins and then at the girl.

"Wow!" he said, "That's exactly what the bracelet costs!"

While wrapping up the bracelet, his eyes welled up with tears. He said to the girl, "You write a card to your sister while I wrap up the bracelet."

He finished wrapping the bracelet, wiped away his tears, and handed the little girl the bracelet.

A few hours later the girl's older sister came into the store holding the bracelet in her hand.

"I'm terribly embarrassed," she said. "My sister should not have come here. She shouldn't have taken this bracelet without paying."

"What are you talking about?" the store owner asked.

"Are you kidding? This bracelet costs hundreds or maybe thousands of dollars. My little sister doesn't have that kind of money — she doesn't even have ten dollars! It's obvious she didn't pay for it."

"You couldn't be more wrong," the storekeeper replied. "She paid me in full. She paid 7 shekels, 80 agurot, and a broken heart."

"I want to tell you something," continued the man. "I am a widower. I lost my wife some years ago. People come into my store every single day. They come in and buy expensive jewelry, and all these people can afford it. But when your sister walked in, with her 7 shekels and 80 agurot — for the first time since my wife died, I felt what love really means."

During the High Holy Days, we come to the Almighty and we want to buy something very expensive. We want to buy life. The best life possible. It's the most expensive bracelet in the jewelry store. But we cannot afford it. We don't have enough money to pay for it. We don't have the merits. We've been saving up all year, but all we have is 7 shekels and 80 agurot.

We come to God, we empty out our pockets, and we give him whatever we have. We tell Him how much we love our family, our community, our Judaism. We want to be the best we can be for them. We want to be the best we can be for God. God owns the jewelry store. He has the diamond bracelet we want, but none of us really has enough to pay for it. All we have is love.

God says, "Thank you so much for visiting My store; thank you so much for your mitzvot. It's more than enough. You don't know how long it's been since I've felt what love means."

He sees how much we love Him and how much we yearn to improve, and He says, "You know what? You have touched my heart. You can have what you want; you have paid in full."

When we think of the Yamim Noraim (High Holidays) as unsophisticated, it is because we overrate ourselves as well-heeled sophisticates. But how does what we need out of life compare with what we have to offer God. It's not an equal playing field. All of us are little kids walking into the jewelry store picking out the most expensive bracelet. We are the op-ed armchair critics discussing the relative merits of keeping just one Shabbat.

Rosh Hashana is so real exactly because it is so simple. The underlying message is that, in actual fact — life is not 3D chess; it is simple 2D chess.

If we are looking for complexity, we are missing the point. In the end it is the simple things that matter. Love. Health. Trying to be a good person. We need Rosh Hashana to get back to basics. And once we are there, we can consider some of the complexities.

Rebbe Naḥman of Breslov writes that simple faith is the most powerful faith of all. All the philosophy and theology in the world will never result in simple faith. Only simple things can do that.

WE CAN REALLY MAKE A DIFFERENCE

first published September 10, 2015

This past Tuesday after shaḥarit (morning services) I shared a short piece from Maimonides' legal work, *Mishneh Torah*, with those who had joined us for prayers. The piece I shared is widely known and quoted, debated, and discussed, and appears in the third chapter of Maimonides' monumental *Hilkhot Teshuva* (*Laws of Repentance*).

Basing himself on a Talmudic source, Maimonides states that a person who has performed more of God's commandments than he has transgressed God's restrictions is a tzaddik, a righteous individual. If the opposite is true, however, the person is considered a rasha, an evil individual. And if the balance between good deeds and bad deeds is exactly 50–50, the person is considered a beinoni — neither righteous nor evil but hovering somewhere in between the two.

This rule doesn't just apply to individuals, says Maimonides. If an entire country has more merits than iniquities, it will be considered a righteous country, while if a country is more sinful than virtuous it will be considered a wicked country, with all that this entails.

The point Maimonides seems to be making is that just one mitzvah or one sin can literally tip the balance, resulting in real consequences. In other words, it is not an accumulation of good or bad deeds that leads to a particular outcome. Rather it could be one seemingly unimportant act that determines one's identity and ultimate fate. Proverbially, the tiny weightless straw added to the heavy burden on a camel's back might just turn out to be what causes the camel to collapse.

Many of the rabbis who expound on Maimonides' monumental composition are uncomfortable with this notion. It seems too black and white, too simplistic. Life is so much more complex and turning human existence into a binary system that seeks to align human fate with single acts, and the fate of countries with such finely tuned calibrations, doesn't fit in with the way the world seems to work.

Although such objections make sense, this week I had a reality check enabling me to see the world from Maimonides' perspective, when I joined 1,200 people who traveled to Washington, DC from all over the United States as part of an AIPAC-led effort to lobby our elected officials on the issue of the Iran nuclear deal, and to convince waverers to vote against the deal.

Some weeks ago, together with Rabbi Alan Kalinsky of the Orthodox Union's West Coast office, and Rabbi Kalman Topp, senior rabbi at Beth Jacob Congregation of Beverly Hills, I went to the local California office of Congressman Ted Lieu, to discuss the Iran Nuclear Deal issue with him.

It was evident from our discussions that Lieu was under phenomenal pressure from the White House and the State Department to side with the deal, but also that he instinctively found himself doubting what he was being told about the deal and what he was being asked to do.

Our visit and similar visits by others, along with the many hundreds of phone calls he received, eventually tipped the balance, and on Wednesday morning he informed our delegation in Washington, DC that he would vote against the deal if the issue was debated on the House floor. We gave him a standing ovation.

The reason I mention this is that I'm sure every single person who lobbied Congressman Ted Lieu, all of whom no doubt felt strongly on the issue of this dreadful deal, surely thought to themselves, "What difference can I make? I am only one person!" In the end, though, it was all of us who bothered to lobby — ordinary people like me and my colleagues, and all the others who beat a path to Ted Lieu's door, one by one — that made the difference.

Lieu's office tallied every phone call, and his staff took notes during every meeting. And, as a result of all of our efforts, individual effort by individual effort, he decided to vote with his conscience and oppose the deal. Had we not made that effort he might have chosen to do what was easier and surely better for his long-term political prospects — to side with his party on this issue, and to support the president.

It doesn't stop there. In Washington you really get the sense that one person can make a difference. One senator voting one way, or another can make the difference between a bill passing or not passing. One congressman can make the difference between a veto-proof majority and a majority that can be ignored by the executive branch.

Individuals count. Individual acts count. Each person can make a difference. A difference in our lives, for our families, for our country, and for the world.

In Parshat Nitzavim, Moses begins his monumental address to the Jewish nation very curiously (Deut. 29:9):

אַתֶּם נִצָּבִים הַיּוֹם כֻּלְּכֶם לִפְנֵי ה' אֱלֹהֵיכֶם רָאשֵׁיכֶם שִׁבְטֵיכֶם

זִקְנֵיכֶם וְשֹׁטְרֵיכֶם כֹּל אִישׁ יִשְׂרָאֵל

You are all standing here today in front of God:
your leaders, your tribes, your elders, your officers,
every member of the Jewish nation.

What point is Moses making? Why bother specifying the groups if he could have just said, "Every member of the Jewish nation is standing here today"?

Evidently that was his point. As part of a group, we often rationalize that we don't count. Our individual contribution seems to be immaterial. Similarly, when we consider how we should act in our daily lives, we dismiss the opportunity of doing something good. We ask ourselves: "What difference will it make?"

In the same vein, we can think to ourselves that sneaking in something not so good doesn't matter either — after all, overall, we are good people, so what difference will it make?

But every act is important, and every person is important. If each of us would only treat each act as the one that could tip the balance and think of ourselves as the one person who could alter fate, the world would be a much better place, and all of our lives would be so much more meaningful.

You and me — we can really make a difference. And as we head into a new year, that's what we need to keep uppermost in our minds.

LONDON BRIDGE IS FALLING DOWN

first published September 25, 2014

This past summer our family did a very American thing — in late July, we went on a 1,000 mile road trip. We drove all the way from Los Angeles to the Grand Canyon, and then back to Los Angeles via the Hoover Dam and Las Vegas.

In researching routes for the trip, we decided that on our way to the Grand Canyon we needed to stop somewhere overnight.

There are not that many choices of places to go between Los Angeles and the Grand Canyon. In the end, we opted for a town called Lake Havasu City, which none of us had ever heard of or knew anything about.

As it turns out, Lake Havasu City, Arizona, is famous for one thing and one thing only. As crazy as it sounds, this remote Arizona retirement town is home to the original London Bridge that spanned the River Thames in central London, from the 1830s until London's local government decided they needed a new bridge to replace it in the mid-1960s.

Enter Robert Paxton McCulloch (1911–1977), an aging American millionaire, who had made his fortune inventing and manufacturing chainsaws. McCulloch had decided to build a new town on the shores of Arizona's Lake Havasu, and, to propel it to fame and notoriety, he resolved to buy London Bridge and import it from England, so that it could become the town's centerpiece.

McCulloch purchased the bridge from the City of London in 1967. He then had it dismantled brick by brick and transported to Los Angeles via the Panama Canal. Finally, he had it trucked to its new home in Arizona, where it was completely reassembled. The project cost him four million dollars and took four years to complete, and as a result, London Bridge, in all its Victorian engineering glory, can now be found in sun-parched Arizona.

I'm guessing that McCulloch wanted to leave a lasting and resounding legacy. He wanted his name to resonate long after he was dead and buried. I thought about that when I saw the bridge, looking completely out of place and quite forlorn in the middle of this sleepy town, and, as I gazed at the wrought iron and the masonry that makes up the bridge, I was struck by the utter futility of McCulloch's act.

If anything I have ever seen in my life has made me think about what I am doing here in this world, why I was born, the futility of so much that we do in life, it has been seeing that bridge in Arizona. I cannot get the image out of my head, and in particular, it helped me to understand a strange Talmudic passage that had always puzzled me.

The Talmud in Eruvin (13b) records a debate between the two great late Second Temple period schools of Jewish learning, Beit Shammai and Beit Hillel.

> **For two-and-a-half years Beit Shammai and Beit Hillel debated. One said, "It would have been better for man not to have been created than to have been**

created." And the other said, "It is better that man was created rather than had he have not been created."

The topic of this debate makes no sense when you consider who these interlocutors were. Beit Shammai and Beit Hillel were not two schools of Greek philosophy. They were two centers of Jewish legal studies, with rabbis and students discussing and deciding Jewish ritual law. Why were they debating this arcane and — in terms of practical application — useless topic? And more importantly, why would the debate have taken two-and-a-half years to resolve?

The Talmudic passage continues as follows:

At the end they voted and decided that it would have been better had man not been created. However, now that man had been created, he should check his deeds [in other words, in case he has sinned, and has to repent]; or another version has it like this: he should carefully consider his deeds [in other words, decide carefully before doing any action].

What is going on in this Talmudic passage? The argument, the vote, the conclusion, and the advice, are all completely incomprehensible. If it would have been better had we not been created, why bother examining or considering our deeds? And if examining or considering our deeds could justify our existence, why would it have been better not to have been created?

There is another related topic that has long vexed both philosophers and anthropologists. It is the debate over the default nature of human beings. Is human nature intrinsically good, or is it intrinsically evil?

If, for example, a newborn baby would not be conditioned or educated at any point from birth through adulthood, or exposed to circumstances that might steer it in a particular direction, how would that person turn out? Would he or she naturally evolve into a selfless adult, with morals and a sense of justice? Or would it turn out to be an immoral, or amoral, selfish, and self-serving adult?

Of course, this experiment is pure theory, hence the debate. But it is nonetheless a troubling question.

Judaism has an answer to this question, and I would propose that this answer is the definitive answer. Human beings are born with an animal body, a selfish physical entity intent on survival by whatever means necessary — just like every other animal. The difference is that humans also have a soul that resides within them, a soul that contains all the ingredients of good, of divine justice, and morality.

Consequently, every human is a living contradiction, neither bad nor good. Instead, we are creatures with an inclination for survival that may result in us harming others due to selfishness, but we are simultaneously possessed of a powerful potential for altruism and selflessness. All we need to do is take charge of ourselves and allow our souls to be in control.

In this material world we are at a tremendous disadvantage, calibrated to desire physical things and to act selfishly, and yet we have been given the power to overcome these desires, with our souls able to overrule our animal instincts to do good, so that we are greater than the sum of our physical parts.

Let me compare this idea to something we can all relate to — the physical force called gravity. Gravity affects us all; we cannot escape it. Nevertheless, with every step we take, and every time we move, we defy gravity. Even though gravity is something we cannot escape, we still have the power to overcome it if we want to, without which we would not be able to function for even a minute.

The same principle applies to our animal instincts. We can't escape them, but we can constantly overcome them. And this was the main point of the debate between Beit Shammai and Beit Hillel. The fundamental underpinning of Judaism is the performance of mitzvot, as without mitzvot our existence would be pointless. What they were looking to find out was whether our existence is pointless even if we do mitzvot.

Why should we be born to battle our own animal instincts? Maybe it would have been better never to have been born at all? After all, why should Beit Shammai and Beit Hillel discuss and debate the laws of Shabbat observance, for example, or the dos and don'ts of ritual impurity, if there is no point in getting it right?

After this fundamental debate had raged for two-and-a-half years, Beit Shammai and Beit Hillel finally agreed that our existence is indeed pointless — but only if what we do is just about performing the act of mitzvot. Just going through the motions and discharging one's Jewish duty, in the same way that circus animals do the tricks they are trained to do, is utterly futile. It can't be right and would not have been worth God's effort. Only if we insert meaning into our acts and do them because we are defying our animal instincts rather than embracing them, do our lives have any meaning.

Observing Shabbat only matters if it is focused on building our relationship with God. The same applies to keeping kosher. The same applies to the laws of ritual purity. The same applies to charity. The same applies to interpersonal relationships. It is a constant battle, but it is that battle that makes human existence worthwhile.

Seeing London Bridge in Arizona made me realize that no matter how grand the gesture, no matter how spectacular the physical act, everything we do that is aimed at leaving a material legacy, even if it is not on such a grand scale, is ultimately futile.

Most people have never heard of Robert Paxton McCulloch, and even those who have heard of him, regard his decision to bring the London Bridge to Arizona as farcical. And yet, we are all like McCulloch, unless we choose not to be. Our acts only become worthwhile if we inject them with meaningfulness. That is the only way that we will endure beyond our lives, lasting into the spiritual realm long after our physical lives are over.

On Rosh Hashana, we resolve to inject our mitzvot with energy, spirituality, and meaningfulness, so that they turn from physical acts into soul-energizing deeds that will make our existence meaningful. The format of Rosh Hashana and Yom Kippur is geared specifically towards this plan. We are charged with doing three things — teshuva (repentance), tefilla (prayer), and tzedaka (charity).

Teshuva is checking one's deeds — our existence is not justified unless we reflect on who we are and how we can improve ourselves. Tefilla and tzedaka mean that we need to consider our deeds before we act.

By resolving to act appropriately both in our relationship with God, and in our relationship with our fellow humans, being on this world suddenly begins to make sense.

Teshuva is a very personal thing — it is private and complex. Tefilla and tzedaka are public manifestations of our relationship with God and man, and they come together best in a community setting where they are combined with each other, and where one cannot exist without the other.

FINDING TRUE MEANING IN UMAN

first published September 22, 2014

I n 2010, at the invitation of a dear friend of mine, I went to Uman for Rosh Hashana. Uman is a tiny town in rural Ukraine that had no permanent Jewish population for almost a century. Nonetheless, it remains renowned within the Jewish world as the burial site of Rabbi Naḥman of Breslov, the enigmatic Ḥasidic leader who died of tuberculosis in 1810 at the age of 38.

Reb Naḥman left behind a legacy of teachings that continue to engage and impress all those who study them. Ranging from folk stories to kabbalistic insights, from ethics to an earthy philosophy, it is clear he was possessed of a brilliant mind and an incredible insight into the human struggle to balance the harsh realities of routine existence, and the striving for a meaningful relationship with God.

Although he only had a small following when he died, and despite not being succeeded by a replacement leader, his legacy has lived on as a result of a deathbed promise to personally intercede in the "Heavenly Court" on behalf of any true penitent who visited his gravesite to recite ten specific chapters of Tehillim (psalms) on Erev Rosh Hashana.

So, for the past 200-plus years, despite the ridicule and even hostility of other Ḥasidic groups, Breslov Ḥasidim have made their way to Uman for Rosh Hashana, to honor the memory of their departed leader and to celebrate the festival at his gravesite.

My friend was pushing at an open door as I had long been attracted to this pilgrimage. My first exposure to Breslov teachings was during my teenage years, through my close association with the late Rabbi Shlomo Carlebach (1925–1994). Already then I began to read the works of Reb Naḥman, and I particularly identified with his focus on joy and resilience as a way to overcome the stresses and strains of life.

At that stage, though, I was unaware of the pilgrimage. Indeed, it was only after the fall of the Berlin Wall in 1989 that the annual Uman pilgrimage really began to attract wider attention. Every year more people would go, and what started out as just a few hundred people every year eventually evolved into many thousands.

By the time I went to Uman in 2010, the number of pilgrims was estimated at 25,000. I understand that the number is now closer to 30,000.

When I got back from Uman, I recorded my impressions of the visit in an article for London's *Jewish Chronicle* newspaper. These were my thoughts then — and they remain a timeless message that endures year after year:

> **Rabbi Naḥman of Breslov was reviled in his lifetime, even by his own family — one contemporary Ḥasidic leader is said to have guaranteed paradise for any antagonist of Rabbi**

Naḥman. Nevertheless, his teachings and message are embraced across the spectrum of Jewish life, and he is revered by Jews of every level of observance.

It was this exact thought that crossed my mind last week as I joined a record crowd at his gravesite in Uman, Ukraine, for the annual Rosh Hashana pilgrimage. More than 25,000 men — the event is exclusively male — travelled from outside Ukraine to spend this auspicious festival in close proximity to Rabbi Naḥman's last resting place.

What struck me first and foremost was the range of different types of Jews who made the effort to be there. No doubt there are other Jewish religious events that attract many thousands, and which are, in their own way, both impressive and moving. Take Meron at Lag B'Omer, or the Kol Nidrei service at the massive newly built Belz synagogue in Jerusalem. But I am certain that these events cannot compare to spending Rosh Hashana in Uman.

At Meron, you are attending as an individual or as part of a small homogenous group within the larger crowd. At Belz, or at any similar large gathering, unless you are one of the many regular members of the community, you will undoubtedly feel like an outsider, even if you may be struck by the solemnity and awe of the occasion.

In Uman, there is no such thing as an outsider. Whoever you are, and wherever you are on the religious compass, you will be embraced and welcomed by everyone else who is there. And you will find yourself doing the same to them. Uman belongs to nobody, and so it belongs to everybody. What a way to spend Rosh Hashana, when, according to our tradition, we are judged by God on the basis of how we judge others.

At one point, as I led the prayers, the hundreds of people at our minyan spontaneously joined hands and danced; singing the same words, with the same tune. A Sephardi in full Yemenite garb went by hand-in-hand with a Satmar ḥasid from Williamsburg. A long-haired Israeli sporting a Na-Nach kippah and a yeshiva boy from New York. And so, it went on. No two people were alike. But all were singing with identical enthusiasm.

Rabbi Naḥman's message of religion through joy, self-criticism and introspection, through non-judgmentalism, and eternal optimism, is reflected in this spirit of unity. Perhaps it doesn't last much beyond the return journey home and no doubt Rabbi Naḥman would have been the first one to admit that.

That is why people come back year after year, and why new people join them. Because, as Rabbi Naḥman says, just because the world isn't perfect, and each one of us isn't perfect, doesn't mean we should stop trying to reach for the stars. And Rosh

Hashana in Uman, it would seem, has become the perfect crucible to try, and then to try again.

YOM KIPPUR

THE IMPOSSIBLE IS POSSIBLE

first published September 9, 2021

Every Yom Kippur, in synagogues across the world, there are people who you never see at any other time of the year. In my view, this is a testament to the power of Jewish identity. I find it truly amazing that Jews who rarely if ever come to shul, choose the most serious day of the year to make an exception. There seems to be an instinctive understanding in the soul of every Jew that their Judaism is a serious matter, and if one comes to shul at all, it should be for something meaningful.

And then — we don't see them again until next year! But it's not just them. The challenge of Yom Kippur is something that affects all of us, even if we are regular shul attendees.

Yom Kippur is meant to be an agent of change, but in reality we all imagine ourselves to be immune to change. Although we would love to shed our bad habits — after all, we all want to be more spiritual, more learned, and more meticulous about our Judaism — we nonetheless still manage to convince ourselves that it's never going to happen. We all want to improve, but we somehow believe that self-improvement is impossible. We tell ourselves that we're just the same this year as we were last year, and it is more than likely we will be the same again next year, and the year after that.

So why bother with Yom Kippur at all?

As with so many Jewish questions, the answer lies in an unconnected digression. At the beginning of the Talmud, the very first discussion focuses on determining when a day commences (Berakhot 2a). If you ask any child when the day starts, they will tell you that it begins in the morning — but curiously, that is not the correct answer. In the secular world, a day begins at midnight — a rather strange notion, dating back to the Romans, who insisted on calculating their days using noon as the main reference point. Midnight is exactly halfway between one noon and the next, so it became the start of the day.

The Jewish day also doesn't start in the morning, but nor does it start at midnight. Instead, it begins immediately after dusk when the sky goes completely dark. The Talmud explains that this designation is based on the creation narrative in Genesis. At the conclusion of each day of creation, the Torah describes the day that had passed as "vayehi erev vayehi boker" — "it was evening, and it was morning" — which confirms that the Torah considers the night to have come before morning, and not the other way around. But although this provides us with a Torah source for why a day begins at night in Jewish law, it offers no explanation for the logic behind it.

The three daily prayers of Judaism are each linked with one of the three patriarchs. The morning prayer is associated with Abraham, the afternoon prayer with Isaac, and the evening prayer is connected to Jacob — which seems to indicate that the morning prayer, *shaharit*, is the first one, as Abraham is the first of the patriarchs.

But Rabbi Judah Loew, the celebrated Maharal of Prague (1526–1609), explains why the evening prayer, maariv, is the pinnacle of Jewish daily prayers (*Netivot Olam, Netiv Ha'Avodah 3:3*):

> **This [prayer] befits Jacob, as it corresponds to the fact that the world is in the hands of God, and the [uncertainty of] night conveys that the world is in the hands of God, and Jacob was more in the hands of God than the other patriarchs.**

The night is a time when we are at the mercy of the elements — there is no light, and no easy access to resources that can help us survive. It is only with God's help that we can make it to the morning. Jacob is the master of the night, which is why the night prayer is associated with him and not with his father or grandfather.

But how are we to understand this? Is the Maharal suggesting that Abraham, the founder of monotheism, didn't trust that God would get him through the night? Is he proposing that Isaac, who willingly allowed himself to be tied to the altar to be sacrificed, didn't believe that God would help him through the night?

A fascinating Midrash describes the early life of Abraham. As a young man Abraham was brought before the mighty Nimrod, King of Shinar (Mesopotamia), for the crime of having destroyed his father's pagan figurines. According to this Midrash, not only did Abraham refuse to apologize for his crime, but he also brazenly defended his actions.

Nimrod decided to execute Abraham by burning him alive, and he was thrown into a furnace. But God saved Abraham, "because Jacob will be his grandson." The Heavenly court erupted in uproar. "Why should Jacob be the reason for Abraham's miraculous reprieve? Why not Abraham himself?"

In the Midrash, God responds with a very strange statement. "All of Jacob's children are going to be perfect," He says, "as opposed to Abraham — who will have Ishmael; and [as opposed to] Isaac — who will have Esau."

But is this actually true? Were Jacob's children so perfect? Glance through the Torah portions that narrate the story of Jacob's family — you will discover that Jacob's children appear to fall far short of perfection.

Reuben got himself into trouble by interfering in his father's married life. Shimon and Levi tricked and then murdered an entire city (after their sister Dinah became an unwitting elopee with the chieftain's son). Judah abandoned and then almost killed his son's wife. And all of them sold their brother Joseph into slavery. And as for Joseph, he was a shameless telltale who wantonly fell out with his brothers.

Let's face it — none of Jacob's children sound like they were the paradigm of perfection.

The truth is, Jacob's family was not at all perfect — but Jacob had an unbelievable quality: he always saw opportunity in imperfection, and he believed that even when everything seems dark — there is still a light that shines, and a morning to look forward to. It came to him in an epiphany on the day he was forced to run away from his brother Esau, who he knew wanted to kill him.

In a very short space of time, Jacob's entire life had gone from calm to chaos, and from safety to grave danger. Until that moment his life had been the equivalent of the brightest day, but now it was the darkest night. That night he went to sleep with no family, no possessions, and no place to call home. And then, when he woke up, he realized he had made it through the darkest hour, and suddenly it all made sense. At that moment he exclaimed (Gen. 28:16) — אָכֵן יֵשׁ ה' בַּמָּקוֹם הַזֶּה וְאָנֹכִי לֹא יָדָעְתִּי — "surely God is in this place, and I did not know."

Until then Jacob's life had been perfect, but now everything had changed. Nevertheless, God was there with him, and everything was going work out fine. That was when Jacob composed maariv — the night prayer. He discovered that darkness is not an end; rather it can be a platform for a new beginning.

From then on this was Jacob's approach to life. Laban tried to cheat him out of marrying Rachel. No problem. Laban tried to kill him. No problem. Esau was marching towards him to kill him. No problem. Family issues, difficult children, his favorite son dead. No problem.

Jacob encountered challenging situations at every twist and turn, but none of it was a problem, because Jacob was a maariv man — as far as he was concerned there was no such thing as night. Even in the darkest hour the future is bright, which means the present must also be bright.

And that was why God saw Jacob as the ultimate patriarch of the Jewish nation. Feeling great when everything is bright is no big deal. Daylight gives you confidence. But having confidence in the future when everything is dark — that requires real faith.

Which is why, in Jewish tradition, we start our days at night. The beginning of true faith is when everything is dark. So much so, that it was worth saving Abraham to enable Jacob to become our beacon of faith.

Time after time the Jewish nation has emerged from darkness into light. That's why we are known as Bnei Yisrael — Children of Israel — we are descendants of Jacob whose name was Israel because he is our ultimate role model.

When we come to synagogue on Yom Kippur, we may be thinking to ourselves: "What's the point? Nothing is ever going to change. We are who we are, and we will always be the same."

But if that's what we think, it's only because we are not on the same wavelength as our patriarch Jacob. We are limiting ourselves, only seeing opportunity if it shines directly in our faces. Except, that this is not the Jewish way. The Jewish way is optimism and positivity. We always have to believe that the impossible is possible. And then, that's what happens.

TO BE KNOWN AS A JEW

first published September 24, 2020

Exactly a year ago, I traveled to Israel for a meeting with more than thirty Jewish leaders and activists, at the invitation of Israel's President, Reuven Rivlin. The agenda of our two-day mini-conference was to discuss a problem that is increasingly threatening the future of Jewish identity and of the State of Israel — the increasing divide between different groups of Jews, particularly but not exclusively over the subject of Israel and the direction it has taken under its current government.

The meeting sponsor was a group called Our Common Destiny, which is funded by a charitable organization called the Genesis Philanthropic Foundation. This foundation was founded by a Russian Jewish oligarch, Mikhael Fridman, who is a proud Jew and strong supporter of Israel, in spite of the fact that he is not Jewishly observant and did not receive any meaningful Jewish education.

Some years ago, the Genesis Foundation came up with the idea of the Genesis Prize — a kind of Jewish Nobel Prize — described on its website as follows: "The Genesis Prize fosters Jewish identity, inspires Jewish pride, and strengthens the bond between Israel and the Diaspora. The annual one-million-dollar award celebrates Jewish talent and achievement by honoring individuals for their professional accomplishments, commitment to Jewish values, and contribution to improving the world."

The first Genesis Prize laureate was the international businessman and former New York Mayor Michael Bloomberg (2014); the second one was Hollywood actor Michael Douglas (2015); the third, violinist Itzḥak Perlman (2016); and so on.

Then, in 2018, the prize committee nominated the Israeli-born Hollywood actress Natalie Portman to receive the prize. Initially she accepted the honor, but when she heard that Binyamin Netanyahu was going to be presenting the prize she abruptly pulled out, citing her "distress" at recent events in Israel.

To say that Mikhael Fridman was shocked by this development is an understatement, and it was as a direct result of Ms. Portman's very public snub of the Genesis Prize that he decided he wanted to launch a project to prevent such a thing from ever happening again, and this was the catalyst that led to the launch of Our Common Destiny.

Perhaps the vision of Our Common Destiny is utopian and unrealistic to the point of being fantasy, and the road to Xanadu is certainly laden with countless potholes and boulders, but nevertheless the idea is so wonderful and heartwarming — and it is certainly worth celebrating.

First and foremost, we are all Jews, so surely we can find enough that we share in common that we don't need to use differences between us to act as a wedge to keep us completely apart.

But the question we need to ask ourselves is this — what exactly do we share in common to the exclusion of anything that might keep us apart? And once we have found that "thing", how can we use it as a platform to keep us together in every circumstance so that we can be strong together rather than weaker as a result of being a disparate collection of unconnected parts.

Many years ago, I heard an apocryphal story about the creation of a "Tomb of the Unknown Soldier" in Israel. Sometime after the creation of the state, the Prime Minister of Israel approached the Director-General of the Ministry of Defense to discuss the creation of a "Tomb of the Unknown Soldier".

"Every other country has a Tomb of the Unknown Soldier that plays a central role on Memorial Day and military events," he said, "and it is important for Israel to have one too."

The Director-General of the Ministry of Defense called in one of his senior officials and tasked him with the job of creating Israel's Tomb of the Unknown Soldier. Some months went by, and invitations went out to the President, the Prime Minister, Members of Knesset, government officials, foreign diplomats, and senior military personnel — "You are cordially invited to the unveiling of the Tomb of the Unknown Soldier" — with a date and time.

The day arrived, and everyone took their seats at the designated location. The Ministry of Defense official straightened his tie, and slowly and solemnly walked up to the podium to begin his address.

"Ladies and Gentlemen," he began, "I would like to welcome you to the unveiling of the Tomb of the Unknown Soldier, Chaim Shlapevarski. Chaim Shlapevarski was a very great man — a brilliant economist, a first-class historian, a wise philosopher, a profound scholar, a wonderful orator…"

As this preamble progressed, and with each word that was uttered, the Director-General of the Ministry of Defense was turning every color under the sun. Unable to contain himself, he rushed up to the podium and whispered desperately into the official's ear, "What in heaven's name are you talking about? This is the Tomb of the Unknown Soldier! What is all this about Chaim Shlapevarski?!"

The official looked at him quizzically — "What do you mean? You asked me to create a Tomb of the Unknown Soldier… Chaim Shlapevarski was a great man — a brilliant economist, a first-class historian, a wise philosopher, a profound scholar, a wonderful orator — **but as a soldier he was unknown!**"

In my many experiences around the Jewish community and with Jews all around the world — I have met many Chaim Shlapevarskis. They are all brilliant in their fields, whether they are in business, or Hollywood, or academia, or politics. They write books, make films, make money, run governments, and much else. But as Jews, they are often totally unknown (only to themselves, of course).

On Yom Kippur, our primary task is to reconnect to the Jew in us and to drop everything else — as it is the "Jew" inside us that we all share in common, and it is this which we need to put front and center, to the exclusion of anything else that might keep us apart.

The Jew inside us is the commonality that we can use as a platform to keep us united in all circumstances, making us strong together, instead of being weaker as a disparate collection of unconnected parts. I truly hope that after going through Yom Kippur, none of us remains unknown as a Jew ever again.

YOUR PARENTS ARE A GIFT FROM GOD

first published September 29, 2017

A few weeks ago, before Rosh Hashana, I counted how many sermons and shiurim I would have to prepare, starting with Selihot and going through until Shabbat Bereishit. I was delighted to discover that the number was 18, matching the numerical value of the Hebrew word ḥai — which means life. Not just because this somehow correlates to the theme of High Holidays — ḥayyim — but because I had been concerned that for a community to have to listen to 18 drashot from their rabbi might turn out to be life-threatening.

For my Yizkor drasha on Yom Kippur, I decided to talk about my parents. Not stories about their lives, but about them as parents. That's because I miss them, and whenever it gets to a yom tov, I miss them even more. It surprises me just how much I miss my parents, because, in truth, I don't actually need them. Don't be shocked. What I mean is this: At a certain point one doesn't need one's parents anymore. And yet, they continue to retain an emotional hold over us long after they should, whether they are alive or not.

We cherish our relationship with our parents, even as it changes over time. We begin our lives as total dependents, we progress to defiant teenagers, we move on to become more independent — eventually relating to our parents as equals and friends. And ultimately, for many of us, our parents become dependent on us. And then they die, too early, and we are left with a vacuum — a gaping hole in our hearts.

Rabbi Avraham Yitzḥak Hacohen Kook (1865–1935) was the Chief Rabbi of Palestine between 1919 and 1935. When his elderly mother died, she was buried on the Mount of Olives. At the funeral Rabbi Kook cried inconsolably. The people who had gathered for the funeral were quite surprised — of course it was his mother, they thought to themselves, but she was very old — and he was old too. Why was he so upset? Why was he weeping?

Those closest to him decided to ask him why. He looked at them amidst his tears. "Everyone respects me, everyone calls me Rabbi, or Chief Rabbi, or Rebbe — even my wife!" he said to them. "But my mother called me Avreimele. Now that she has died — who will ever call me Avreimele? No one will ever call me Avreimele again!"

Over the past few weeks, and every year over the weeks before and after Rosh Hashana and Yom Kippur, I am forced to think about the loss of my parents in a very stark and unsettling way. In Psalm 27, which we recite twice a day from the beginning of Ellul until Hoshana Rabba, there is one pasuk we say that since my parents' passing I have found profoundly disturbing. This year I decided that I would delve into this pasuk and try to make some sense of it.

כִּי אָבִי וְאִמִּי עֲזָבוּנִי וַה' יַאַסְפֵנִי

**For my father and mother have abandoned/forsaken me,
and God gathers me in.**

I guess King David was trying to comfort himself — and us — with this verse, but it does prompt the question: How is God meant to replace my parents? I can't call Him on the phone and schmooze about politics, or the family, or some other triviality. He's not going to bake honey cakes for me for yom tov, nor will he buy clothes for my kids. He isn't going to go all gooey-eyed when I show him photos of my children, and He won't hug me when I need a hug. How exactly should I feel towards the words "V'Hashem Ya'asfeini"?

You won't find an answer in the classical commentaries. In fact, Rashi's commentary on this verse is particularly disturbing. Maybe what he suggests worked in eleventh-century France, but it certainly doesn't work for me.

For an answer that addresses this issue in a sensitive way you will need to turn to a Ḥasidic master. And not just any master, but to the master of masters: Rabbi Mordekhai Yosef Leiner (1801–1854), the Rebbe of Izhbitze in Poland. He wrote a work that was a masterpiece, called *Mei Hashiloaḥ*, which was published by his grandson after he died.

Before looking at what he says, let me first offer the following thought by way of introduction. I am a big fan of wildlife documentaries. Whether they are about animals, birds, or reptiles — I find that understanding the natural world is the best way of appreciating the concept of "Ma Gadlu Ma'asekha Hashem" — "How great are your works, oh Lord" (Ps. 92:5).

There's one fact that you will discover over and over again if you watch wildlife documentaries — animals are fiercely protective of their young. Just recently I saw a clip of a swan attacking some guy who was trying to free its baby cygnet from a chicken wire fence. The swan went berserk. Swans are mean and miserable looking creatures at the best of times — this one was positively fierce.

But the thing is this: The moment that young animals or birds no longer need their parents, the parents disappear from their lives, at least in any kind of meaningful way. In the wild — there's no mentoring, no photo showing, nor are there any honey cakes for yom tov. It is all strictly about survival. When the kid needs the parent, the parent is there for the kid. But when the kid no longer needs the parent, then the parent is out of the kid's life. And as to the parent needing the kid — that simply doesn't happen!

And so, King David says something very profound — if life was just about survival, my parents would have abandoned me. That's what animals do. But do you know why I am lucky enough to have a relationship with my parents — V'Hashem Ya'asfeini — because it is a gift from God. Having a meaningful, productive, generational relationship with my parents, long after I need them is clear proof of God's existence, and it is a Divine gift of huge proportions.

And this gift from God continues long after one's parents have passed away. Every time I think of my parents — V'Hashem Ya'asfeini. Every time I hear a song and it reminds me of my father — V'Hashem Ya'asfeini. Every time I have a good piece of honey cake and it reminds me of my mother — V'Hashem Ya'asfeini.

The fact that we have a legacy for our children is because we had a relationship with our parents. That is V'Hashem Ya'asfeini — God gathers me in. Every time we come to shul, we give charity, we listen to rabbis giving sermons — God has gathered us in through the relationship we have or had with our parents and grandparents and their ancestors.

There is a haunting story in Elie Wiesel's book *Night*. In 1944, as Yom Kippur approached, the Jews of Auschwitz debated whether or not they should fast. All of them were starving, and each of them close to death.

Elie Wiesel writes:

> **The question was hotly debated... In this place, we were always fasting. It was Yom Kippur all year round. But there were those who said we should fast, precisely because it was dangerous to do so. We needed to show God that even here, locked in hell, we were capable of singing His praises.**

The story is so incredible — why would anyone in Auschwitz even think of fasting on Yom Kippur? The only way to answer that is to understand that all these people had lost their parents and grandparents. How would they remember them if they abandoned Yom Kippur? What type of people would they be if they ate on Yom Kippur? They wouldn't be V'Hashem Ya'asfeini people; they would be animals!

Interestingly, Elie Wiesel tells his readers that he did not fast on that Yom Kippur. His father — who was still alive and with him, knowing that his son needed every morsel of food — forbade him from fasting. In fact, as Elie Wiesel later said, he was only determined to survive Auschwitz because he knew if he died, his father would die.

Later on, when they were in Buchenwald concentration camp, Wiesel's father did die — and Wiesel later said he could still recall the shame he felt when he heard his father being beaten to death and he could do nothing to save him.

V'Hashem Ya'asfeini — our duty on Rosh Hashana and Yom Kippur is to take the gift of our parents and our ancestors and give it to our children. We need to make sure that they grow up in a world of V'Hashem Ya'asfeini. We need to make sure that God gathers our children up. That is why we honor our parents in life, and that is why we remember our parents after they die, even if it causes us pain and anguish. Our children need to learn the lesson of V'Hashem Ya'asfeini so that they, too, can give it to their children and grandchildren.

IT'S LIKE A GAME OF CHESS

first published September 29, 2017

One of the best chess players of all time was the son of a German ḥazzan, a man called Emmanuel Lasker (1868–1941). He was world chess champion from 1894–1921, a genius whose innovative chess moves are studied to this day.

Lasker was a good friend of the renowned physicist Albert Einstein (1879–1955), and whenever the two of them met they would play a game or two of chess. On one famous occasion, Lasker played chess with Einstein, and afterwards, everyone wanted to know whether the world's greatest scientist was also a good chess player.

Lasker smiled. "He's good, but when it comes to chess, he's no Einstein!"

I have never been a particularly good chess player, although the association between rabbis and chess goes back a long way. The medieval bible commentator Rabbi Abraham Ibn Ezra (1089–1164) wrote a poem about chess in the twelfth century, and the fifteenth-century Italian rabbi, Yehuda Aryeh di Modena (1571–1648), wrote a book about chess called *Ma'adanei Melekh*.

Chess offers us an interesting insight into Yamim Noraim, and in particular, Kol Nidrei.

Kol Nidrei is without question both the best known and the most controversial of all Jewish prayers. Its haunting melody was made universally famous by the Hollywood star Al Jolson (1886–1950) — and later by the pop singer Neil Diamond (b.1941) — in the movie *The Jazz Singer*. At the same time, antisemites consider Kol Nidrei to be the perfect example of Jewish duplicity.

Recited at the most auspicious synagogue service of the year, on Yom Kippur night, Kol Nidrei doesn't speak about God and angels or about repentance and forgiveness, nor does it address the beauty of faith — rather, it is essentially a legal declaration:

> **All vows, and prohibitions, and oaths, and consecrations, and promises, and pledges, that we may vow, or swear, or consecrate, or prohibit upon ourselves, from this Yom Kippur until next Yom Kippur, regarding them all, we regret them henceforth — they will all be permitted, abandoned, cancelled, null and void, without power and without standing. Our vows shall not be valid vows; our prohibitions shall not be valid prohibitions; and our oaths shall not be valid oaths.**

The tune may be sublime, but the words are utterly prosaic and mundane. I guess it's lucky nobody understands Kol Nidrei, or if we do, that we think of Aramaic as a language of dramatic liturgy. I mean, how much would that tune move us if we were to chant the words of Kol Nidrei in English?

How does it even make sense that we begin Yom Kippur with a prayer about nullifying promises? A request that over the coming year, no less than seven different kinds of vows should not count and should be canceled? What a strange way to begin the holiest day of the year! Couldn't we have found something more fitting for this special moment? And are the antisemites right? Are the vows we commit ourselves to actually invalidated even before we make them? Is that really who we are as devout Jews?

Which brings me back to chess. I heard this story from a friend of mine a few years ago. At the time he worked at a synagogue in New York as a youth director, and several times a month they had a teen chess club. Over one summer the synagogue managed to secure the services of a chess grandmaster, Dmitri, who instructed the kids how to play chess. My friend was very excited to play chess with Dmitri, and he played against him numerous times over the course of the summer.

The thing is, he had always thought of himself as a pretty good chess player, but Dmitri demolished him time and again. He tried to help my friend as the games unfolded, while they were playing, and my friend said his game improved as the summer progressed — but he still could never win against Dmitri. He just could not beat the guy.

It was the end of the summer, the last game, and after a few moves Dmitri asked my friend, "It looks like you are trying to capture my queen — why are you doing this?" My friend replied, "It's simple — the queen is the most powerful piece on the board; if I can capture the queen, I will have a better chance of winning."

Dmitri smiled. He looked down at his queen, and then looked back up at my friend. Without saying a word, he reached over, took the queen from the board, and handed it to my friend.

"Here, take it," he said. "And while we are pausing the game, are there any other impediments on the board that you think are preventing you from winning?"

My friend thought for a moment, and then pointed to the two rooks. Dmitri removed these two critical pieces from the board and handed them to him without a word.

"Are there any more impediments?" he asked again, "or are we done?"

By this time, my friend was confident that he could demolish Dmitri, now that he had lost his three most powerful pieces. He just shook his head. "No, I'm good."

"Great," said Dimitri, "no more impediments."

And with his remaining pieces — with no rooks and no queen — he proceeded to destroy my friend in ten easy moves.

As we enter Yom Kippur, we are probably asking ourselves, "What are our impediments?" Last year, I promised I would be a different person by the time I got to this Yom Kippur, but it feels like Groundhog Day. Here I am, again! Same time, same place! Why do I feel just the same as last year? What has held me back from reaching my goals? What has held me back from hitting my targets?

For example, I set a goal to study more Torah, on my own and with others, but it didn't happen. I set a goal to spend more time with my family, to pray with more devotion, to be involved with more charities, to lobby more for Israel — and the list goes on and on.

What happened? We all have a list of goals each year, and we all struggle to make meaningful changes that are noticeable and that we can point to. Each Yom Kippur we want to reflect on the past year and think about how much we have grown. What's holding us back from achieving the best version of ourselves possible?

Do you know what the great irony is? It is exactly these goals and resolutions that hold us back. They become the excuse for us not to grow. They are the queens and the rooks and the knights and the pawns. When what we need is the king. We need to be going for the king.

Do you know why we begin Yom Kippur, the holiest day of the year, with Kol Nidrei? It's not about the vows and oaths we make to others. That is just the nonsense that antisemites made up. Kol Nidrei is about the vows that we make to ourselves. We are going to get rid of this queen and that rook, we imagine, and then everything is going to be ok. We make promises, oaths, and vows — and then every one of them is an impediment to our growth. We add layer upon layer of obligation, trapping ourselves in a prison of our own creation. After all, if I say that I'll be somewhere at 8 o'clock, it prevents me from doing anything else at 8 o'clock.

And it's not that we make **actual** oaths — because an oath isn't just something that I say I'll do or that I won't do. My regular routines and my daily commitments are my vows. Perhaps the reason I don't have as much time for Torah study is because I waste too much time on my iPhone replying to WhatsApps and checking social media.

I once heard this great story about a woman who was cleaning an old vase one day and a genie comes out of the vase and tells her he will grant her three wishes.

"What's your first wish?" he asks her.

"I want my husband to only have eyes for me," she replies.

The genie gives a hollow laugh — "Are you kidding? Do you know your husband?"

"What's your second wish?"

"I want my husband to think I am the most important thing in his life."

The genie laughs again. "Really? Your husband? Come on! Get real, lady!"

"Okay, so what's your third wish?"

"I want my husband to wake up every morning and give me 45 minutes of his undivided attention."

The genie is crying with laughter. "Listen lady, I know I'm a genie, but you are setting your sights far too high."

And then, suddenly, the genie gets serious. "Actually," he says, "I think I can help you with all three wishes." And he turns the woman into an iPhone.

Yes, that's right. Technology is our oaths and vows. We have so many "important" distractions that hold us back from doing what need to do and being what we need to be. But our goal in the chess game of life is to capture the king, not to focus on the queen and the rooks. Our goal is to get closer to God. Our goal is to be better people all around. To do more mitzvot, to be holy, to be kinder to others, more tolerant of others, tougher on ourselves — not just in specific settings and situations, but in every situation and every setting. And what's getting in the way of us capturing the king? All of the other impediments! The oaths and the vows.

That's why we start Yom Kippur with the only way we can be successful. Kol Nidrei is about removing all the impediments so that we can reach the ultimate goal of capturing the king.

YOM KIPPUR NOT JUST ONCE A YEAR

first published September 28, 2017

I magine you had never heard of Yom Kippur before, and you would be informed about the existence of a day called Yom Kippur. Suddenly you discover that on this day of the year we are given a unique opportunity to repent and be granted a clean slate.

If I now ask you to tell me which type of person needs to take this annual opportunity most seriously, and who can be more relaxed about it, you would surely respond that those who are diligent about observing mitzvot all year round can relax on Yom Kippur, while all the slackers need to grab this opportunity with both hands, and use Yom Kippur to the fullest extent possible.

And yet, who are the ones who pray the hardest on Yom Kippur and take it the most seriously? Is it the once-a-year guys, or is it the very committed guys?

I think we all know the answer to that. The least committed Jews are the ones who slip into shul for an hour or two, if they come at all, and their attitude towards Yom Kippur is very relaxed.

Meanwhile, the serious ones are in shul all day, and during the weeks leading up to Yom Kippur, they are the ones at seliḥot services early every morning, getting themselves prepared.

How does it make any sense that venerable rabbis, the kind who sit and study Torah all day and never compromise on any aspect of Jewish observance, are the ones who cry their hearts out on Yom Kippur, while the slackers go through Yom Kippur without so much as breaking a sweat, and many of them are not seen in shul again for another year?

The answer is that it is contingent on how we see Yom Kippur. Do we see Yom Kippur as a one-off day, or do we see it as much more than that? If we take an exam, is it just about the time spent taking the exam, or is it about the hours, weeks, and months of investment we have put into the course study to ensure that we get a good grade? When we go to a job interview, or to a crucial business meeting, is it just about the time we spend at the interview or meeting, or do we take into consideration the impact that small amount of time may have on the months and years ahead?

The ones who take the day of Yom Kippur seriously are the same ones who take Yom Kippur seriously all year — they anticipate it, they work their lives around it, and they measure everything they do around the day they know is coming.

And when Yom Kippur arrives, they hope that all the work they have put into it will have paid off — although, despite all that they have already done in anticipation of Yom Kippur, they fear it still won't have been enough.

Meanwhile, the once-a-year guys, sliding up the scale to the once-a-week Shabbat service attending guys, and further up the scale to those who do more but not enough, perhaps cutting lots of corners and making too many compromises — do you know why they don't take Yom Kippur as seriously as they should? It's quite simple. It is because they have made an enormous effort to ensure that Yom Kippur doesn't feature on any other day of the year besides Yom Kippur itself. For them Yom Kippur is one day out of all the many other days of the year — serious perhaps, but isolated. And then they can't understand why they don't feel spiritual on Yom Kippur, and why it is that Yom Kippur doesn't affect them.

Sadly, if you spend your whole year avoiding Yom Kippur, when Yom Kippur arrives it isn't going to be too meaningful. Which is why it is so important to get yourself ready and prepare yourself fully for Yom Kippur, so that when the day happens, it won't just be a chore you need to get through. Instead, it will be the culmination of a program of preparation that will ensure your year ahead is an improvement on the year you have just ended. That is what Yom Kippur is all about.

THE POWER OF COLLECTIVE ASPIRATION

first published October 8, 2016

Earlier this week, I read an op-ed written by a former UK prison warden, who gave his thoughts on the rising problem of radical Islam in British prisons.

To be clear, this former official is not some zealot with an anti-Muslim agenda. In July 2015, he was asked by the British government to officially investigate the Islamic extremism problem in jails, and to make recommendations for dealing with it.

For six months, he visited jails across the UK and in other countries — speaking to prison staff and other stakeholders, including ex-prisoners — in an effort to understand the scope and depth of this growing phenomenon.

His conclusions, although not entirely surprising, are nonetheless alarming. Over and over again he discovered that "a small number of highly charismatic prisoners were given far too much latitude to preach messages of hatred to others and [to] mobilize gangs to dominate and control their environment."

While this is not an unusual situation in the intense atmosphere of a prison, he discovered that the influence and power of Islamist radicals in prisons posed a clear and present threat to UK civilians on the streets of Britain. Although ordinary prison kingpins seek only to exercise power in their own setting, Islamist kingpins, the official wrote, are "intent on trying to convert others to violent anti-British beliefs in support of terrorism," which means that when petty criminals who are Muslim become radicalized and are later released, they are almost certainly potential terrorist time bombs.

As a result of his report the UK government has just announced that dangerous Islamic extremists will from now on be incarcerated in isolated high-security prisons to prevent them from radicalizing others. The report also recommended a ban on radical literature in jails, and the removal of Islamic fanatics from weekly Muslim prayer meetings — to prevent them from influencing other Muslims, or from intimidating them into submission and silence.

Most Muslim prisoners in the UK are not jailed for terrorist-related offenses and have no prior interest in fundamentalist Islam. Many are interested in rehabilitation, or at least have no intention of being influenced by the violent doctrines of Islamic extremism.

But that can change when they come into contact with Islamist radicals whose appeal can have a domino effect across a Muslim prison population. And thanks to the report, Muslim prison chaplains will now be carefully vetted before they are hired, so that a more benign influence can become the norm for incarcerated Muslims.

The op-ed was not only striking in its exposition of the dangers posed by giving radical individuals the power to corrupt others, but also because it highlighted the importance of group dynamics in terms of generating change.

In the early twentieth century, three distinguished mental health professionals on the East Coast of the United States came up with the concept of group psychotherapy. One particularly effective form of group psychotherapy is known as "milieu therapy."

The idea behind this particular version of the group model is to encourage participants to take responsibility for themselves as well as the others within the group, based on a hierarchy of collective consequences.

If one patient violates the group's rules, other group members who were aware of the violation and failed to intervene are "punished" based on a scale that measures their culpability in the rule infringement. The underlying theory is that belonging to a group can either foster individual growth, or — as is most common — it can result in the decline of acceptable behavior across the group, resulting in negative behavioral changes in previously blameless individuals.

The most extreme example of group deterioration can be seen in the incredible success of Nazi antisemitism in pre-war Germany, where ordinary Germans were swept up by the malign influence of individual Nazis within their social groups, until the vast majority of Germans became virulent antisemites who were then complicit in the Holocaust.

Milieu therapy uses this dynamic to generate positive instead of negative change in a group, as it becomes clear to participants that passive association is not truly passive and will result in unpleasant consequences. Meanwhile, positive growth is rewarded across the group, and everyone benefits when individual participants progress in an upward spiral. These milieu therapy groups are just a microcosm of society at large, and the same rules clearly apply in a wider setting.

It is for this reason that on Yom Kippur we say two types of vidui. The Hebrew word vidui is usually translated as "confession" — but it is more accurate to translate the word as "sin acknowledgement," with the caveat that this acknowledgement is an integral part of a self-improvement process. The vidui prayer is said ten times over the course of Yom Kippur, five of those times silently and privately, and the other five collectively as a community.

I am not sure when the formula for this prayer was finalized, or when the decision was made for it to be articulated by everyone at the same time — but the power of this group confession is nothing short of cathartic. It allows us to acknowledge, as a group, that all of us are guilty of something, and that we all want to be part of a group that desires to improve and perfect itself.

On Yom Kippur, we are not just out for ourselves — we are also there for each other, giving our fellow community members a hand so that we are all elevated by the power of collective aspiration. And in the same way that we recognize how one bad apple can drag us all down, we know how beneficial it is when we all aim higher together.

THE DEATH OF RABBI HYMAN KRUSTOFSKI

first published October 3, 2014

Earlier this week it was widely reported that Rabbi Hyman Krustofski had unexpectedly passed away. CNN, *Time*, and *The New York Times* all reported it. In fact, every major news organization covered the story, devoting time and attention to his death.

You may or may not have heard of Rabbi Krustofski, but you will certainly have heard of his son, Krusty the Clown, an iconic character on the long running cartoon show, *The Simpsons*. Yes, you read correctly. Rabbi Hyman Krustofski is a fictional character on a TV show, voiced over by the veteran Jewish comedian, Jackie Mason.

Incredibly, in a week when the Ebola virus hit the United States, when an intruder with a weapon made it into the White House, when Hong Kong erupted with unprecedented protests, and when the United Nations heard competing accounts of Israel and Hamas's role in the Middle East, ink and airtime were used abundantly to report the death of a fictional rabbi who had featured in a quirky cartoon sit-com.

What are we to make of this? What are we to make, generally, of the dumbing down of news and information? Kim Kardashian gets more airtime than President Putin of Russia. A photo of

Justin Bieber punching a photographer in Paris was tweeted around the world in seconds, while the execution in Iran of 37-year-old Mohsen Amir-Aslani for heresy and trumped up charges of rape barely registered. How does that make any sense?

The answer is that it makes eminent sense because most people treat news as entertainment, and unless it is entertaining them, they are not interested. Nobody wants to hear a serious discussion about real news. Analysis is too dense. Context is too obscure. And if the news outlets can manage to make news stories out of the entertainment industry and entertainers — it's a slam-dunk. It allows people to pretend that they are serious — it's a news story after all! — while in fact they are just gaining pleasure through entertainment.

And that is what entertainment is — a source of pleasure. Human beings are constantly seeking ways of making themselves feel good. Entertainment is just one of the routes to pleasure, along with good food and relaxation. If news is entertainment, then it leads to pleasure.

You might be wondering, if entertainment and giving pleasure is the goal of news organizations, why would they report wars and violence? The answer — sadly — is that war stories are also considered entertainment, in the same way that horror movies are considered entertainment. People are stimulated by the mayhem of war, and they are titillated by violent murder.

The treatment of wars as entertainment is, incidentally, the reason why many wars — such as the one recently fought by Israel against Hamas in Gaza — are perceived in the way that they are, with negative public sentiment directed at the wrong party.

Clearly, if war is presented very superficially and simply to entertain, public reaction is bound to be ill-judged and shallow.

All of this will help us understand the laws associated with Yom Kippur. Every year I am asked, by one person or another, why it is that we must refrain from eating and drinking on Yom Kippur, as well as from other basic aspects of daily life. Surely, we would concentrate better on the prayers and on the awesomeness of the day itself if we could have some food, just as we do on every other festival and Shabbat? By starving ourselves all that will happen is that we will crave food. What is the point of that?

While this might be true, eating on Yom Kippur would mean missing the whole point of the day. On this incredible day of reflection we desist from indulging in our pressing need for physical stimulation, to drive home the message that if you want to get serious, by which I mean **really** serious, you must strip away all the fluff and the externals, in the first instance to demonstrate to yourself how needy and dependent you actually are, and also so that you can focus exclusively on what it is you are doing in your life, and how you can create a meaning out of your existence, in a setting where stimulation is proscribed.

If that is your aim for Yom Kippur — to get to grips with the real you without any distractions — then the 25-hour break from a cacophony of meaningless stimulants — news, phones, TV shows, food, drink, and the list goes on — seems like a very good idea. It will give you the time and mental space to focus on what really matters.

So why not have Yom Kippur more often? The answer is that we are, after all, humans, drawn to stimulants of every kind. And there is nothing wrong with that. It is the way God created us. We need stimulation to help us function more positively.

But an annually scheduled daylong break from those stimulants will certainly help us reconsider and reevaluate which stimulants we seek out during the rest of the year, and what we seek to get from them. We might choose to be stimulated by a meaningful relationship with God, and productive and healthy relationships with our families and friends, instead of choosing to be stimulated by a news report of the death of Rabbi Hyman Krustofski, or by stimulants of a similarly flippant nature.

SUKKOT

THE WORLD'S MOST REMARKABLE FRUIT

first published October 6, 2022

It is fair to say that the etrog fruit used by Jewish communities across the world as part of the four species during the festival of Sukkot is one of the world's most remarkable fruits. Cryptically described in the Torah as pri etz hadar (literal translation: fruit of the hadar tree) and referred to in English as a "citron" (or by its Latin name, citrus medica), this unprepossessing member of the citrus family has long been the object of fascination for horticulturalists.

Where did it first originate? Why are there so many different iterations of citron — some that are the size and appearance of a pomelo, others that are dark green and tiny, and yet others that look like a bumpy lemon? And how are we to reconcile the various Talmudic interpretations narrowing down the options of which fruit to use for Sukkot leaving the citron as the only option?

One of the great controversies of modern rabbinic literature is whether the different available varieties of citron are purebred, or whether at some point one or another of them was crossbred with lemons or some other citrus fruit, rendering them unfit for use. Interestingly enough, until the late sixteenth century, there is no discussion regarding hybrid etrogim in any of the halakhic literature.

The Shulḥan Arukh records detailed laws about etrogim and the four species (O.H. 648-649), but the issue of hybridization — known in Hebrew as murkav — does not come up at all. It was only subsequent to the publication of the Shulḥan Arukh that this issue exploded onto the scene.

The controversy led to a nineteenth-century pronouncement by the rabbinic luminary, Rabbi Moses Sofer (1762–1839; *Hatam Sofer*), proclaiming that once an etrog plant has been contaminated by the introduction of another citrus fruit, via graft or any other method, no descendant emanating from the original etrog tree can ever be used for ritual purposes.

Rabbis were suddenly lumbered with the problem of identifying and eliminating hybrid etrogim, and they consequently suggested all manner of telltale signs to weed out the fakes — but none of these signs has ever proven entirely reliable, as Rabbi Sofer himself admitted in his responsa (O.H. 207). Etrog growers, particularly those in the Greek island of Corfu, all claimed to have the purest variety of etrog, totally beyond any suspicion of hybridization, while they denounced all other varieties as illegitimate.

And then there were those who entirely dismissed the idea that a murkav etrog was disqualified for use on Sukkot. The deeply revered kabbalist, Rabbi Shlomo Eliezer Alfandari (1826?–1930), defended the use of hybrid etrogim in his book *Limmud Zekhut*, going as far as to say that ordinary lemons might be kosher to use on Sukkot for the Four Species.

In 1933, Rabbi Avraham Yeshaya Karelitz (1878–1953) — universally known as the *Ḥazon Ish* after his magnum opus — arrived in Palestine, soon emerging as a leading halakhic authority of the era. Rabbi Karelitz was particularly appalled by the ubiquitous availability of murkav etrogim in Palestine, all of them widely promoted and used by devout Jews over Sukkot. Determined to identify the purest pedigree of etrog, he settled on a particular variety — the "balady citron" — and arranged for these to be grown under special supervision. This variety of etrog now bears his name and is known as the Ḥazon Ish etrog.

And yet, according to at least one source — namely, Rabbi Moshe Hacohen Illovitzky, a close confidant of Rabbi Karelitz who is quoted in *Pe'er Hador*, the official five-volume biography of the Ḥazon Ish — Rabbi Karelitz conceded in a letter written later in life that he had been mistaken to believe he could correctly distinguish between hybridized and non-hybridized etrogim, implying he had begun to doubt the purity of his own chosen variety.

In a groundbreaking 2005 study, titled "The Search for the Authentic Citron," five horticulturalists researched the long history of the etrog fruit, and used modern scientific methods to see if evidence of hybridization could be established once and for all, in any or all of the varieties available.

"It is well accepted that the citron was the first citrus fruit to reach the Near East and the Mediterranean," the study begins. Archeological evidence of etrogs exists from the second century BCE — surprisingly lemons and oranges only started to arrive up to 1,000 years later. The study confirms what the Ḥatam Sofer and the Ḥazon Ish had already conceded: "Even today, with all the modern, molecular techniques, there is no way of … establishing the never-grafted nature of a citron tree."

More stunning is the revelation that despite the prevalence of grafting throughout etrog-growing history, no doubt employed by growers to improve the strain of one or another of the varieties of etrog, "the results of the genetic analysis are unequivocal and do not leave much room for interpretation — in spite of diverse geographical origin and the considerable morphological variation in fruit size and shape, presence of pulp and persistence of style, all the citron types examined revealed a high degree of similarity."

Rabbi Abahu in the Talmud offers an explanation for why the etrog is not specifically named in the Torah but is instead identified as pri etz hadar (Sukkah 35b): אַל תִּקְרֵי "הָדָר" אֶלָּא "הַדָּר" דָּבָר שֶׁדָּר בְּאִילָנוֹ מִשָׁנָה לְשָׁנָה — "don't read it as 'hadar' (beautiful), but rather as 'haddar' — [namely] the object that dwells on its tree from year to year." Indeed, whatever the time of year, there are always ripe etrogs on the citron tree, as well as others that are just beginning to form or ripen.

But I think the lesson goes far beyond that simple interpretation. If you think about it, this unique fruit — which serves no purpose other than its ritual use for Jews during Sukkot — has not only endured for millennia, but despite attempts to hybridize it into something else, the etrog has remained true to its origins, and is as pure today as when it was first identified by the Torah.

What strikes me most about this stunning piece of information is that there could not possibly be a better metaphor for the Jewish people than the etrog. After thousands of years, and despite dozens of varieties and every possible attempt to destroy or compromise Jewish identity, the Jewish people have prevailed, and the Jewish nation continues to remain utterly faithful to its origins. As it turns out, we are the ultimate etrogs of history.

FROM SUEZ TO AFGHANISTAN

first published September 15, 2021

After watching the recent Afghanistan withdrawal debacle unfold, I could not help but be reminded of the Suez Crisis of 1956 — with a sense of foreboding and terror about what the future holds for those who treasure the freedoms and comforts of the Western world.

Truthfully, it wasn't the shocking scenes of Afghan citizens desperately running alongside a US military cargo plane at Kabul airport that I found so discomforting, although that image has seared itself on my mind forever. Nor was it the shocking revelation that the US military has left billions of dollars' worth of military hardware in Afghanistan, weaponry that is now controlled by an evil terrorist regime.

For while it is true that these aspects of the withdrawal do send a chill down my spine, they are not the cause for my doomsday premonition. Rather, it is the specter of Suez that hangs over Afghanistan which gives me sleepless nights and makes me fear for the future of the free world.

The Suez Crisis of 1956 is best remembered for the precipitous downfall of its main cheerleader, UK prime minister Anthony Eden (1897–1977), until then one of Great Britain's most highly regarded politicians and statesmen. The crisis began on July 26,

1956, after Egypt's populist president Gamal Abdel Nasser (1918–1970) nationalized the Suez Canal, one of the world's most important waterways, then owned by the Suez Canal Company, a commercial entity controlled by French and British interests.

Nasser's provocative decision had been precipitated by an American and British decision not to finance the construction of Aswan Dam, a consequence of Egypt's growing ties with the Soviet Union. Nasser was furious and took his revenge by seizing control of the canal with the idea that Egypt could use revenue from the thriving shipping trade to pay for the dam's construction.

But Britain and France were determined to thwart Nasser's unilateral seizure of their asset, and decided that Nasser had to be taught a lesson. They secretly planned a military campaign together with Israel, to regain control of the canal, and to effect regime change in Egypt.

After a pre-agreed Israeli invasion of the Sinai in late October, and the inevitable conflict between Israeli and Egyptian forces which followed, the Anglo-French alliance declared the military confrontation a casus belli, and in early November sent their armies to occupy the canal, wresting control of the territory from the Egyptians.

But the Suez campaign turned out to be a gross miscalculation. US president Dwight D. Eisenhower (1890–1969) — who had not been informed of the plan in advance — was horrified, believing that the Anglo-French invasion would be widely perceived as an egregious example of Western imperialism, driving Egypt and other Arab nations into the arms of the Soviet Union, who were eagerly looking for a foothold in the Middle East.

The US administration, in a rare show of cooperation with the Soviets, secured a UN resolution condemning the invasion while simultaneously refusing to sell oil to the British, whose supply of oil was severely curtailed by the blockage in Suez — all of which forced the British and French armies into a humiliating withdrawal. Eden, once celebrated as Winston Churchill's right-hand man and as the wisest of diplomats, was compelled to resign his premiership with his reputation in tatters.

At the time, besides for Eden's dramatic fall from grace, the Suez Crisis outcome was widely perceived as an unequivocal success. The United States, with the help of the United Nations, and by using its considerable leverage with the UK, had succeeded in preventing wholesale bloodshed, while the international economy emerged largely unaffected, possibly even improved, as a result of the internationally sanctioned resolution.

Both the United States and the Soviet Union had behaved responsibly, acting together to ensure that this kind of foreign military adventure — which only benefited superpowers, while less adept countries took the brunt of hostilities — would no longer be tolerated by the new international order. Everyone breathed a sigh of relief.

But how wrong they all were. An emboldened Nasser went on to use his victory against Great Britain in particular, and the weakness of the West in the face of his belligerence in general, as proof that if the mouse roars loud enough, the mightiest lions will slink away.

Eden was utterly convinced of this awful consequence, telling an interviewer in 1967 that he was "unrepentant" for having initiated the Suez campaign, and that he believed Nasser was a postwar incarnation of Hitler. Forcing the West into retreat had simply encouraged him and other Arab leaders to arm their countries which had, in turn, gravely threatened peace in the region.

Eden's biographer, D. R. Thorpe, was far more blunt. In his book *Eden: The Life and Times of Anthony Eden* (London, 2003), he wrote: "Had the Anglo-French venture succeeded in 1956, there would almost certainly have been no Middle East war in 1967, and probably no Yom Kippur War in 1973."

The difference between the humiliating climbdown and troop withdrawal by Great Britain in 1956, and the shameful fiasco of the US withdrawal from Afghanistan in 2021, is that by 1956 the British Empire was already in steep decline, and while the Suez Crisis may have been the catalyst for a faster descent into oblivion, it brought into sharp focus just how toothless the once-mighty British tiger had become.

By contrast, the United States of America is ostensibly still the world's mightiest superpower, a position it has held for decades, and to see it disgraced and sent scuttling out of a country, leaving an unholy mess in its wake, reveals just how ephemeral and evanescent that power really is.

Historians will one day look back at the Afghanistan withdrawal and cite it — as they do the Suez withdrawal for Britain — as the moment when the penny dropped, and the American king was seen with no clothes.

The Jewish calendar cycle includes a festival called Sukkot, celebrated each year in the early autumn. We build a temporary outdoor structure, using leaves or branches as a roof. For an entire week this hut becomes our home — we eat in it, we spend family time there, and many of us even sleep in the sukkah.

Custom demands that we decorate our sukkah — and the interior of some sukkahs can be elaborate and even ornate, with beautiful drapes and artistic images covering the walls, and fabulous decorations suspended from the ceiling. But then, once the Sukkot week is over, each sukkah is dismantled and the lovely interior that was our home for seven days is gone.

One of the most frequently asked questions about Sukkot is why it takes place in the fall, and not during the spring, when the weather is more suited to the outdoor aspects of the festival. Answers are abundant, but the answer that has always struck me as particularly sharp is the one suggested by Rashi's grandson, Rabbi Shmuel ben Meir (*Rashbam*; 1085–1158).

He suggests that God deliberately chose the fall, after the harvest is over, exactly at a time when an agricultural society feels most successful and complacent. The storehouses are full, life is good, and there is nothing to be worried about. It is exactly now that God asks us to leave the comfort of our homes and spend some time in a temporary dwelling — although, despite their ramshackle transience, we are expected to decorate and make them as nice as our permanent homes, or even nicer.

And then, after being in them for a week, we dismantle them completely, and they're gone.

As we approach the winter, God wants us to be aware just how temporary our livelihood and security really is — or can become; it's here one day and gone the next. Because, in the final analysis, it is not our status, our homes, our possessions, or our strength that give us security — it is God. And all those things can be gone in the blink of an eye.

All of us in the Western world are endlessly dazzled by our prowess and self-assessed superiority, as we navel-gaze and shoot the breeze on every topic besides for our own existential vulnerability, while at the same time the barbarians are at the gate waiting to turn our harvest festival into the harshest winter we have ever experienced.

That's why we need Sukkot — so that we spend time reflecting on just how quickly our world can turn upside down and be gone, with the edifice that is our home taken apart, leaving us to face the elements without the protection we took for granted.

It is this Sukkot phenomenon that should have been the strategic takeaway of the Suez Crisis. Had that been the case, the Afghanistan situation might have unfolded quite differently.

And this time the stakes are far higher, which is the reason I am so worried. Let us all hope and pray for a mild winter, and that spring comes much earlier than expected.

WE ARE THE CHOSEN PEOPLE

first published October 1, 2020

"Imagine." It is John Lennon's most iconic song. The music video for the song begins evocatively with John and his wife Yoko walking through the mist in their large garden. Birds chirp in the background as their feet crunch the gravel with every step. It is a scene of soft tranquility with an added air of mystery. And then, suddenly, the soft piano chords begin to play.

The lyrics are so familiar, and when we hear the opening piano riff start to play we can all immediately sing along with the words.

> **Imagine there's no heaven**
> **It's easy if you try**
> **No hell below us**
> **Above us only sky**
> **Imagine all the people**
> **Living for today...**
>
> **Imagine there's no countries**
> **It isn't hard to do**
> **Nothing to kill or die for**
> **And no religion too**

Imagine all the people

Living life in peace…

You may say I'm a dreamer

But I'm not the only one

I hope someday you'll join us

And the world will be as one

Imagine no possessions

I wonder if you can

No need for greed or hunger

A brotherhood of man

Imagine all the people

Sharing all the world…

You may say I'm a dreamer

But I'm not the only one

I hope someday you'll join us

And the world will live as one

You may think it's odd for a rabbi to quote an iconic pop song. Truthfully, I'm not bothered. First of all — this is not just any song, it's "Imagine" by John Lennon. And secondly, it is without any doubt the best-known "peace" song of the 60s and 70s, preaching universal love, equality for all, non-violence, and of course world peace.

Whatever we may think of John Lennon and some of the more radical aspects of the peacenik movement, there is a part of us that wants to buy into the core message of this song. Surely it represents a perfect world — no war, no arguments, no discord, not even petty disputes about possessions. And although we live in an imperfect world, with the lyrics of this rousing song Lennon gave us a glimpse of what a perfect world could look like.

Well actually — and forgive me for being a party-pooping iconoclast! — I'm quite sure that he didn't. To begin with, let me contrast the lyrics of "Imagine" with a prayer we say numerous times over the festival period, beginning on Rosh Hashana and Yom Kippur, and then again over Sukkot: Ata Beḥartanu Mikol Ha'amim — "You chose us from all the nations; You loved us, You desired us above all other people; You sanctified us with your commandments; and You drew us near to your service." This prayer is the ultimate celebration of the fact that God turned the Jewish nation into His Chosen People.

And this theme of "chosenness" reappears on numerous occasions in Hebrew scripture. I can quote you countless verses throughout Tanakh that reflect this idea — telling us that the Jews are special, the Jews are chosen, the Jews are unique — am segulah, am ha-nivḥar, am kadosh.

Troublingly, this idea seems to fly in the face of a universal God. How is it that the God of all humanity has chosen to reveal Himself uniquely to one nation? What about equality for all? And I hardly need to remind you that our enemies and detractors have often used this foundational aspect of our national identity to criticize and vilify us.

And especially for those who love Lennon's "Imagine" there is an uncomfortable truth here — we cannot possibly reconcile our Jewishness with the worldview painted in the idealistic lyrics of that song. How can we be good Jews and subscribe to the utopia Lennon describes?

The answer is simple — we can't. Although, actually, that's not a bad thing. In fact, it's a good thing — because being the Chosen People does not mean we are racist, or arrogant, or special — at least not special in the sense that white supremacists might describe themselves as such. Moreover, the idealized world painted by Lennon in his cherished song would be a world that is the very antithesis of what God wants. Rather than being a utopia, it would be a nightmare.

Search through the entire Torah, Talmud, and Midrashim, or indeed in any Jewish source — and you will be struck by an incredible fact. It appears we Jews do not believe that we were chosen for any special privilege. Nowhere are we promised the Kingdom of Heaven to the exclusion of gentiles. Nor are we promised special treatment by God to the detriment of others.

If anything, the contrary is true. We are told that we need to serve, or else we will fare very badly. And in return for a life of unending commitment we are told that our lives will be OK. It seems that being chosen means we were chosen to serve, and potentially to suffer the ordeals true service might entail.

In the movie *Fiddler on the Roof*, the central character, Tevye, comments: "I know, I know. We are Your Chosen People. But, once in a while, couldn't You just choose someone else?"

The point is this. Our ancestors took something on at Mount Sinai — they declared "Na'aseh Venishma", "we shall do, and we shall obey." They meant that they would do everything and anything that Judaism demanded of them. They undertook an exacting code of morality, law, and discipline — more than any of the contemporary nations — then as now.

Drawing on the sentiment behind Tevye's cue, many Jews have indeed opted not to be so special after all, and have rejected observing mitzvot and ultimately, they have rejected their Jewish identity. But to do that hardly makes sense if being chosen is such a privilege.

In which case, what does it mean to be chosen? It means that God chose us to do everything that made creating the world worthwhile. And like all relationships, the closer you are, the more intense it is.

If someone hears about a random kid who has misbehaved, they won't be too concerned. But when it's their own child who has misbehaved it is very different. And when a person hears that their kid has done well, they celebrate. Your child's success intensifies your feelings of love.

Our special relationship with God is just the same. It is subject to highs and lows because we are His children: when we do well, we bask in His love, and when we do badly, we elicit a negative reaction.

Chosenness means responsibility. It means something is expected of us. And it requires a consciousness that is reflective and on the ball. This is the chosenness of being God's Chosen People.

The pretty chords and softly sung words of Lennon's anthem blind us to the fact that if the world was ever the way he describes it, it would be an utterly dreadful place. Universal love is not love at all.

Imagine I would say to my wife (and by the way, I don't recommend that you try this): "Darling, do you know how much I love you? I love you just as much as I love every other woman on the planet." How long do you think it would take her to throw me out? By choosing my wife I am expressly and without equivocation rejecting every other woman on the planet. That is not regressive, nor backward. It is beautiful.

But this kind of exclusive commitment comes with responsibilities. We know very well what it means, and we also know that the alternative is ridiculous and unworkable. And it explains why God is referred to as a jealous God in the Ten Commandments. Rather than describing some petty human emotion, the Torah is using a human emotion to help us understand our chosenness.

If a husband is not jealous about his wife, or a wife is not jealous with reference to her husband, then their relationship is not a relationship of chosenness. God could never allow us to have any other "gods" in our lives, because we are His Chosen People. Jealousy is the perfect human emotion to help us understand that.

Lennon suggests a world where there is "nothing to live or die for." I can't imagine a world more boring than that. The most invigorating thing of all is the fact that there is good and evil, right, and wrong, and that there are things in our lives worth dying for.

It is worth dying to protect my children, or my value system, or my loyalties. The utopia of universal equality as described by Lennon in "Imagine" is not a utopia at all. It is a nightmare. In fact, it has been tried and it failed — in an experiment called the Soviet Union — which ended up being a colossal failure. Indeed, such a dream is the antithesis of God's plan for humanity.

Which is why being the Chosen People is nothing to be ashamed of. We must celebrate it, and every time we say or hear the words Ata Beḥartanu Mikol Ha'amim we should remind ourselves that we need to live up to our chosen role, and not fool ourselves into thinking that we are special or better than everyone else.

Rather than it being a privilege, being chosen is a challenge. Our task, as those who are chosen, is to live up to that challenge.

SUKKAH FIT FOR A RABBI

first published October 10, 2019

Unless you are an aficionado of Jewish law, the name *Pri Megadim* will mean very little. Nonetheless, it happens to be the title of a very important work authored by Rabbi Joseph Teomim (1727–1792), a rabbi from Lemberg, then a market town on the eastern limits of the Austro-Hungarian empire, now known as Lviv, in Western Ukraine.

Rabbi Teomim came from an extremely distinguished rabbinic family and was a great rabbinic scholar in his own right, although he struggled to make a living as a rabbi. But that all changed when he began to publish what would soon become one of the most influential works of Jewish law ever written.

Pri Megadim primarily focuses on explaining and unpacking three earlier commentaries on the Shulḥan Arukh, which is the definitive halachic code — namely, *Turei Zahav*, *Magen Avraham*, and *Siftei Kohen* — adding omitted information, and offering insights into the background and legal principles underpinning their views.

Rabbi Teomim thoroughly annotated these works and in general offered a well-researched backdrop to the Jewish laws that they covered, so much so that his work has become a mandatory study aid for anyone seeking formal ordination as a rabbi and any position of rabbinic authority.

All of this is by way of introduction to Rabbi Teomim's fascinating halakhic opinion regarding the supremacy of rabbinic law in Judaism, an opinion he illustrated via an obscure discussion about a sukkah.

According to the *Pri Megadim*, if the rabbis who established halakhic guidelines mandated the performance of a Torah mitzvah in a particular way, telling us exactly how it should be performed, then the failure to meet these rabbinic requirements would totally negate the observance of the mitzvah, as if it was never performed — even if by Torah standards the mitzvah had actually been observed.

For example, according to rabbinic law, if a sukkah is so small that one is forced to eat off a table that remains outside the sukkah, one has not discharged one's sukkah obligation at all. And although this stringency was only introduced by the rabbis, while Torah law considers such a sukkah fully kosher, since by eating in this sukkah one has disregarded a rabbinic law, according to Rabbi Teomim one has not even fulfilled one's Torah obligation.

Puzzlingly, this idea seems to contradict at least one opinion in the Talmud. In tractate Sukkah (23a), Rabbi Meir is recorded as allowing a sukkah to be constructed on top of a live animal, while his perennial interlocutor Rabbi Yehudah does not. The Talmud explains that this dispute centers on a verse in Deuteronomy (16:13): חַג הַסֻּכֹּת תַּעֲשֶׂה לְךָ שִׁבְעַת יָמִים — "you shall observe the festival of Sukkot for seven days" — namely, a sukkah must be available to use for the entire seven-day festival period.

In Rabbi Yehudah's opinion, since one is not allowed to get onto an animal on Shabbat and festival days, a sukkah constructed on an animal's back is not just invalid for the festival days and the intermediate Shabbat, but for all seven days of Sukkot. But Rabbi Meir disagrees; in his view the prohibition of climbing onto an animal is only a rabbinic law, and you cannot undo a Torah obligation on the basis of a rabbinic restriction.

On that basis, it would appear that according to Rabbi Yehudah, a rabbinic prohibition **can** negate the ability to observe a Torah law, in accordance with the view of the *Pri Megadim*, and Rabbi Meir's opinion is that a rabbinic prohibition does not. And while the rabbis determined that in a halakhic dispute between Rabbi Meir and Rabbi Yehudah the law goes according to Rabbi Yehudah, it is strange that the *Pri Megadim*'s halakhic principle seemingly contradicts this senior Talmudic sage, and that he does not see fit to reconcile himself with Rabbi Meir's opinion.

But actually, on reflection, we can rescue the *Pri Megadim* from the indignity of this glaring blunder. Firstly, it is possible that the rabbinic insistence on having a table inside one's sukkah is a specific requirement for a sukkah, and Rabbi Meir might very well make an exception to his leniency if one failed to uphold a rabbinic prohibition that directly relates to the observance of the law itself.

Meanwhile, the prohibition of sitting on an animal on yom tov applies to all festivals, not just Sukkot, and has nothing whatsoever to do with the validity of a sukkah. Rabbi Meir would not accept dismissing a Torah-mandated mitzvah on the basis of a general rabbinic restriction unrelated to that specific mitzvah, and that is why he allows a sukkah to be used even if it is on an animal's back, and even though that sukkah may not be used on the first days of the festival or during the intermediate Shabbat.

What I love most about this debate and discussion — and particularly about the *Pri Megadim*'s assertive stance — is the reverence it demonstrates for rabbinic law, which has been the backbone of Jewish identity since the dawn of Jewish nationhood.

Maimonides writes that the Torah itself established the centrality of rabbinic input into Jewish law, with the verse (Deuteronomy 17:11): לֹא תָסוּר מִן הַדָּבָר אֲשֶׁר יַגִּידוּ לְךָ יָמִין וּשְׂמֹאל — "you must not deviate from any word that they tell you, neither right nor left" (MT Neg. Mitzvot 312).

It is a fact that all those Jews who have favored relying purely on scripture as the source for Jewish law — such as the Sadducees, the Boethusians, and the Karaites — have long since evaporated as identifiable Jewish groups, having bound themselves up with an ossified and ultimately self-destructive form of Judaism that undermined any hope for their future.

Only Rabbinic Judaism, with its strong focus on a carefully managed evolutionary halakhic system, has managed to sustain itself over millennia, bequeathing a living, breathing, dynamic Torah to each emerging generation, who have in turn handed it down to the next.

And so, as we sit in our sukkah this year, with a table firmly inside it for us to eat off, we would do well to reflect on the remarkable ancient tradition that we have been lucky enough to be born into. Our identity as Jews only has meaning because of it.

A TRUE MAN OF FAITH

first published November 9, 2017

One of the key teachings of the book of Genesis is that each of the three patriarchs represents different elevated characteristics to which we should all aspire. Abraham, who is our first ushpizin guest on Sukkot, is always presented to us as a perfect paradigm of two characteristics: faith and kindness. He was the first person to self-generate the concept of a creator God, and throughout his life he was tested by God, to see if his faith was firm and unshakeable. Remarkably, he passed every test with flying colors.

There is some disagreement as to what these ten tests actually were, but clearly they were all geared towards exercising his faith muscles, so that by the time Abraham got to the final test — the Akeida, which everyone agrees was the tenth test — he would be ready for it.

I have always struggled with this concept of a monolithic patriarch. Human beings do not have one-dimensional personalities. They may be predominantly one thing or another, but human beings are not angels, nor are they computers or robots. They don't always act one way. In fact, what would be the point of faith without doubt?

And it's not just this aspect of matching the patriarch with the attribute idea that bothers me, because there's something else as well. The facts. Of course, we should never let facts get in the way of a good story, but we are not talking about an after-dinner speech, or a magazine article. This concept is fundamental to our understanding of our origins. It must line up with the facts.

Let's look at the facts, as recorded in the Torah. How can Abraham be considered such an incredibly faithful man if as soon as he arrived in Canaan and discovered that the country was in the midst of a famine, he immediately gave up and went to Egypt? Why didn't he believe in God? Why was he worried that Sarah would be kidnapped? Why does he challenge God about destroying Sodom if God has told him that Sodom needs to be destroyed?

And what about the kindness? Would a kind and gentle man lead a military campaign against four mighty kings? Would a kind and gentle man banish his wife Hagar and his son Ishmael? Then there are his canny negotiating skills with Ephron, and his concern that Eliezer might not follow his instructions, which leads him to force an oath on his trusted servant.

What we have here is a very nuanced individual, full of personality, full of surprises — sometimes passive, sometimes aggressive. Occasionally he reacts one way, and at other times he reacts completely differently. He seems unpredictable, and he certainly does not appear to be the primary example of unadulterated faith and pure kindness. So, what are we to think?

I am certainly not the first one to ask these questions, nor am I the last. The most ancient commentaries addressed them, some of them more satisfactorily, some of them less so. And usually, these questions about Abraham are asked and answered in the context of one particular incident, and not in an attempt to come up with a comprehensive answer.

Allow me to share a Sukkot story that offers an illuminating path to understanding Abraham.

In the old country there was this very poor Jew who loved the festival of Sukkot. Throughout the year he would put away a couple of rubles each week so that he would be able to buy the best and most expensive etrog when Sukkot came around.

One year, there were floods, storms, transport problems — whatever it was that could cause for there to be no etrogs in those days. Indeed, there were no etrogs in his town that Sukkot, not for any price.

A week before Sukkot he heard that in a nearby city there were a handful of etrogs for sale for 500 rubles or more. The price was far too high — he didn't have 500 rubles — so he resolved, sadly, not to have an etrog that year. He told his wife that he wouldn't be getting himself an etrog, and that was it.

Then, on the day before Sukkot, after morning prayers, just as he was putting his tefillin away, he suddenly had a thought. He wouldn't be needing his tefillin for the next ten days, until after Simḥat Torah. If he sold his tefillin today and combined the money with the money he had saved the whole year — he would be able to afford the 500-ruble etrog!

He immediately ran out of the shul and sold his tefillin. He then rushed across to the neighboring town and bought the most beautiful etrog he could find.

Utterly delighted, he came home with the etrog, and wanted to show it to his wife. But she wasn't around, so he placed the etrog down on one of the counters in the kitchen, so that she would see it as soon as she came in. Meanwhile, he went outside to finish putting up his sukkah.

After the sukkah was up, he came back into the house, and saw that his wife had returned.

He said to her, "Honey, I managed to buy an etrog — and not just any etrog — it's really beautiful."

"How did you manage to buy one?" she asked.

"I sold my tefillin."

"But what are going to do after yom tov?"

"I will worry about it then."

"Are you crazy? Tefillin you need every day of your life, an etrog is for seven days a year — what were you thinking?"

The man sat her down. "As I was taking off my tefillin this morning," he told her, "I realized that the mitzvah of the day is not tefillin, it's etrog. The mitzvah for the next seven days is etrog, so I need to worry about etrog. After Sukkot, the mitzvah of the day will be tefillin, so I'll worry about tefillin then."

She smiled at him, "OK, so let me see your etrog."

He said, "It's so beautiful," and he ran over to the counter to show her the etrog, but it wasn't there.

"The etrog was right here, did you see it?"

His wife turns white. "What??"

He says, "I put it right here for you to see."

She starts stammering, unable to speak.

He says, "Honey, what's wrong?"

Eventually she answers. "I was making a salad for yom tov; I needed a lemon and lemon juice for the salad. I looked around and I saw a lemon, a beautiful yellow lemon on the counter. I started to squeeze it, but there wasn't much juice coming out. So, I cut it up, and squeezed the pieces into the salad, and I threw it in the trash. I never dreamed it was an etrog, you told me you didn't buy an etrog. I thought it was a big lemon."

She started to cry, she felt absolutely terrible. Her husband looked at her, and he was quiet. Then he walks over to her, gives her a big hug, and says to her "Honey, I cherish you, I treasure you, I love you."

She says to him, "Are you crazy? Aren't you angry with me? Aren't you going to shout at me? I robbed you of your most precious thing of the year, and after you had even sacrificed your tefillin for it?!"

He looks at her and says, "Let me tell you something — yesterday the mitzvah of the day was to put on tefillin. Today, in the morning, the mitzvah of the day was to buy an etrog. Right now, the mitzvah of the moment is to be here for you. To be sensitive to you. To be kind to you." And he hugged her again.

My friends, our biggest mistake is to imagine that perfect Judaism is some monolithic construct. A model. In fact, if we aren't careful, we can become addicted to that model, that fantasy of perfection.

And if the model is gone, we feel our Judaism has been destroyed. This etrog Jew understood what it means to be a Jew. A Jew with real faith. It means being a Jew every moment, in the moment. There is a moment when the mitzvah is tefillin. Then there is a moment when the mitzvah is etrog. Then, in the next moment, there's a new mitzvah — it's the mitzvah of loving your wife.

If you stay in tefillin mode, then you lose the etrog moment. If you stay in the etrog moment, you lose the loving your wife moment. Because if you are addicted to the Judaism fantasy, the moment your etrog is taken away, you have nothing. Your whole world is shattered. But if that happens, you have no tefillin, no etrog, and no marriage — and actually, you have no God. You have nothing.

But if you are in the moment, even if you don't have tefillin or your etrog, you do have your marriage, and you do have God.

And that's how we need to understand Abraham. Abraham was not confined to a construct. He was someone whose faith in God was in every moment, and for every moment. And not every moment or every situation is perfect, or the same. Circumstances change, we change, other people change — it's summer, its winter, we were younger, now we're older.

Abraham knew that sometimes his profound belief in God demanded one reaction, and at other times it demanded a totally different response. The one constant was not the self-defeating fantasy, it was his utter faith in God in every individual moment.

All of us can get caught up in a version of the Judaism fantasy. We may even try to prop up that fantasy and keep it going. That's because we don't have the courage to live in the moment.

We need the inspiration of Abraham who was not some boring one-dimensional man of faith. Abraham's faith was the faith of someone who engaged it in good times, and in bad. That's what it means to be a true man of faith, and that is the lesson of Abraham.

(With thanks to Rabbi Y.Y. Jacobson for sharing the wonderful story in this article)

THE CHOICE IS IN OUR HANDS

first published October 5, 2017

Themtext he haftara we read on Shabbat Ḥol Hamoed Sukkot is highly unusual, and very dramatic. It is a narrative from the Book of Ezekiel (Ez. 38:18–39:16) describing the devastating battle between Gog and Magog that will precede the Final Redemption. As a prophecy, it is both graphic and fascinating, although, on the face of it, it seems unconnected to the festival of Sukkot.

The Talmud (Meg. 31a) records a discussion regarding the portions of Torah and Prophets one should read on festival days and directs us to read this passage on this particular day. In explaining this strange directive, the great medieval Babylonian rabbinic authority, Rabbi Ḥai Gaon (939–1038), writes that the war of Gog and Magog is relevant to Sukkot as it will occur during the month of Tishrei. But even if this is true, it does not adequately explain why we need to read this selection during Sukkot.

The passage itself is easily summarized, but its meaning is clearly much more profound than the plain translation of the text. Ezekiel's prophecy predicts that Gog will come to attack the Land of Israel, and God will respond in such a powerful way, that the ensuing destruction of the anti-God forces will act as a final and everlasting proof of His might and omnipotence. But although Gog will ultimately be killed and his forces obliterated, before that happens many will have died, and he will have brought devastation to Israel.

Rabbeinu Saadia Gaon (882–942) devotes considerable attention to the traditions regarding the arrival of the Messiah, one of which is that those killed during this great war will not be revived during tehiyat hameitim (resurrection of the dead). This prediction seems harsh, although there is an alternative source that offers a "get-out clause" — the Talmud (Shab. 118) records that those who always eat Seudah Shlishit (the third and final meal of Shabbat, just before it ends) will find salvation from several disasters, including the ill effects of the war of Gog and Magog.

In reality, both sources are just the tip of the iceberg. They introduce us to the remarkable impact this prophecy has had on Jewish theology, despite the fact that Gog and Magog are almost entirely absent from the Hebrew scriptures besides for two oblique references. Magog is mentioned in Genesis (10:2), in the list of Japheth's descendants, and in 1 Chronicles (5:4) Gog is mentioned as one of the grandsons of Reuben, although it is unlikely that this Gog is the same Gog as the one mentioned in Ezekiel. And yet the Talmudic and Midrashic sages interpret many seemingly unrelated prophecies as referring to the war of Gog and Magog.

Avot de-Rabbi Natan, for example, records the ten occasions that scripture refers to God descending to Earth; the war between Gog and Magog — during which God's "legs" are described as standing on the Mount of Olives — is one of them. The source for this is in Zachariah, but although the passage there refers to a battle at the end of days, neither Gog nor Magog are mentioned.

Evidently, the war we read about in Ezekiel 38–39 is not merely "a war," but "**the** war" — the battle that will finally establish the existence and rulership of God for eternity.

The great rabbinic luminary, Rabbi Aryeh Leib Gunzberg (1695–1785), author of *Sha'agat Aryeh*, charts the order of the Messianic era as derived from Maimonides' description of this period which he renders at the end of his seminal work, the *Mishneh Torah*. According to this timeline, the Messiah will only arrive after the battle of Gog, and, following his arrival, God will blow a shofar to gather in the exiles.

But if that order is correct, it is very troubling. Particularly over the past 70 years, but also during the preceding century, there has been an ingathering of exiles which has resulted in a concentration of Jews that far outstrips anything we have seen for almost two thousand years. Today, the largest concentration of Jews in the world lives in Israel, and it won't be long before more than half the Jews of the world will live there.

If we are to take Maimonides at his word, this return of the exiles cannot be the real one, because the war of Gog has not yet happened — as is evident from the fact that God's eternal and almighty rulership has not yet been established beyond any doubt for all the inhabitants of earth.

But this is only a problem if the order and details of the Messianic Redemption as recorded by Maimonides and Rabbi Gunzberg are set in stone. But that is not the case at all. In actual fact there are multiple paths, and multiple orders, and while all of them are possible, none of them takes precedence over any other. They are all true in the sense that they could all happen, but at the moment of execution, only one of them will.

That being the case, perhaps it is possible to avert the horrors Gog and Magog in ways other than eating the third Shabbat meal. Perhaps any steps we take towards making God's rule known to the world, and towards highlighting and avoiding any ruler who would brazenly challenge God and attack God's people, are steps we can also take to save ourselves and others from the death, destruction, and suffering of the war of Gog and Magog.

Which is why we read this particular haftarah during Sukkot, which has God's role in our lives as its central theme. We celebrate a successful harvest granted by God, we pray to God for rain, and we throw ourselves at God's mercy by sitting in a sukkah for seven days.

Sukkot is a God-recognition festival in every aspect of its themes and observances. This haftarah reminds us all that one way or another, the course of human history will ultimately lead to universal recognition of God's power and His special relationship with the Jewish people.

But although the course of events that lead to this universal recognition could include an awful Gog-Magog type war, when we celebrate Sukkot, with all the joy in God-recognition activities it includes, we remind ourselves that rather than going down the Gog-Magog route, we must strive to bring about the recognition of God in ways that mimic the themes and joy of Sukkot, thereby saving ourselves and others from the devastation of the alternative prophecy. The choice is in our hands.

SPIRITUAL ELEVATION IS A PROCESS, NOT A SWITCH

first published October 3, 2017

With each passing year, the sukkah companies endeavor to make it ever easier to build your sukkah. All you need to do is buy a kit from a sukkah store. And now you can find all the construction instructions online — presumably because they know that you've already lost the paper instructions before you got home from the store.

"Don't worry!" the YouTube video promises, "Even a novice can put up the sukkah in less than 15 minutes."

This declaration is accompanied by a time-lapse video of a white-shirted yeshiva guy putting up his sukkah in a hyper-speed enhanced 32 seconds, while upbeat klezmer music plays in the background.

The Talmud devotes a dense and lengthy tractate to the construction of a sukkah. Those familiar with it will tell you that the rules are complex and complicated. Actually, the rules sound like something out of a Jackie Mason routine. The sukkah can't be too short, but it can't be too tall. It doesn't need four walls, but it needs more than two. That doesn't mean it needs three — two-and-a-half walls is good, but not two-and-a-quarter walls. You can't have too much sun coming in through the roof, but too much shade is also no good. You get the drift.

Which makes the Talmud's assertion (Avoda Zara 3a) that building a sukkah is a mitzvah kalla — a simple commandment — all the more intriguing.

The passage there is discussing what will happen when the Messiah arrives, and the nations of the world come face-to-face with their long and bitter history of mistreatment of the Jews, along with their refusal to acknowledge God's designated religion. Each nation will present its case as to why they should be included in the Messianic redemption, but their excuses will all be dismissed.

The nations will then request one last chance to start afresh and make amends, proclaiming to God:

Offer us the Torah anew and we shall obey it.

To which God will respond…

Oh, foolish ones, he who took trouble to prepare for the Sabbath can eat on Sabbath. But he who has not troubled to prepare for Sabbath, what shall he eat on Sabbath? <u>Nevertheless, I have an easy commandment called "Sukkah"; go and carry it out.</u>

Immediately, all of them will go and construct a sukkah on their rooftops. But God will cause the sun to burn over them like the height of summer, and they will all trample down their sukkahs and depart…

This passage is extremely bizarre. Building a sukkah properly is not "easy," as the passage suggests it is. It is complicated and challenging. Besides, if it gets too hot, observing the mitzvah becomes impossible, and is no longer mandated. Why does God ask the nations to observe Sukkot, only to make it uncomfortable for them by raising the temperature? And why tell them it is an easy commandment?

The early modern rabbinic luminary, Rabbi Abraham Ḥayyim Schor (d. 1632), offers a remarkable insight into this curious Talmudic tale. He points out that although there are certainly simpler Jewish observances than sukkah, none of them have the one crucial quality that only a sukkah has.

When you are sitting in a sukkah, it is as though you are observing everything else that is written in the Torah. And while there are other ways one can do this, they are either more costly, or they require more commitment, or they require greater expertise. Making and then wearing tzitzit at all times is one example; another example is observing Shabbat.

When the Talmud refers to sukkah as an "easy mitzvah," the suggestion is not that building a sukkah is easy. Rather, it means that a sukkah can provide those who use it with an expedited route to God. In the end-of-days scenario depicted in the Talmudic narrative, the nations are looking for exactly such an opportunity, to make up for lost time, so that they can participate in the Messianic redemption.

While this explanation is compelling, how exactly does a sukkah encapsulate the essence of everything which God seeks from humanity, and what is the Talmudic narrative trying to teach us? Clearly none of what is described in the narrative has happened, and it may never happen — so what is the underlying message?

Perhaps the message is this. Ultimately, the purpose of creation is for material things to recognize God despite the handicap of being physical, and therefore detached from the Divine. The Midrash describes the process as follows: "God covered Himself up and created the world," which means that God shields the physical world from His light.

As we advance through life and develop spiritually, rather than revealing His light to us all in one go, God exposes us to it little by little, so that we are not blinded or overwhelmed.

Sukkot occurs immediately after the High Holidays when we go through a spiritual detox. But while that might prepare us for God's light, we are still not quite ready to be subjected to blinding, burning sunshine. We need a little more shade than light as we emerge from utter darkness. Shifting from physical to spiritual is a process. We may get there in the end, but it cannot be rushed.

Even emerging from the house is unwise if we are not properly prepared. As God says to the nations in the Talmudic narrative, "He who has not troubled to prepare for Sabbath, what shall he eat on Sabbath?" But the nations are impatient; they have no time for process. They want it all, and they want it all now.

This Talmudic passage is an eye opener for spiritual seekers. Too much, too fast — and you will crash and burn. If you demand instant results, you are guaranteed disappointment, and the opportunity will be lost. Sukkot is there to remind us that God created us to be marathon runners, not sprinters.

It is all about the process. We are on our way, and we will all get there. But it must happen in carefully managed stages.

A MATTER OF PERSPECTIVE

first published October 10, 2014

I t is all a matter of perspective. To some, Christopher Columbus (1451–1506) is the heroic explorer who discovered the New World. To others, he is the man who "played a pivotal role in the worst genocide humankind has ever known"— as was stated by Kshama Sawant, a city council member in Seattle, where this week it was decided that Columbus Day should double up as Indigenous Peoples' Day.

Sawant's stand was vehemently opposed by Lisa Marchese, a lawyer affiliated with the curiously named Order Sons of Italy in America, as well as with the Italian-American Chamber of Commerce of the Pacific Northwest.

Columbus's Italian origins — he was born in Genoa — has motivated Americans of Italian origin to oppose Native Americans who advocate for Indigenous Peoples' Day to replace Columbus Day so that they can celebrate the culture that disintegrated as a result of the European invasion.

"Italian Americans are deeply offended," Marchese said.

The most fascinating aspect of this storm in a teacup is that neither Columbus Day nor Indigenous Peoples' Day are recognized public holidays in Washington State. And yet, despite this, people are willing to spend time and expend energy, and even trade insults, to ensure that their side is victorious in a fight where the winners have won nothing, and the losers are no worse off than they were before the fight began.

The saga of modern-day Native Americans fighting the descendants of Italian immigrants over the legacy of a fifteenth-century adventurer who accidentally landed in the Bahamas in 1492, and who may or may not have precipitated the decline of the indigenous culture of the Americas, brought to mind the most famous verse in *Kohelet* (Eccl. 1:2): הֲבֵל הֲבָלִים אָמַר קֹהֶלֶת הֲבֵל הֲבָלִים הַכֹּל הָבֶל — "Vanity of vanities, said Kohelet; vanity of vanities, all is vanity."

This verse, written millennia ago, perfectly summarizes the human condition. The incredible efforts expended by human beings over matters that are, for all intents and purposes pointless, often defies comprehension and explanation, but — as *Kohelet* goes on to point out — "there is nothing new under the sun."

Human beings seem compelled to campaign and battle over issues that ultimately amount to very little for anyone, while the really important stuff is often ignored or marginalized.

Kohelet is read on Shabbat Ḥol Hamoed Sukkot or on Shemini Atzeret. It seems an odd choice of scripture to be associated with a festival that we proclaim as z'man simḥateinu — the time of our joy. It is, on the face of it, a deeply pessimistic and downbeat tract, consisting of a narrative that catalogues human folly and the fragility of human existence.

How is this theme appropriate for the one Jewish festival when we are expected to be blissfully happy and cheerful? It might be argued that if ever there was a spirit dampener, *Kohelet* is it. The author seems intent on pressing home the point that nothing is worth doing, and whatever you have already done has been an utter waste of time. None of this chimes with the spirit of joy.

Although, as it happens, Sukkot is probably the most appropriate time to read *Kohelet*. Hot on the heels of Rosh Hashana and Yom Kippur, Sukkot is the great equalizer. Rich and poor are forced to leave their homes and subject themselves to relative discomfort in a temporary, leaf-covered booth for seven days.

Even the most sophisticated sukkah is open to the elements, and those who use the sukkah are going to be subjected to wind, or heat, or rain, or all of the above as the festival unfolds.

The idea behind the sukkah is that we should take the lessons of the High Holidays and put them into practice. How could we better demonstrate that the lessons we claim to have learnt during fervent prayers in the synagogue on Rosh Hashana and Yom Kippur — lessons of humility and commitment to God at all costs — have truly been absorbed and put into practice? Consequently, we shun the physical comforts and familiar routines of our homes and displace ourselves into a temporary space that is less comfortable and less appealing.

What is most remarkable about this annual adventure is that if it is done in the correct spirit, it works. If our prayers were heartfelt, and our resolutions genuine, we will embrace the sukkah as the perfect vehicle by which to show that we were not merely paying lip service on Rosh Hashana and Yom Kippur, but rather we were intent on living up to the ideals embodied by those awesome days.

Nothing is more liberating than knowing that you do not really need very much to be happy. The lower you set the bar, the easier it is to achieve bliss. People who need their creature comforts, and who collapse as soon as their comfort zone is breached, will remain chronically unhappy. People who can forgo the convenience of their homes and enjoy a seven-day sukkot experience are the ones who are most likely to be happy.

In which case *Kohelet* is the perfect partner to Sukkot. It urges its readers to understand the futility of material pursuit, and the superficiality of human wisdom, so that in as much as each and every one of us is lucky enough to have material comfort and intellectual achievement, we will rejoice with what we have, despite its limitations, in the knowledge that everything we have is truly a blessing.

Facing up to the truth about our limitations is a recipe for happiness, not a route to depression. That is the message of the sukkah, and that is the message of *Kohelet*. It is certainly not the message of Columbus Day or Indigenous Peoples' Day, nor of those who fight about which one is more important.

FINDING YOUR BURIED TREASURE

first published October 8, 2020

What is the festival known as Shemini Atzeret really about? Why do we need an extra day of yom tov?

The Midrash offers a wonderful suggestion. God is reluctant to let us go, the Midrash explains, and we are reluctant to let go of God, so we continue for another day, before embarking on the long winter until the spring, when the festival season starts again with Pesach.

In California we don't have cold winters. In fact, being a weatherman in California is probably the best job on the planet. How wrong can you ever be? Although, I remember my late father saying, with a twinkle in his eye, that he wished he had become a weatherman. In what other line of work can you be so consistently wrong and still keep your job?

I don't know if the following story is true — but it could be. One year, in late October, a tribe of Native Americans on a remote reservation asked their chief if the coming winter was going to be very cold or just mild. Truthfully, he had absolutely no idea — but he didn't want them to know that. After all, he was meant to be the expert, his people's oracle. Just to be on the safe side, he told the tribe that the winter was going to be cold and that they should collect plenty of firewood to be totally prepared.

But the chief wanted to make sure that he didn't make a fool of himself, so after a few days he drove to a public phone far away from the reservation village and called the National Weather Service to ask them if the winter ahead was going to be cold.

"Yes, according to our information it looks like this coming winter is going to be cold," the meteorologist told him. Feeling vindicated, the chief went back to his village and told the tribesmen to collect more firewood.

The following week he called the National Weather Service again, anonymously of course. "Does it still look like we are going to have a very cold winter?" he asked. The man at National Weather Service was firm — "Yes, it's going to be a very cold winter this year."

So, once again the chief went back to his people and ordered them to collect every scrap of firewood they could find. Two weeks later he called the National Weather Service one last time, just to be completely sure.

"Are you absolutely positive this winter is going to be super cold?" he asked. "Oh, categorically," was the response. "In fact, it looks like it is going to be one of the coldest winters we've ever had."

"Really? But how can you be so sure?" the chief asked.

The weatherman paused for a moment. "It's simple," he said, "we're so sure it's going to be freezing cold this year because we've heard that the Native Americans are collecting firewood like crazy!"

Shemini Atzeret feels like a yom tov where everyone is clueless about what's going on, and we are all looking for some kind of guidance from somewhere — anywhere! — as to what we should be doing. Like the Native American chief asking the meteorologist, and the meteorologist looking for clues from the Native Americans — it's almost as if we are going around in circles to work out the facts regarding Shemini Atzeret. What exactly should we be doing?

In one of his most striking stories, Rabbi Naḥman of Breslov describes a poor Jewish tailor living in Ukraine who persistently had the same dream in which he discovered a buried treasure in Vienna, at the foot of a bridge over the Danube River.

But there was a problem with his dream — the tailor had never been to Vienna, nor even Austria — he lived in a little village in Ukraine and had never ventured more than a few miles from his home.

But after the same dream kept reoccurring, he told his wife about it and that he wanted to go to Vienna to get the treasure. She looked at him for a moment and sighed. "Well, I guess if you had the dream so many times it must be true, and the treasure must be there — just go to Vienna and find it!"

The tailor travelled to Vienna — and sure enough he found the bridge just as he had seen it in his dreams. But there was a problem — the exact spot where the treasure was buried in his dreamworld, in the real world was guarded by two fierce looking Austrian soldiers.

Not sure what to do, the tailor hovered around the area for a couple of days, waiting for the soldiers to go off on a lunch break or something, so that he could dig for the treasure. But the soldiers found his loitering a bit strange, and eventually they arrested him and brought him in for questioning.

"What are you doing at the bridge? Are you a Russian spy?"

"You will never believe me if I told you why I'm here," he replied.

"Try us!" they said.

The tailor revealed his dream to them and explained that he had come to Vienna to find the buried treasure. The soldiers burst out laughing. Still chuckling, one of them says to the tailor: "Do you know something? Last night I had a dream that under the house of a Jewish tailor in some little village in Ukraine there is a fabulous treasure. Do you think I'm crazy enough to go all the way to Ukraine to find it?" And they let him go.

The tailor journeyed home, and as soon as he got back, he dug under his house — just to see, maybe the soldier's dream was right after all. Remarkably, after digging for a few minutes, he discovered a fabulous treasure buried right under his house.

Rabbi Naḥman of Breslov uses this story to convey something to us that we all already know. Whatever we do and wherever we go looking to find that treasure, the most precious treasure is always much closer to home — inside us. It is not buried in Vienna, or anywhere else, it is wherever we are right now, in the heart of our lives. We just need to dig for it, and we'll find it.

Ellul, Rosh Hashana, Aseret Yemey Teshuva, Yom Kippur, Sukkot, shofar, apples, honey, davening, fasting, lulav, etrog, sitting in the sukkah — all of these things are very important, but at the same time they are also all very distracting. It's a roller coaster. We need a bit of time to reflect, to remember, to savor.

In fact, we need a time that is specifically designated for digging up the treasure that is already underneath our own house, so that we can use the strength it gives us to keep us going through the winter months, until Pesach — when the whole cycle starts up again. And that is what Shemini Atzeret is all about.

THE SECRET OF SIMḤAT TORAH REVEALED

first published September 26, 2018

There is a maxim in Jewish ritual law which prohibits mixing two distinct expressions of joy, a rule known as "Ein Me'arvin Simḥa Besimḥa" (Mo'ed Katan 9a). This means, for example, that weddings are proscribed during ḥol hamoed, so as not to eclipse the joy of the festival.

And yet, Simḥat Torah, which is not mentioned anywhere in the Hebrew Scriptures, has been superimposed onto the festival day of Shemini Atzeret. Surely by conflating Shemini Atzeret with Simḥat Torah we are diluting the joy of a mandated festival day? It seems odd, at best, that this paradox has been enshrined in our calendar.

Before trying to unlock this puzzle, let me explain our obligation to be joyful on festival days. Each of our festivals has particular requirements, put there to direct our celebration.

On Passover we eat matzah, maror, and the lamb sacrifice. Shavuot has the special offering of bikkurim and the festival showbread. On Sukkot we wave the arba minim (four species), and reside in a sukkah.

All these obligations share one objective — to remind us why we are celebrating the festival so that we can experience the appropriate joy and happiness. Strangely enough, Shemini

Atzeret seems to have no mitzvah to call its own, and there is no indication in the Torah to tell us what we are expected to use as the trigger for joy.

The Talmud (Sukkah 55b) notes that seventy separate sacrifices were offered at the Temple over Sukkot, corresponding to the "seventy nations of the world." On Shemini Atzeret, however, there was only one offering, "corresponding to the one [chosen] nation."

While the non-Jewish world seemingly has a role to play throughout the festival of Sukkot, on Shemini Atzeret only the Jewish nation is the focus, and we are only required to bring a solitary offering. The joy and happiness of Shemini Atzeret is more self-contained, without any need for accessories and artificial enhancements.

On each day of Sukkot, we invite one of our illustrious biblical ancestors to join us in the sukkah — Abraham, Isaac, Jacob, Moses, Aaron, Joseph, and David. Each one of these ushpizin guests represents our attempt to repair a particular characteristic we wish to remove from our identity, a trait that connects us to the nations of the world.

Similarly, on each day of Sukkot we wave the arba minim in six directions, protecting ourselves from damaging influences that can invade our space from every side.

And on the final day of Sukkot, Hoshana Rabba, as we hold the arba minim in our hands, we circle the Torah seven times, and implore God to protect us from any potential danger.

The explicit focus of Sukkot is to mitigate the threat to our viability from the unknown beyond, and the joy we experience on

Sukkot directly correlates to our victory over every potentially damaging alternative. But on Shemini Atzeret we no longer seek protection; our safety is generated by the festival itself.

There is a beautiful Midrash in *Yalkut Shimoni* that gives us a powerful backdrop to the Shemini Atzeret festival:

> **After the seven days of Sukkot are done, God says to Israel, "Now you and I will rejoice together", and when Israel hears this, they begin to praise God, saying (Ps. 118:24), זֶה הַיּוֹם עָשָׂה ה' נָגִילָה וְנִשְׂמְחָה בוֹ — "This is the day that God has made, we will rejoice and be happy with it."**

The Midrash goes on to say that the ambiguous pronoun "it" at the end of the verse is not a reference to the festival day. Rather "it" refers to the Torah, which the Jews will use on that day to celebrate their unique relationship with God.

The joy of Shemini Atzeret is not associated with any historic event, nor are we required to perform a particular mitzvah. The joy of Shemini Atzeret is meant to reflect our relationship with and love of God's Torah.

The feeling of longing that we have for a loving, meaningful relationship with God transcends individual mitzvot, and instead encapsulates the whole Torah, along with everything it contains and imparts. It is about our love of God's word over and above the details of each mitzvah — and it is this aspect of our identity that distinguishes us from the other nations of the world, clarifying why Shemini Atzeret belongs exclusively to the Jewish nation.

Someone once shared a compelling insight with me about the dichotomy between Jewish penitence and the repentance processes prevalent in other religious faiths. Those who adhere to other religions are induced to repent out of fear for God's retribution, but Jews cleanse themselves of sin so that they can renew the relationship they have with God, unencumbered by the baggage of iniquity and material distractions.

By the time we reach Shemini Atzeret we no longer need a specific mitzvah. The clarity of our relationship with God is at its zenith, and we do not require a crutch to support it, nor a ladder to reach it.

That is why Shemini Atzeret is the perfect time to celebrate and dance with our precious Torah scrolls. People mistakenly believe that the reason for the Torah-oriented celebration on Shemini Atzeret is because this festival happens to coincide with the conclusion of our annual Torah reading cycle. In fact, exactly the opposite is true. We deliberately conclude and recommence the Torah cycle on Shemini Atzeret because Shemini Atzeret is the most appropriate date in our calendar for this moment to occur.

Which means that dancing and singing with Torah scrolls on Shemini Atzeret is not the imposition of an intruding element of joy into the festival. As it turns out, Shemini Atzeret and Simḥat Torah are identical — the ultimate celebration of our unique relationship with God.

CHANUKAH

first published December 10, 2020

O ne of the most celebrated military victories in the history of war took place in 1560. It was the culmination of a military encounter known as the Battle of Okehazama, a decisive confrontation during the civil war which had erupted in sixteenth-century Japan as a result of warlords battling for control of the entire country.

One of the less prominent warlord families was the Oda clan, not considered frontrunners as potential victors in the messy war.

The family was led by Oda Nobunaga (1534–1582), a capricious and erratic 26-year-old, widely believed to be mentally unstable.

It all began in 1560, when Imagawa Yoshimoto — who headed the far more powerful Imagawa clan — embarked on a campaign to take Kyoto, then the capital of Japan. To get to Kyoto, his army needed to cross through Owari, which was controlled by the Oda family.

The Imagawa army numbered as many as 40,000 men, while Oda Nobunaga had just 3,000 soldiers in his militia. All of Nobunaga's generals told him that he had to surrender unconditionally and allow the Imagawa army uninterrupted passage. But Nobunaga ordered his men to construct a dummy army, while he snuck up on Yoshimoto's troops in a flanking maneuver.

Yoshimoto's men were in the midst of celebrating various recent victories, and many of them were drunk, believing that there was no danger from the Oda forces. Fortuitously, a thunderstorm masked the Oda army's approach, and they were able to ambush the unprepared enemy, catching them off guard.

Yoshimoto's men fled in every direction to avoid being slaughtered, leaving their leader unprotected. Meanwhile, Yoshimoto thought the commotion was a drunken squabble between his own men and was killed before he even knew what was happening. Incredibly, the vastly outnumbered Oda army won the battle in less than two hours.

Another military victory considered as remarkable as it was unpredictable, was the Battle of Austerlitz in 1805, which is also called the Battle of the Three Emperors. It was one the greatest victories for Napoleon (1769–1821), with 68,000 of his *Grande Armée* troops defeating almost 90,000 Russians and Austrians, forcing Austria to make peace with France in the Treaty of Pressburg, and preventing Prussia from joining the anti-French alliance. Using an array of brilliant tactical maneuvers, Napoleon managed to divide the enemy forces into two, which allowed the French army to wreak havoc and decimate their adversaries.

These examples are just two out of countless similar military victories that stunned all of those involved when they happened and continue to be cited as examples of tactical genius and the lucky confluence of circumstances which saw an underdog emerge victorious.

But, what interests me more than the victories themselves is the subsequent fate of the conquering protagonists — viz. Oda Nobunaga and Napoleon Bonaparte.

Nobunaga is considered the first "Great Unifier" of Japan, due to successfully bringing most of Japan under his control. Then, in 1582, he was unexpectedly set upon by one of his allies, and in the ensuing skirmish committed ritual suicide rather than fall into the hands of enemy forces.

Napoleon's incredible victories during the eponymous Napoleonic Wars saw him emerge as one of the most powerful leaders Europe has ever known — but hubris saw him pursue goals that eventually resulted in his ignominious downfall, initially seeing him dispatched into exile in Elba in 1814, and eventually to St. Helena in 1815, where he died — possibly after being poisoned — in 1821.

There's an unmistakable message here, and it is one that resonates deeply with the central theme of Chanukah — namely the miracle of the oil. Truthfully, the oil miracle seems rather minor when compared with the incredible military successes of the Maccabees against a Seleucid Greek army, which was far better equipped than the Jewish rebels and vastly outnumbered them.

But soon afterwards, the military victory of the Maccabees against Antiochus IV Epiphanes was a pyrrhic footnote. The Maccabees installed themselves as a royal house that came to be known as the Hasmonean dynasty, and before long they differed very little from the Hellenized Jews and their Seleucid sympathizers they had so vigorously opposed. Over the next century, the Hasmonean dynasty degenerated, and it eventually disintegrated completely at the hands of Herod the Great, an Idumean upstart and brutal dictator who had married into the Hasmonean family.

To celebrate the military victory on Chanukah would be to miss the point completely. Which is why the relatively minor aspect of the Channukah story — namely, the ritually pure olive oil that lasted for a full eight days, the time needed before new oil could be pressed and processed — became the central theme of the festival. The military victory was ephemeral, quickly eclipsed by evolving circumstances; but the faith victory, which allowed Judaism to survive and thrive into the future — was something that remained meaningful long after the spoils of war were distant memories.

In both Vayeishev and Mikeitz, the two Torah portions that coincide with Chanukah, we are introduced to Joseph, the only one of Jacob's sons referred to by the sages of the Talmud as Ha-Tzaddik (the righteous). While he is certainly worthy of this epithet, his brothers surely deserved to be similarly addressed. And yet, they are always referred to just by their given names, with no added title.

The message is simple. While Joseph was one of his era's most powerful political leaders, with the entire wealth of mighty Egypt under his personal management, it is not this feature of his life's achievements that had any enduring value. Rather, it is the fact that he was righteous, considerate, generous, and loyal, and that he was profoundly faithful throughout his rollercoaster life.

The riches of ancient Egypt have long since evaporated, but Joseph's virtues endure, evident in those who remain inspired by his example to rise above the material success and temptations of their lives, and to retain a devoted commitment to God.

As we light the Chanukah lights and recite the blessing aimed at He "who performed miracles for our ancestors in those days, and today," we must remind ourselves that great military victories soon become irrelevant in the wake of evolving circumstances, but the victory of faith in God is a miracle that always outlasts temporal success.

INSANITY IS NO EXCUSE

first published December 26, 2019

A couple of weeks ago, during the early hours of Saturday morning, Anton Redding, a 24-year-old man from Pennsylvania, rampaged through Nessah Synagogue in Beverly Hills, just a few blocks away from our own synagogue, and home to a flourishing Persian Jewish community, some of whose members are also members of my shul.

Redding, who has been variously described as being from Millersville, Mohnton, and Lancaster — all of which are suburban towns southeast of Harrisburg, PA — was arrested in Kona, Hawaii, just a few days later and arraigned in court, where he entered a plea of not guilty, and he is now in jail until his next court hearing on January 30.

Almost immediately after the incident was discovered on Shabbat morning, our synagogue security team was informed of what had happened by the Beverly Hills Police Department. We naturally took all the necessary precautions, as at that stage Redding was still on the loose and no one could be sure of his next move.

But news soon filtered through that this outrage was the act of a "crazy guy" who was not necessarily an antisemite, and although he had undeniably trashed furniture as well as desecrated Torah scrolls and prayer books at Nessah, there seemed to have been no premeditation, and he had peculiarly also left certain unmistakable Jewish icons, such as Israel's flag, completely undisturbed. Additionally, he had not spray-painted swastikas or profanities, the staple indicator of antisemitic vandalism acts in synagogue and Jewish cemetery attacks.

The senior rabbi of Nessah, Rabbi David Shofet, has since gone on the record to say that "although this vandalism and crime… may prove to be the act of a lone man of disturbed mind, we should all be vigilant, united, and responsive to the rise of antisemitism in our country."

His statement projects the idea that we might somehow think that the behavior of a solitary madman is not connected to the issue of rising antisemitism in the United States, and that we therefore need to be warned not to sigh with relief if Anton Redding proves to be suffering from a mental illness which resulted in his nocturnal act of sabotage at one of our local synagogues.

Truthfully, and with respect, Rabbi Shofet is only half-right, and besides, the issue is too important to leave it at that. Because Rabbi Shofet did inadvertently hit upon a very important point — a point that we must all become acutely aware of, take very much to heart, and absorb into the fiber of our beings: namely, that antisemitism, and, indeed, racism or prejudice of any kind, is a mental condition.

In the 2016 book *Are Racists Crazy?*, the authors — historian Sander Gilman and sociologist James Thomas — considered the question of whether a psychological or psychiatric diagnosis is a useful way of dealing with racism or antisemitism, or whether addressing it this way simply shields racists and antisemites from any blame. And their book is hardly the first attempt to address the issue — this debate has been raging for decades and has proved to be highly controversial.

In 1934, the American Jewish Congress organized a public mock trial of Adolf Hitler at Madison Square Garden in New York City. According to the eminent medical professor, Lewellys Barker (1867–1943), acting as chief witness for the prosecution, Nazism had to be defined as a "psychic epidemic," and, as he told the audience of 20,000, "to understand Hitler and Hitlerism, one is compelled to enter the domain of psychopathology."

Once again — as was noted then and has been noted since — the problem with this thesis is that it somehow gets Hitler off the hook, and indeed the psychopathology argument was quickly dropped once Nazi hostility to Jews turned violent — after all, no one wanted Nazi murderers to be exonerated on the basis of an insanity plea.

Unfortunately, however, the problem did not disappear. In 1981, an elderly white man in Kansas, Anthony Simon, shot his Chinese American neighbor Steffen Wong. Charged with two counts of aggravated assault while using a deadly weapon, Simon's defense team claimed he suffered from "anxiety neurosis" as he was afraid of "Orientals", whom he considered to be a deadly threat because of their "expertise in martial arts".

Even though the court acknowledged that this defense argument was a "distortion of reality" — in other words, patent nonsense — Simon was acquitted on both counts, and his case has consequently become a legal precedent used to defend racists claiming mental illness.

As far as Jewish law is concerned, there is no practical difference if someone commits a violent act because they are suffering from a "racism mental condition" or not. If a person objectively understands that violence is wrong, then they are always liable for any violent act they commit, whether or not their target is, in their warped worldview, an undesirable, or some kind of perceived but misplaced threat.

The proof for this can be found in the way rabbinic literature refers to the antihero of Chanukah — Antiochus IV Epiphanes (215 BCE–164 BCE), king of the Seleucid Greeks, and antagonist of the Jews in Judea in the period leading up to the Hasmonean Revolt. Known as "Epiphanes", which means "God Manifest" in Greek, he was also called Antiochus IV "Epimanes", Greek for "the crazy", a wry play on words.

Apparently, Antiochus would often disappear from his palace only to be found later reveling with ordinary folk, or in artisanal shops, chatting and discussing art with metalworkers. Courtiers would frantically search for him to no avail, eventually finding him wandering around in disguise or drinking with common people whom he had never previously met. But all this bonhomie camouflaged an evil sociopath, who thought nothing of murdering and persecuting thousands of Jews simply for practicing their faith.

Rather than giving him a pass because he was Antiochus "the Mad" who could argue that he was not in control of his actions because he suffered from "anxiety neurosis" whenever he saw a Jew, rabbinic literature refers to him simply as אַנְטִיוֹכוּס הָרָשָׁע — "Antiochus the Wicked". If he could function in daily life as an ordinary human being, then he would be judged by his actions, and not on the basis of some specious psychological evaluation.

Anton Redding is no different. Nor should any other antisemitic attack on Jews or their property be judged on the basis of psychopathology. Notwithstanding the fact that a perpetrator of violence against Jews may be crazy, they are nonetheless responsible for their antisemitism, and must be punished accordingly. And, as it turns out, this is one of the intrinsic messages of Chanukah.

> *(On November 19, 2020, Anton Redding entered a guilty plea to one felony count of vandalism of religious property. He was sentenced to 220 days in county jail and five years of formal probation. He was also ordered to complete a 12-month residential treatment program and to pay $166,604 restitution to Nessah Synagogue.)*

AND FINALLY, THE MIRACLE OF CHANUKAH

first published December 7, 2018

Y ou will be forgiven for having never heard of Chaim Selig Slonimsky (1810–1904). A minor celebrity in nineteenth-century Eastern Europe, he was an avuncular man with solid credentials as an astronomer and scientist, notorious for his traditional Jewish appearance, and particularly for his expansive white beard.

In an age when secular studies were universally frowned upon in strictly Orthodox circles, Slonimsky was considered safe — a committed observant Jew who excelled in the world of science, but whose convictions were firmly in the right place.

Legend has it that Slonimsky somehow stumbled on the formula for duplex telegraphy in 1859, but rather than patenting it, he filed his discovery away, telling his wife "Now let us see how long it will take **them** to figure it out!"

And although American scientist Moses Gerrish Farmer (1820–1893) had successfully demonstrated a rudimentary form of duplex telegraphy in 1856, it was not until 1871 that Joseph Barker Stearns (1831–1895) figured out a serviceable version that was almost identical to Slonimsky's proposal, and his system was then further improved upon, and more importantly, commercialized, by Thomas Edison (1847–1931) in 1874, paving the way for the modern telephone.

Remarkably, Slonimsky's innovation would never have come to light had Soviet dictator Joseph Stalin (1878–1953) not tried to use it as part of an anti-American propaganda campaign in 1952, when a pair of distinguished Russian scientists published a paper which essentially said, "Russia got there first!"

Slonimsky's stellar reputation in the traditional Jewish world took a severe knocking in late 1891, when he published a short article in his newspaper, *Hatsefira,* which questioned the veracity of the celebrated miracle of Chanukah, namely the discovery of a container of uncontaminated oil for the Temple menorah which should only have lasted 24 hours, but which lasted a full eight days, the time period required to produce new oil.

Citing Maimonides' omission of the particular words in the Talmud that convey the narrative of this miracle (see M.T. *Hil. Hannukah* 3:2), Slonimsky suggested that Maimonides was clearly of the opinion that the "miracle" of Chanukah was not in fact supernatural. Rather, the victorious Hasmoneans lit the Temple menorah each night in front of the crowds celebrating their God-assisted triumphant victory, but once people had left, the priests extinguished the flames so that enough oil remained to light up the menorah each subsequent night until new oil was produced.

Slonimsky's article set off a firestorm of protest among traditional rabbis, and countless articles and pamphlets were published to refute his thesis. Critics claimed Slonimsky was an irredeemable heretic and challenged him to recant.

But he was unintimidated and responded defiantly, refusing to retract even the smallest detail of his radical proposal. Ultimately the excitement died down, and Slonimsky went on to live to a ripe old age, dying in Warsaw more than a decade later at the age of 94.

Slonimsky's detractors were certainly right about one thing — that his dismissal of this story would lead to a general ambivalence towards both the festival of Chanukah and towards the authenticity of Talmudic legends. As recently as this past October, an article appeared in the *Huffington Post* under the headline "The Truth(s) About Hanukkah," in which the (Jewish) writer trivializes every aspect of the festival, and particularly the miracle story.

Nevertheless, it is an unavoidable fact that the account of the miraculous oil was first recorded hundreds of years after the Hasmoneans stormed Temple Mount and reclaimed the sacred site for the Jews. If it had happened immediately following the victory, why was it not included in the two contemporaneous accounts of the rebellion against the Greeks — Maccabees I and Maccabees II? While both these books speak of the Temple having had to go through a ritual cleansing process, neither of them mentions anything about a single cruse of oil lasting eight times as long as it should have. Surely this emblematic miracle was worthy of at least a single reference?

As if this is not puzzling enough, one must also wonder why we choose to focus on what is such a minor miracle, notwithstanding its supernatural aspects, when the headline story is surely the astonishing victory of a ragtag bunch of rebels against a professional army of trained combatants? Why did the Talmud feel the need for another hook to hang this festival on, when the success of the Hasmoneans was itself so extraordinary?

Numerous scholars have grappled with these questions and have come to different conclusions to the one Slonimsky suggested. Rabbi Dr. David Berger, for example, notes that Maccabees I has no record of any miracles whatsoever, while Maccabees II is brimming with miracles far more impressive than the long-lasting oil. On that basis, the omission of the oil miracle in a book totally devoid of miracles is hardly surprising, while the absence of a minor miracle in a book containing numerous superlative miracles is similarly predictable.

Other scholars point out that the Bi'mei Matityahu prayer, which summarizes the Chanukah story and was composed far earlier than the account in the Talmud, focuses exclusively on the military victory and omits any mention of the oil having lasted longer.

My own thoughts on this matter are rather more prosaic. When the victory was still fresh in people's minds — and bearing in mind that the victors were all highly devout — the miracle of the oil, while undoubtedly noteworthy, took second place to the incredible — and miraculous — success of the Hasmoneans against the Hellenists' bid to destroy Judaism.

But after the fall of Jerusalem to the Romans, and the later brutal crushing of the Bar Kokhba revolt, the sages of the Talmud sought to refocus the Chanukah festival onto what had previously been seen as more of a minor detail — namely, a miraculous demonstration of God's personal imprimatur on what had occurred.

Perhaps the miracle of Chanukah was ingeniously revived by the sages of the Talmud to bolster a festival that might easily have evolved into a God-free event, no different to the frequent anniversary celebrations of ancient military victories prevalent at the time. By celebrating the miracle of the oil, we are assured that this festival remains religious, and we are compelled to acknowledge Divine involvement in what was essentially a military victory against the Greeks.

This important point may have eluded Slonimsky, but to me it stands out loud and clear.

A VICTORY FOR TRADITIONAL JEWS

first published December 7, 2016

In the months leading up to the recent US election, numerous pundits expressed concerns about a Donald Trump presidency, were he to win. Among the many reasons cited in support of these concerns was his fondness for a populist rhetorical style that, over the many months of the campaign, succeeded in mobilizing a dark corner of the electorate associated with racism and antisemitism.

As the election drew nearer, this concern morphed into personal accusations of racism and antisemitism against Donald Trump himself, undoubtedly part of a wider strategy to mobilize progressive forces to vote against him on Election Day.

Even after Trump won the election, the antisemitism accusations continued, allegations that rose to a deafening crescendo when he appointed Breitbart supremo Steve Bannon to his White House team as chief strategist and senior counselor.

The denunciations of Trump and Bannon do not require my rebuttal. There have been numerous others who have adequately addressed these charges and repudiated them, whether you buy into their repudiations or not. The point I wish to address is the seemingly boundless anti-Trump enthusiasm of so many leaders and opinion-formers in the Jewish-American community, who confidently assert that to be pro-Trump amounts to a rejection of Jewish values.

On September 14, 2016, for example, an article by Daniel Kirzane, a Reform rabbi from Kansas, appeared in *The Forward* with the headline "Why I'm a Jew Against Trump." It began, "Never in the history of American politics has a man so antagonistic to Jewish values achieved as much acclaim as Donald Trump has."

Although Kirzane conceded that Trump is not an antisemite, this point was marginal to his thesis, which proclaimed that any political rhetoric amounting to incitement against minorities rendered the personal convictions of the person uttering them irrelevant, as anything that could be construed as the targeting of minority groups is the epitome of "un-Jewish."

Besides for the fact that this is simply not true, it would seem that Kirzane and his ilk are very eager for all of us to live in a minority dictatorship. The smaller the group, the more its views must be respected, even venerated. Mainstream values honed over centuries and millennia are of no concern, disposable and irrelevant to those who wish to accommodate minority interests to uphold an ideology they tell us is far more lofty and superior.

The general public has become so accustomed to the arguments behind ubiquitous campaigns for the advancement of progressive ideals that many have either jumped aboard or been browbeaten into complicit silence. Those who have the audacity to swim against the tide are either vilified or accused of endangering the whole structure of democracy and freedom that progressives argue must be protected at all costs.

I could not disagree more. The moral relativism and unraveling of ethical standards advocated by the progressive left is a minefield posing a grave danger to democracy and freedom — greater than any of us really understands. Although promoted as a natural evolutionary process, what we are witnessing unfolding is a social experiment that undermines the very freedoms it purports to uphold.

The Chanukah story is usually presented as a Jewish war against the Greeks. The anti-hero Greek king, Antiochus IV Epiphanes (215 BCE–164 BCE), is portrayed as a heartless dictator who imposed anti-Jewish decrees on Judea and was ultimately overthrown in a revolt led by the Maccabean priestly family.

The truth, however, is rather different. Two rival Jewish high priests, Jason and Menelaus, vied for Greek support by trying to outdo each other in their attempts to Hellenize Judaism and Jews, most of whom were hostile to these changes but who felt themselves powerless to counteract the hijacking of everything they held sacred by a political elite more interested in holding onto power than in the needs or interests of the majority.

Sound familiar?

In the end, despite the active support of a powerful Greek army, the Hellenizers were rooted out and the Jerusalem Temple was reclaimed by representatives of this previously voiceless traditional group, who immediately acted to reintroduce unadulterated Judaism to this holiest of shrines by finding and lighting the Temple menorah.

The Talmud recalls that the Maccabees found just one container of uncontaminated oil with which to light the Temple menorah, and although the oil in the container should have lasted only for a single day, the lights miraculously burned for eight days, by which time a new batch of oil had been produced to use going forward. To commemorate this miracle, we observe Chanukah each year for eight days.

Rabbi Joseph Karo (1488–1575), author of the definitive code of Jewish law Shulḥan Arukh, points out that the miracle actually lasted for only seven days, as the oil they discovered was enough to last the first day. In which case, why do we celebrate Chanukah for eight days and not seven?

Hundreds of answers have been suggested in what has become a rabbinic sport. My own suggested answer is that the miracle of the first day was the victory of traditional Judaism over the overwhelming and seemingly unbeatable forces of modernization and progress that had eroded Judaism to such an extent that its most public representatives had become almost indistinguishable from the dominant Greek cultural influences of the era.

The Maccabean family later evolved into the Hasmonean royal dynasty and ultimately proved to be as problematic as the Hellenizers they had overthrown. Nevertheless, the victory of traditional Judaism over a progressive agenda endured and out survived them, as well as all the vicissitudes faced by Jews in every subsequent period. This is a miracle that is truly worth celebrating on the first day of Chanukah.

The Trump presidency represents much more than the victory of a political novice over a deeply entrenched political establishment. Whether you agree with them or not, and what they represent are not necessarily Jewish values, those who voted for Trump embody a counterrevolution that has attempted to press the reset button so that a "minorities agenda" is no longer the only voice heard in the corridors of power.

And while not everyone feels comfortable celebrating the victory of Donald J. Trump the man, as a Jew I am ready to embrace the victory of traditional values over a corrosive progressive agenda that dominates Western thinking, and whose outcome is rather more worrying than its cheerleaders would ever concede.

WHAT WE CAN LEARN FROM ANTISEMITES

first published December 30, 2016

All of us who care deeply about Israel have been fuming ever since hearing or reading about US Secretary of State John Kerry's recent set piece speech on the Middle East Peace Process. According to Kerry, the biggest problem for the world right now is the construction of houses for Jews on land that isn't theirs, even if it is theirs, but apparently it isn't legally theirs (confusing, I know).

According to Kerry, Israel illegally occupied the West Bank in 1967, and that occupation is the root of every evil known to man. Crucially, if the West Bank is vacated of every Jew, including the Old City of Jerusalem, then finally the world will be able to rest at ease — and we will have "peace in our time" (or something to that effect).

Frankly, I find the international community's obsessive focus on West Bank settlements very weird. Besides for the fact that the world is burning in front of our eyes, Israel is hardly the only "illegal" occupier on the planet. Let's face it, Russia has illegally occupied Crimea, and China has illegally occupied islands in the South Seas. And yet, there are no Security Council resolutions. In fact, there is barely any international reaction at all.

And to those who might say: "But those occupations only happened recently, and Israel has been occupying the West Bank for almost 50 years" — let's deal with first things first, and then let's address Crimea and the Pacific islands.

Because let's face it, who are we fooling? After all, the United States occupied California in the 1840s, which means that all of us who reside in Los Angeles are living on occupied Mexican land, which is, in actual fact, Native American Tongva land. So, where is the outrage? Where are the UN resolutions? It is all hypocrisy, utter hypocrisy.

Some people have suggested that the explanation for this unfair obsession with Judea and Samaria is that it is blatant antisemitism. But if that's the case, I'm quite confused — because we keep on reading that Kerry and his boss President Obama are not antisemites. They love Jews. They are surrounded by Jews. Everyone they deal with is Jewish. Their lawyers. Their accountants. Their stockbrokers. The guy who sells them their cars. The guy who cuts their hair. How can someone be an antisemite if they are surrounded by Jews?

Actually, it's not that puzzling. Consider this: We talk a lot about ahavat Yisrael — namely, how important it is for Jews to love each other. And we all buy into the idea of the unity of the Jewish nation and that we need to care for every Jew. It's a Jewish mantra: Kol Yisrael areivim zeh lazeh — "every Jew is responsible for every other Jew." Which means that every Jew is expected to love every other Jew, and take care of every other Jew, and care about every other Jew — right?

But is that really the case? Ask a Jew about the guy he sits next to in shul, or about the Jew who lives on his street.

"What do you think of Goldstein? I'm thinking of investing money with him."

Or: "Goldstein's daughter was suggested for my son — do you think it's a good shidduch?"

"Goldstein? Are you crazy? The man is a crook, a scoundrel, a thief, don't go near him."

"Ok, and what about Greenberg? I heard he is a good accountant. Should I use him?"

"Did you say Greenberg — the man is an immoral amoral fraud. I haven't spoken to him for 30 years, and I will never speak to him again, as long as I live."

"Aha. And what about the Jewish People?"

"Ahhh, Klal Yisrael — am kadosh — a holy nation. Am hanivḥar, the Chosen People. I love the Jewish People."

"But what about Goldstein and Greenberg? Aren't they part of the Jewish nation you love so much?"

"Thieves. Frauds. Crooks. I hate them."

Meanwhile, when you speak to a gentile antisemite, it's the exact opposite.

"What do you think of the Jews?"

"The Jews? Disgusting people. They control the media. They murder babies. They are communists, capitalists, militarists, pacifists. Scum of the earth."

"And how about your accountant, Moishe Goldberg. Is he a disgusting person?"

"Moishe Goldberg? He's the finest person I've ever met. Honest. Cultured. Trustworthy. And a real gentleman."

"And what about Jack Cohen, your attorney?"

"Jack is a genius, and so accommodating. I love the guy."

"And what about the Jews?"

"Jews — they are the source of all the world's ills, from global warming to nuclear proliferation, to rampant unemployment and exploitation of the working classes."

You may think it's funny, but it's so true. So how do you figure it out?

The answer is quite simple. Moreover, it explains both the story of Chanukah and the story of Joseph. In Parshat Vayeishev, Joseph goes looking for his brothers. He meets a man on the road who tells him nas'u mi'zeh — his brothers have "gone away" (Gen. 37:17). Rashi explains that the man Joseph met was not a man at all, but rather he was an angel, and what he was actually telling Joseph was that his brothers had abandoned any sense of brotherhood they may have ever had, along with any familial unity that bound them together with him. They had literally "gone away."

Clearly, however, the angel did not say this explicitly and it was a coded insinuation, otherwise Joseph would not have continued with his journey to meet his brothers. Although, if Joseph was oblivious to the angel's roundabout message, why did the angel bother saying it to him at all?

Rashi has an interesting insight into the different levels of prophetic vision in his commentary to a verse in Exodus (11:4).

Moses usually prophesied using the words: כֹּה אָמַר ה׳ — "So did God say" — and the later prophets always prophesied using this exact same introductory phrase. However, Moses did occasionally begin his restatement of God's words with the phrase: זֶה הַדָּבָר — "**This** is the word [of God]."

Rabbi Judah ben Bezalel Loew (1526–1609), the Maharal of Prague, offers a compelling explanation for the difference between these introductions. If the introductory phrase begins with the Hebrew word "koh", it means that what follows is a prophecy limited to the time and place it was uttered. But if the Hebrew word "zeh" is used, it means that the prophecy is eternal — not timebound to the day it was delivered.

Which means that whenever anyone refers to a "zeh" prophecy, in whatever time or place they may be throughout history, it will still be true, it will still be relevant, it will still be fresh, and it still will be real.

Rabbi Shmuel Bornsztain of Sochaczew (1855–1926), in his remarkable *Shem MiShmuel* commentary, explains that Joseph's brothers' decision to kill him, or to sell him into slavery, may have made sense in the context of their particular time and place, but it was not reasonable in any kind of universal strategic sense. What the angel was hinting at when he met Joseph and said nas'u mi'**zeh** — was that his brothers had become timebound and parochial, and they had abandoned the eternal "zeh" element for the sake of expediency and the needs of the moment.

And although Joseph did not realize what the angel meant at the time, in retrospect he got the message. The brothers' decision to discard their brother was a fleeting moment in time, but in the final analysis it had no enduring ramification. Ultimately it would be Joseph's dreams, and his vision of presiding over his family, and over the mission of the Jewish nation that would emerge from his family, that would prevail.

The message of זאת חֲנוּכָּה — the passage we read from Parshat Nasso on the last morning of Chanukah — is the same. Why is it that this one victory of the Hasmoneans against the Greeks generated a festival that has been celebrated all over the Jewish world every year for over 2,000 years? Why do we celebrate the menorah miracle and not the military victory? And why is the primary focus of Chanukah about Chanukat HaMishkan — the dedication of the Temple — and not about national pride?

The answer is that the Hebrew word "zot" shares the same root as the Hebrew word "zeh" — which means that the message of Chanukah didn't end with the military victory. Chanukah commemorates the eternal nature of the Jewish people, and that victory has lasted long beyond the Hasmoneans, even enduring as a centerpiece of Jewish life after the Temple was destroyed.

Individual Jews may be good or bad, but the Jewish nation — the embodiment of God's presence in this world — is far greater than the sum of its individual parts. Antisemites don't necessarily have a problem with individual Jews — Goldberg is a great accountant, Cohen is a great attorney, and their individual existence doesn't threaten the equilibrium of their gentile clients. But "The Jews" — by which they mean the oldest and most enduring people over the length and breadth of human history, this "People of the Book" that continues to exist and thrive, and who feel passionately about the land of that ancient book as if they were thrown out of there yesterday — antisemites just cannot accept their existence under any circumstances.

Meanwhile the Jews themselves are human just like everyone else. They live in intense, close-knit communities, sometimes too close for comfort, and, regrettably, they can end up harboring ill-feelings towards their neighbors and fellow community members. But every Jew who understands what it means to be a Jew knows that the Jewish nation is evidence of God's existence, and that the survival and success of the Jewish people is crucial and valuable at every level.

The pattern is so clear. When Joseph was thrown in the pit and humbled — he knew that this was just a bump in the road. When the Greeks took over the Temple, the Hasmoneans knew it was just a short-term aberration. And when John Kerry tries to undermine the Jewish connection to Jerusalem, Bethlehem, Hebron, Beit El, Shekhem — even if he is fresh in from a haircut by his Jewish barber and lunch with his Jewish lawyer — he, too, is just another antisemitic bump in the road.

The Jewish people will continue to succeed and thrive long after John Kerry is off the speakers' circuit and a footnote in history books. Even then, we will still be celebrating Zot Chanukah — the message of "zeh", of an eternal Jewish presence as evidence of the existence of God. And that is exactly the message of every twinkling menorah candle spreading the light of our everlasting mission.

THE MOMENT WHEN EVERYTHING CHANGED

first published November 27, 2013

The Torah portion of Miketz is always aligned with the festival of Chanukah, which means that the commentaries all try to find a connection between the two, some of which are rather more tenuous than others.

Nonetheless, it cannot be an accident that Miketz and Chanukah are inextricably bound with each other, year after year. That being the case, looking for a common denominator between the two makes sense, as the convergence is clearly significant.

One area of focus is the accusation by Joseph that his brothers were spies (Gen. 42:9–14). Naturally, Joseph's brothers firmly denied the charge, but this only seemed to make Joseph even angrier. Despite their insistent claim that they were simply a group of brothers who had come to Egypt looking for food during a famine, Joseph continued to accuse them of spying, and of being liars and fraudsters.

It was only at a later stage that Joseph calmed down, replenishing their food and money and sending them back to Jacob without harming them in any way. What had changed? Why did Joseph initially act so harshly? And why did he soften his attitude later on?

The answer can be found in Gen. 42:21. While talking among themselves, the brothers admitted — probably for the first time — that everything that was going on with Joseph (who they had not recognized) was undoubtedly the result of their mistreatment of their younger brother Joseph so many years ago:

וַיֹּאמְרוּ אִישׁ אֶל אָחִיו אֲבָל אֲשֵׁמִים אֲנַחְנוּ עַל אָחִינוּ אֲשֶׁר רָאִינוּ צָרַת נַפְשׁוֹ

בְּהִתְחַנְנוֹ אֵלֵינוּ וְלֹא שָׁמָעְנוּ עַל כֵּן בָּאָה אֵלֵינוּ הַצָּרָה הַזֹּאת

They said to each other: 'We must be guilty with regard to our brother, as we saw how distressed he was when he begged us, and we did not listen; that is surely the reason we are going through such distress ourselves.'

Joseph was eavesdropping on this conversation among the brothers and was able to understand what they were saying without them realizing it. It was the beginning of the process that allowed him to reconcile with his brothers. Suddenly there was an admission of wrongdoing — an acknowledgment that the suffering they were going through was a direct result of their behavior towards him all those years ago.

Earlier on in the story, when the brothers had insisted that they were innocent of all guilt and honest to a fault, Joseph was infuriated by their arrogance and self-delusion. But when they began to be introspective and admitted that their behavior in the past had been far from perfect, his attitude towards them softened, and the healing process began.

The story of Chanukah took place after years of religious and societal decline in the Land of Israel. Hellenized Jews had aligned themselves with the Greeks and taken over control of the country. Even the Jerusalem Temple's high priests were Hellenists, and partial to paganism. It seemed as if God had abandoned the Jews: the Jerusalem Temple was defiled; Torah-true Jews were persecuted; and Judaism was almost certainly doomed to oblivion.

It was only when Matityahu, the elderly patriarch of the priestly Maccabee family, came to the realization that it was up to him and the few others who were concerned for the future of Jewish life to take action, that miracles began to happen — the strong were overcome by the weak, and the many were conquered by the few.

We all struggle to deal with challenges and unpleasant circumstances. Usually, all it takes to change things around us is an admission that the power to trigger such a change is in our hands. If we can admit to our mistakes and understand our own role in the circumstances of our lives and how we can impact the present and future, the change that we need for things to be better will happen, and the process that will eventually lead to that result can commence.

Joseph's brothers were able to rehabilitate themselves and undo the evil they had perpetrated against their brother, because they were willing to own their past and to assume responsibility.

Matityahu and his sons were able to change the course of Jewish history because they were willing to assume responsibility for what needed to be done to get the nation and country back on track — and they went right ahead and did it.

Great people are the ones who bite the bullet and stare fate in the eye. It is this lesson that is one of the most powerful messages of Chanukah, and it is this lesson that can explain Chanukah's proximity to the portion of Miketz.

PURIM

MY BROTHER BENZI, AND HOW TO BE KIND

first published February 25, 2021

My late brother Benzi died in a car accident in 2008. Although he is principally remembered for his superlative philanthropy — and it is true, his philanthropy was exceptional — my own recollections of him revolve around his incredible sensitivity and compassion.

Truthfully, his phenomenal generosity — which amounted to many millions of dollars given away to charity every year — was merely a byproduct of his unlimited kindheartedness and his boundless empathy for the needs of his fellow human beings. And this characteristic was evident long before he had made his first million, and even afterwards; his kindliness played out in how he distributed his money to those in need.

In the mid-1980s my grandfather from Holland became involved in the rescue of a group of teenage Jewish boys from Iran. These traumatized adolescents, who had endured a challenging and life-threatening journey from Iran into Turkey, and then across Europe to Holland, were "temporarily" housed in Amsterdam until their legal status could be resolved. For about a year, Benzi flew from London to Amsterdam every weekend to spend Shabbat with them — to boost their spirits and to keep them in touch with their Jewish heritage.

A few years ago, I bumped into one of the boys. He has since become a top-tier physician and lives in Los Angeles. He told me that some of the group had been wild and out of control when they were in Holland, and at one point some of them had fallen out with the supervising adult at the apartment where they were being housed.

When Benzi arrived that weekend, he discovered that a few of the boys were missing.

"Where are they?" Benzi inquired.

"They're sleeping rough, we don't know where they are," was the reply.

Concerned about their welfare, Benzi immediately went out to find the missing boys, and eventually discovered them in a local park. He gave them food, chatted with them, sang with them, and told them amusing stories — he was a marvelous raconteur.

After a couple of hours went by it began getting dark. The boys told Benzi to go back to the apartment to get some rest and said that they would see him again in the morning.

"Nonsense," he said, "if you're sleeping in the park, so am I. Actually, I've never slept in a park before — so it should be quite an experience."

He lay on a park bench and closed his eyes.

"Why are you sleeping here?" the boys asked him, quite shocked. "Why don't you sleep in the apartment?"

"No, no, it's good here. I want to be with you guys."

Benzi was adamant — he was staying in the park. The back-and-forth went on for a few minutes, until the boys relented and said that if he went back to the apartment they would sleep there too, just so that he wouldn't sleep rough.

Reluctantly, Benzi conceded, and they all went to the apartment to sleep the night. Even 30 years later, this story was fresh in the mind of the now 40-something "boy" who had witnessed it. Tearfully, he told me that Benzi was one of his life's greatest heroes.

And here's another story about Benzi — it happened many years later. Someone had come to London from Israel to collect money for his son, who needed a lifesaving operation. He had heard that Benzi was generous, so he sought an appointment with him, and got to see him late one night.

"How much money do you need?" Benzi asked.

"We need $40,000."

"How much have you raised?"

The fellow was embarrassed. "About $3,000."

Benzi left the room and returned a moment later with a mobile phone.

"Here you are," he said.

The guy looked at him quizzically and Benzi smiled at him.

"While I write you a check for $37,000, please call your wife and tell her you've just raised the rest of the money. She probably hasn't slept for months because she is so worried about your son, and she is also worried about whether you'll be able to raise all the money needed for the operation. Every second she is worried and in pain is terrible for her. I don't want you to wait to call her until after you've left my house with the money. So go on, call her now."

Benzi was a truly amazing person, but what is particularly special about this type of empathetic kindness is that it is intrinsic to the Jewish concept of tzedakah — which means so much more than just charity.

It is also reflected in the rather curious narrative we read on Purim, about the rescue of the Jews from genocide via the intervention of Queen Esther and her cousin Mordechai.

The story of Purim as recorded in Megillat Esther includes a variety of seemingly irrelevant details. Why, for example, is there such a comprehensive description of Aḥashverosh's parties and revelry? Who cares? Kings and princes party all the time — why give us every detail? And why is the description of how to celebrate Purim so detailed? And why are the mandated Purim celebration obligations so different to those of other Jewish festival celebrations? Why the feasting? Why the need to give charity and gifts?

The explanation is straightforward. The world we live in is dominated by the material — all our senses are tuned in to the physical, material world. Materialism is instinctive. We are programmed that way and it is literally in our DNA.

Oddly enough, though, it is this very aspect of the human condition that dominates the unfolding narrative at the beginning of the Megillah.

Aḥashverosh reacts to his success and power by partying and having a good time — he throws a party to end all parties. Then, when his wife doesn't listen to him, he simply gets rid of her and finds another one. And when someone offers him cash to murder a bunch of people — he says, "No problem, let's kill some people and make some money."

The sad thing about all of it was that at that early point in the story the Jews were no different. They were also slaves to the physical, material world, totally obsessed with their needs and desires. The question hovering in the background was: How would the Jews differ from Aḥashverosh if they came out on top, and were as victorious and as successful as he was?

And the answer to this question would surely be a defining moment. If the Jews used their material triumph as a route to the Divine, that would prove they were not mere materialists, like Aḥashverosh and Haman. Not that feasting is intrinsically bad, but if it is done only to experience material pleasure, what is the point of being the Chosen People?

If we feast to show our thankfulness to God, if we give food gifts to our friends to acknowledge Divine benevolence, if we give money to the poor to reflect God's love of charity — then our materialism is not a demonstration of how great and mighty and powerful we are, but rather it reflects how we recognize that all our success is God's success.

This is the reason that the details of Aḥashverosh's parties and revelry are so crucial to the Purim story. Without them we could not begin to understand the end of the story, which details how the Jews reacted to their victory and success, using the very same material aspects of the human condition to get closer to God rather than to abandon Him.

Aḥashverosh's mindless parties are counterbalanced when we turn our material success into vehicles of spirituality and Godliness. Everything about Purim revolves around using materialism to connect people to each other — even though all of our Purim obligations could be done while staying aloof.

We could feast on our own — or we can party together in harmony and affection, connecting with each other for the sake of God.

We could give gifts to patronize or impress others, or we can give them because we want other people to have what we have, and we want to show that what God gives us we can share with others.

We could give charity merely by sending a check in the mail, or we can find someone with an outstretched hand and give them the money personally.

The message of Purim is that we need to truly connect — unselfishly! — with our friends, with our neighbors, with our community, and with those in need.

Purim is about warmth towards others and concern for others — in other words, about being the exact opposite of Aḥashverosh and Haman. That is what Purim is all about, and that is also the legacy of my late brother Benzi z"l, whose yahrzeit each year just after Purim forever connects his memory with this pivotal Jewish message.

DON'T SET YOURSELF APART

first published March 5, 2020

Over the past few weeks, I have noted a major shift in the Jewish world. This shift relates to the Ḥaredi (ultra-Orthodox) community in America and the startling decision by their most respected leaders to put up a slate for election to the World Zionist Organization (WZO). But before I delve into this astonishing development, let me give you some background history.

Since the advent of the Zionist movement in the late nineteenth century, the Ḥaredi Jewish world has been at best suspicious, and at worst openly and aggressively hostile, towards Zionism. In 1900, just three years after the First Zionist Congress, a book called *Ohr Layesharim* was published by ultra-Orthodox activists in Warsaw. This book articulated a firm rejection of Zionism, which the authors contended was just another version of Reform Judaism.

Ohr Layesharim also contained dozens of letters condemning Zionism, written by a broad spectrum of the most prominent rabbis of the era, including Rabbi Ḥayyim Soloveitchik of Brisk (1853–1918), and Rabbi Shalom Dovber Schneersohn of Lubavitch (1860–1920), among many others.

Antipathy towards Zionism, and particularly towards Zionist leaders, formed the backbone of the Ḥaredi attitude during the pre-state era. And although there were different factions among Ḥaredim, each with their own approach — such as Agudat Israel, who were willing to work with Zionists without formally recognizing them as authentic representatives of Judaism; and the Munkatcher Rebbe, Rabbi Ḥayyim Eleazar Shapira (1868–1937), who would not contemplate showing Zionism or Zionists any kind of recognition or even acknowledgement — broadly speaking, the Ḥaredi world maintained its stance, namely, that Zionism was created by heretics, and therefore, in every iteration, it continued to be an outgrowth of heresy.

To be fair, the secular Zionist leadership were no less antagonistic. They considered Ḥaredim to be backward obscurantist reactionaries, and they worked ceaselessly to undermine the influence of traditional rabbis and leaders across the Jewish world, hoping to realign Jewish identity with secular Zionist nationalist ideals.

The first years after the creation of the State of Israel did nothing to repair this rift. Although Agudat Israel were signatories to Israel's Declaration of Independence in 1948, by the early 1950s it had become clear that the newly established state's senior leaders, such as David Ben Gurion (1886–1973), had little respect, if any, for the needs and concerns of the small, but very determined, strictly Orthodox community. Every issue that came up quickly evolved into an existential battle, compounding the entrenched Ḥaredi view that openly endorsing the State of Israel was a dereliction of the Jewish faith.

In 1952, Agudat Israel's elected representatives resigned from Ben Gurion's government, and they subsequently refused to join any coalition government with secular Zionists for many years, preferring to advocate for the interests of their constituents as outsiders within the system, rather than as full-fledged members of the Zionist project.

But that all changed in 1977, when Menachem Begin (1913–1992), scion of Zev Jabotinsky's Revisionist Zionist ideology, won the Israeli elections after almost 30 years as leader of the opposition.

Immediately after his stunning victory, the Prime Minister-designate was asked what style of leadership he intended to pursue in his new job, to which he immediately responded, "a Jewish style." True to his word, Begin wooed the Ḥaredim, with whom he had sat in opposition for decades, and correspondingly, the Ḥaredim, guided by their remarkable rabbinical mentor, Rabbi Eleazar Menaḥem Man Schach (1899–2001), agreed to join a Zionist-led government.

The precedent was set, and since that time the Ḥaredim in Israel have become ever more deeply embedded into Israel's mainstream. But what had become the norm for Israel was not reflected in the Diaspora — at least until now.

Which leads me to the WZO. The WZO was founded in 1897 at the First Zionist Congress in Basel, for the purpose of promoting the Zionist agenda across the Jewish world. In order for it to be truly democratically inclusive, the WZO included an elected body called the World Zionist Congress (WZC), made up of representatives of Jewish groups spanning the spectrum of Jewish identity. Since 1897 the WZC has gone through various phases, and today it is comprised of 500 delegates who meet in Jerusalem once every five years.

The WZC meeting enables elected delegates, two-thirds of whom are not Israeli citizens, to exert ideological influence on Israeli society and to further a global Jewish agenda, and of course, to allocate financial and other resources to various organizations and projects in Israel. The 38th WZC meeting is scheduled to meet in Jerusalem this coming October, and current ongoing online elections, which end March 11, will determine the size of the various delegations.

A few months ago it dawned on Haredi leaders in America, as it had already some years earlier on American Religious Zionist leaders, that the secular and progressive Jewish world in the Diaspora, and particularly in the United States, had been able to overrepresent itself within the WZC, thereby determining the use of funds for projects in Israel, pushing a biased — and some might say insidious — agenda that has, as its openly-stated aim, the destruction of Torah-true Judaism and of traditional Jewish values in Israel.

Although this group does not have a significant constituency in Israel, as a result of their disproportionate numbers on the WZC, they can, for example, influence educational programs all over the country, either to block projects they disagree with, or to promote and fund programs that are in keeping with their progressive agenda.

In the past few months, the Haredi community in the United States has mobilized itself in an unprecedented way. Previous concerns about joining a key Zionist organization such as the WZO have been discarded in favor of participation, to ensure that the structure of Jewish life in Israel — a country that is home to roughly half of all Jews in the world and upon whom the future of Jewish life and identity depends — is not compromised.

Ḥaredim are being actively encouraged by their most senior rabbis in Israel and the United States to vote for the first ever WZC Ḥaredi slate — "Eretz Hakodesh" — led by my friend Rabbi Pesach Lerner, formerly the Executive Vice President of the National Council of Young Israel and currently president of the Coalition for Jewish Values.

Fired up to fight off the threat from WZC slates backed by J-Street and other such destructive groups, the Ḥaredi leadership has decided that after more than 120 years of sitting on the sidelines, the future of Judaism and Jewish life is too precious, and hiding in an ivory tower is no longer a viable option for anyone who cares about Jewish continuity and the safety and integrity of Jewish identity in the State of Israel — whether you are a Ḥaredi living in Israel or a Ḥaredi living in the Diaspora.

Which brings me to the festival of Purim. This festival is often painted as a Jewish victory over genocide, with Haman's planned holocaust being miraculously thwarted by Mordechai and Esther's intervention. But truthfully, this rather superficial reading of the Purim legend misses the point entirely.

Before her dangerous liaison with King Aḥashverosh, Esther appealed to Mordechai to gather together all the Jews of Shushan, without any differentiation, and to unite them into a cohesive group that prayed together and toiled together for Jewish survival. Only by joining up with each other, with all of them working for the same purpose and towards the same goal, addressing the crisis side by side with other Jews doing the same thing, could the threat from Haman be averted.

There are even opinions that view Mordechai as partly to blame for Haman's plans, which only came about as a result of Mordechai's extremism, namely Mordechai's refusal to bow down to Haman, which could be construed as an overly zealous act. According to Jewish law there was no problem for Mordechai to bow to Haman, even if he was wearing a pagan symbol or effigy. Mordechai was bowing to the man, not the effigy.

Rabbi Isaac Samuel Reggio (1784–1855), the Italian bible commentator known acronymically as "YaShaR", maintains that Mordechai should have bowed down to Haman, as it was the king's law, and moreover Haman was considered by the populace to be a human being, not a god. He points out that Abraham, the founder of monotheism, had no problem bowing to an ordinary human (Gen. 23:7 and 23:12), and nor did Jacob, who bowed down to Esau (33:3 and 33:7). Jacob's sons similarly bowed down to Joseph, before he revealed himself as their brother — and further examples of great biblical men and woman bowing to mortals abound throughout the Hebrew scriptures.

To be clear, the implication that Mordechai's overenthusiastic zealotry triggered the catastrophe is a minority opinion; nonetheless, what this view aims to teach us is that the kind of zealotry which sets one apart from everyone else can turn out to be counterproductive and may even lead to catastrophe.

In the end, we must realize that we are all in this together, and, as someone who was born and brought up in the Ḥaredi world, seeing this seismic shift that has resulted in Ḥaredim as part of the

WZC has been a formative moment — and it is a moment I feel we must all acknowledge and celebrate.

To modify a hardened view that has been embedded in a collective psyche for well over a century requires bravery and vision. And if it results in more unity of purpose among Jews who love Israel and care for its Jewish future, then just like the almost undetectable miracle of Purim, we can truly point to it as the Hand of God.

JUST REMEMBER, IT'S PERSONAL

first published March 2, 2020

Each year, on the Shabbat before Purim, we are instructed to recall the abortive attempt by the nation of Amalek to eliminate Jews from the face of the earth. This incident is the first recorded attempted genocide in history.

Truthfully, there is an inherent irony in this directive. On one hand we are being asked to vividly remember this seminal event in our nation's history, but on the other, we are also being asked to obliterate any memory of it. Surely the best way to forget this unpleasant incident and its perpetrators would be to omit the entire incident from our historical narrative.

Had this story been excluded from the official record in the Torah — by now, over 3,000 years later — we would neither need to remember it, nor would we need to forget it. By reminding us of what happened each time we read this passage, we are compelled to consider the evil Amalekites, and rather than eliminating any memory of this long-extinct nation of brutal warriors, we evoke them again and again, year after year.

There is another anomaly in the three-verse instruction that forms the basis of this Torah-mandated directive, and it is an anomaly that may have escaped your attention. The commandment to remember and never forget what Amalek did is recorded entirely in the first-person singular (Deut. 25:17): זָכוֹר אֵת אֲשֶׁר עָשָׂה לְךָ עֲמָלֵק — "remember what Amalek did to **you**…"

How strange that this directive is individualized. Surely it would make far more sense to recall this incident collectively. And this anomaly is amplified in the haftarah that we read for Parshat Zakhor, which recalls the one and only attempt in Jewish history to discharge our obligation to obliterate the Amalekites. King Saul and his army went into battle with Amalek and were victorious against them, but then Saul loses his nerve and decides not to kill Agag, the Amalekite king, despite clear instructions by God for him to be executed.

And once again, the entire narrative in this episode is in the first person singular (1 Sam. 15): לֵךְ וְהִכִּיתָה אֶת עֲמָלֵק — "Go and kill Amalek." Saul seems to be the key player at every stage, and subsequently the entire debacle is laid squarely at his feet.

How is this fair? It almost appears as if he was set up for a catastrophic personal and professional failure — a failure that ultimately cost him his monarchy. Why? The obligation to obliterate Amalek was not his alone — it was everyone's obligation. Why is this missed opportunity pinned solely on poor King Saul?

It is no coincidence that the answers to these questions are found in the portions leading up to Purim: Terumah and Tetzaveh. Throughout the chapters describing exactly what was needed to build a sanctuary, the word that is used most frequently is וְעָשִׂיתָ — "and **you** shall make" — in the first person singular. Which leads to the question — why were the instructions for the sanctuary's construction not given in the plural?

Tetzaveh begins with an instruction for Moses to light the Menorah, and once again this instruction is totally personal (Ex. 27:20): וְאַתָּה תְּצַוֶּה אֶת בְּנֵי יִשְׂרָאֵל וְיִקְחוּ אֵלֶיךָ שֶׁמֶן זַיִת זָךְ כָּתִית לַמָּאוֹר לְהַעֲלֹת נֵר תָּמִיד — "And you shall command the Israelites to bring you pure olive oil, crushed for the light, to keep a constant lamp burning." Why would God have personalized this mitzva to Moses?

My late grandfather, Uri Yehuda 'Adje' Cohen — after whom we named our youngest son Uri — was an active member of the Dutch resistance against the Nazis during the Second World War, and his exploits as a daring underground fighter are recorded in numerous Dutch history books.

In the early 1970s, Opa Cohen moved from Rotterdam to Amsterdam, at around the time that the Dutch government began to recognize war heroes with knighthoods and other state honors, as a way of promoting their heroism to the younger generation born after the war.

One day in the mid-1970s my grandfather received a phone call from a Dutch government official, who told him that he had been chosen for a knighthood. When my grandfather asked him why he was being honored, he was told that the Queen of Holland felt that it was very important for the war years never to be forgotten and that it was imperative for those who had helped in the war against the Nazis to be honored as part of that process.

Without pause, my grandfather told the bewildered official, "Please send a message to the Queen that I have no interest in this honor, and if she truly wants to remember the things I did, she will arrange for the Dutch government to fund a grant to build a new Jewish school in Amsterdam — that is the way my fight against the Nazis will never be forgotten."

Within months, my grandfather had received the grant, the school was built, the royal family attended the opening, and to this day the Amsterdam "Cheider" remains a thriving school that has educated hundreds and possibly thousands of Jewish children for well over 40 years.

Wiping out Amalek and remembering Amalek are not just instructions about the physical obliteration of Amalekites — which in any event is impossible, as we can no longer definitively identify who they are. Rather they are instructions aimed at ensuring that the group of people the Amalekites wished to wipe out can thrive and shine as the nation of God's mission.

None of us could become vigilantes and hunt down Amalekites, but each and every one of us can become community builders, and Torah studiers, and supporters of Jewish education and Jewish continuity.

And the point is this — it is not a collective instruction. That would be too easy. When asked to build the sanctuary, it was the duty of each and every Jew to be involved — some as leaders, some as artisans, and some as donors. But no person could say: "It's OK, the community will take care of it, they don't need 'me' in particular."

When it comes to ensuring a victory over Amalek, all of us must remember that it's personal. Every one of us is important, and moreover, if we fail, our failure is not just a personal failure — it affects everyone.

So — no pressure — but you'd better get out there and do your job.

A RESOURCE TO COMBAT ANTISEMITISM

first published March 9, 2017

The United States has recently been subjected to a surge in antisemitic activity that has been described as unparalleled in its depth and breadth. Bomb threats against Jewish Community Centers, desecrated cemeteries, offensive graffiti, and social media ugliness, are among the many hundreds of recorded incidents over the past several months.

Some of the people who have written about this phenomenon have pointed out that there has not been organized violence against Jews or their institutions, despite numerous threats, and that the one person arrested for making hoax bomb threats was not, as was widely expected, a white supremacist from the far-right, but an African American leftist out-of-work journalist acting out a grudge against his ex-girlfriend.

I grew up in Europe, where antisemitism was far more open and prevalent than it is in the United States, and violence against Jews may have been infrequent but it was certainly not unheard of. Consequently, what has surprised me most about this recent antisemitism upsurge has not been the antisemitism itself, but the genuine shock it has triggered in Jewish America. It is almost as if American Jews have come to believe that antisemitism could only ever be an extremist's ideology, and that no right-thinking, middle-of-the-road American could ever harbor derogatory views about Jews.

It is this collective denial that has resulted in an increasing campaign to blame President Trump and the Republican Party for the antisemitic surge. The thesis neatly associates Trump with extremism and extremists, an association that its proponents argue has empowered the fringe radicals who hate Jews to feel emboldened in their views. But this idea is ultimately superficial and self-serving, as it fails to acknowledge the dangers posed to every one of us by the "antisemite next door," whose disdain and suspicion of Jews may be masked by courteous neighborliness but is as real as the antisemitism of the shaven headed supremacist.

It is also far too easy to fall into the trap of turning the president into an unwitting or even calculated catalyst for the antisemitism we are witnessing, as many liberal-minded Jews have done; or, contrarily, to blame the upsurge of anti-Zionist and anti-Israel rhetoric on the left over the past decade as the factor to blame for the normalization of antisemitism in today's America, as many more conservative-minded Jews have done.

The battle against antisemitism, and against any existential threat to Jews, can only ever be successful if that antisemitism is properly understood, and any action taken against it is apolitical, surgical, and decisive. Getting caught up in political mudslinging or handwringing angst is not just futile, but a sure path to self-destruction. In part it means that we don't really believe antisemitism could ever become a mainstream problem, and that as long as the radical proponents of antisemitism are identified and rooted out — whether those radicals are Breitbart bigots or progressive activists — we will all be safe, and we will be able to sleep soundly. Sadly, this is simply not true at all.

The story of Purim is a wonderful resource when looking for a model of measured but effective reaction to an outbreak of antisemitism in a country where Jews live in safety and security. There was ostensibly no antisemitism in ancient Persia. The leading Jew, Mordechai, was a palace official, and the Jews of Shushan were on the guest list at King Aḥashverosh's celebratory party. And yet, lurking below the genteel veneer of social tolerance and a fully integrated society was a burning hatred for Jews that was ripe for exploitation by an individual with elevated access and a viable plan.

When news of the decree to annihilate Jews reached Mordechai, he sent a message to Esther to immediately go to Aḥashverosh and lobby for the decree to be repealed. Esther refused, on the basis that she had not been summoned, and any attempt to gain an audience with the king without an invitation was dangerous. But Mordechai insisted, adding that although he was certain the Jews would ultimately be saved, if Esther did not do her part right away, she would not be there when the moment of salvation arrived.

All of this happened in Nissan, a full eleven months before the genocide was scheduled. In which case, Esther's argument made perfect sense. What was the point of putting her life in danger **now**? Surely there was plenty of time until the execution of the decree, and at some point during that time the king would call on her, enabling her to address the issue.

But Mordechai maintained that it was imperative for her to see the king immediately. As far as he was concerned this was not a situation where one could wait for the "right moment".

How did Mordechai know that to be the case? Why did he see things so differently from the way Esther perceived them?

The answer is that Mordechai understood from Esther's initial response that she did not feel she was in any kind of personal danger. As far as she was concerned, her life was just fine, and it would remain fine. It is only when a person's life is on the line that they act with urgency and take risks. But when their life is not in any immediate danger, even if they see the desperate need of others, the sense of urgency is just not there.

When you are in a car on your way to the airport, late for a flight, and the driver of the car, or the predicted time on the GPS, tells you that you will be there in twenty minutes, you will nonetheless remain anxious and frequently check the time, fearing that you're going to miss your flight. Meanwhile, your companion, whose life will be unaffected if you miss your flight, remains calm and unconcerned, confident that you will get to the airport on time.

Mordechai's message to Esther was that she needed to feel the danger personally, and to act accordingly. And for us, it must be exactly the same. Our reaction to any threat must never be complacency. We must never get distracted by other considerations, as this will only delay making sure that we execute an effective response to the problem.

In the final analysis, the threat of antisemitism today is much wider than we realize, and it affects every Jew — however safe they might feel. If we are to beat the odds and save the day, our reaction must be urgent and focused — because the alternative scenario is utterly unthinkable.

THE MEMORY OF PURIM CAN NEVER BE LOST

first published March 24, 2016

One of the most frightening aspects of old age is the potential onset of Alzheimer's disease and dementia. Dementia is a dreadful illness. Active, successful people slowly descend into a vacuum of helplessness, as their memory recedes and eventually fails them completely. Close family and friends become strangers, and the past — even the recent past — disappears into an abyss of emptiness. It is agonizing for those who go through it, and unbearable for those who love them. It seems that the only thing left is a shell, and the personality that had characterized the Alzheimer's sufferers throughout their lives is gone forever.

Or so we thought. Professor Susumu Tonegawa, a scientist from MIT, has discovered that Alzheimer's patients' memories may not be lost after all. Instead, sufferers have lost the brain mechanisms to retrieve them, even though they are still there. That being the case, the memories could theoretically be rescued by stimulating nerve cells to grow new connections.

And believe it or not, this idea is not just a wacky theory — it has worked in practice, albeit, so far only on mice. In research experiments on two different strains of mice, scientists at MIT used a technique called "optogenetics," which uses light to activate cells that are tagged with a unique photosensitive protein.

The mice with Alzheimer's-like symptoms were stimulated with light and, incredibly, their lost memories of fear-invoking situations resumed, and when they were exposed to those conditions after the optogenetic treatment the mice once again displayed a fear response.

The optogenetic treatment functions by helping neurons regrow small buds called dendritic spines, which form synaptic connections with other brain cells. Currently there is no way for this technique to be used for human memory retrieval, but the success of this research creates realistic hopes for future therapies that will work in humans. As Professor Tonegawa put it: "The important point is, this a proof of concept... even if a memory seems to be gone, it is still there. It's a matter of how to retrieve it."

There is a strange reference to memory in *Megillat Esther*. After the story of Purim is over, and the Jews have been victorious against the Haman-inspired genocide, the text instructs the reader on how this miracle should be commemorated so that it will be recalled for all time:

. . . וְהַיָּמִים הָאֵלֶּה נִזְכָּרִים וְנַעֲשִׂים בְּכָל דּוֹר וָדוֹר

וִימֵי הַפּוּרִים הָאֵלֶּה לֹא יַעַבְרוּ מִתּוֹךְ הַיְּהוּדִים וְזִכְרָם לֹא יָסוּף מִזַּרְעָם

These days should be remembered and observed in every generation, and the days of Purim will never vanish from among the Jews, and their memory will never be lost from among their descendants.

The Babylonian Talmud (Megillah 7a) deliberates whether *Megillat Esther* was written with prophetic vision; two of the rabbis base their affirmative view on the end of this verse, which seems to predict that Purim would remain a fixture of Jewish life forever.

The Jerusalem Talmud, using this same verse, goes even further than its Babylonian counterpart, and suggests that besides for the Torah itself, only *Megillat Esther* would endure as a sacred text among Jews right until the advent of Messianic redemption.

This rather stunning prediction presents a twofold problem. Firstly, why would *Megillat Esther* even be considered as a contender for this enduring legacy, rather than any of the other books from Hebrew Scriptures?

Secondly, we ourselves are witness to wanton and widespread ignorance about Purim and *Megillat Esther* among contemporary Jews, no doubt all of them descendants of the Jews saved in ancient Persia who were included in the prophecy.

So, was the prophecy wrong?

Megillat Esther, the bible document which records the origins of Purim, is unique in that it is the only episode in ancient Jewish history included in the Hebrew Scriptures that took place after Joshua's conquest of Canaan, but not in the Holy Land. It is a story of Jewish salvation and redemption on foreign soil, and even more curiously the narrative is devoid of any reference to God or miracles. It is a story of the Jewish Diaspora, written about Jews who are in the midst of assimilation, and for Jews who might yet be affected by assimilation.

Megillat Esther and Purim are there to remind us that there is a Divine hand that guides our destiny, and although we may not be aware of it, that hand is always there in the background.

The Talmud is not suggesting that *Megillat Esther* and Purim will never be forgotten. It will certainly be forgotten — and it has already been forgotten by many. Rather, the Talmud is telling us that the memory will never be lost — it just needs to be retrieved. With the right optogenetic treatment, the connectors that succumbed to centuries of collective Alzheimer's disease will reconnect every Jew to their roots, and to their identity.

The powerful Purim narrative, with its echoes of countless other attempts to destroy us, can inspire every generation of Jews to believe that while we might be the Chosen People, that does not in any way mean that God intervenes directly and overtly every time we find ourselves in trouble. The miracle is actually far more subtle. It is found in the fact that no attempt to annihilate Jews has ever succeeded, nor will any attempt succeed in the future.

That is what makes *Megillat Esther* a prophetic work. And that is exactly what we all have embedded on our hard drive, indelible, and for all time. The fact that our enduring destiny is suppressed in many Jewish minds only means that those who are aware of it must work harder to find the suitable therapy to reconnect as many Jews as possible to God through the memory of Purim, and through this important message of *Megillat Esther*.

SOME REMARKS MADE OVER BREAKFAST

first published March 5, 2015

National Prayer Breakfast is an annual event that has been held in Washington, DC on the first Thursday of February every year since 1953. It is an innocuous gathering, meant primarily to generate a positive frame of mind, and to associate that feel-good factor with faith and prayer. Every president of the United States since Dwight D. Eisenhower has addressed National Prayer Breakfast each year of his presidency, and President Obama was no exception.

This year's NPB took place last Thursday, and the gathered guests, including the Dalai Lama, heard President Obama offer his observations on, and suggested resolutions for, the recent surge of violence against innocents carried out in the name of religion, with particular reference to the "Islamic State of Iraq and Syria" (ISIS).

Before offering his views on how to deal with this problem, the president inserted a couple of sentences to historically contextualize the ISIS phenomenon. "Lest we get on our high horse and think this is unique to some other place," he said, "remember that during the Crusades and the Inquisition, people committed terrible deeds in the name of Christ. In our home country, slavery and Jim Crow, all too often was justified in the name of Christ."

The president's analogy, and its careful wording, drew my attention for several reasons. Firstly, the use of the word "we" — "Lest **we** get on our high horse..." — is incredibly misleading. No one sitting at that breakfast belongs to a Christian group that either promotes terrorism or supports violence. The Christians who terrorized and murdered Jews and Muslims, and very often other Christians, with the warped belief that this is what God demanded of them, vanished as a threat long before anyone in that hotel ballroom sat down to breakfast.

It is also worth noting that there were numerous atrocities during the Crusades that were perpetrated by Muslims. In any event, what exactly was the president trying to say with the word "we"? Was he suggesting that Christians today carry guilt for crimes committed in the name of Christianity centuries ago? If he was, it is an utterly preposterous proposition.

But the more troubling aspect of his contextualization was the way it attempted to get radical Islamists off the hook. He seems to have been suggesting that while ISIS murderers are indeed appalling people, this is only a reflection on them as individuals, but not on their faith, because violence in the name of religion is not confined to Islam — Christians are also guilty of it. It is individuals who are violent — not a religious group as a whole — he was saying, because if it is true that all religions and creeds contain violent people, that proves it is people who are violent, not any particular belief system.

Now, if this is actually what the president meant to say, and his words were not just another rhetorical attempt to mitigate the damage ISIS is doing to the Islamic brand, his remarks reveal he does not actually believe in the concept of religion. Religion is not just about a personal faith in God. Religion — in other words being a Jew, or a Christian, or a Muslim, or indeed belonging to any faith group — is about being part of a God-belief system, and a God-believing society. It makes no sense to belong to a religious grouping and to simultaneously claim that an element of your group or its beliefs is an aberration. If you do make that claim, either you do not really belong, or there is something profoundly wrong with the group.

Our enemies historically recognized Jews as a group, united as one through thick and thin. This week we welcomed the month of Adar, during which we celebrate the festival of Purim. When Haman proposed his genocidal plans to Aḥashverosh in ancient Persia, he described the Jews as follows:

יֶשְׁנוֹ עַם-אֶחָד מְפֻזָּר וּמְפֹרָד בֵּין הָעַמִּים

There is one nation that is spread out and scattered among the other nations.

It was this quality, this strength, this cross-identification, that disturbed Haman so much. Wherever they lived in the Persian Empire, every Jew identified with every other Jew in every other part of the empire.

Ultimately, it was this bond that was Haman's downfall. When the time came to fight back, every Jew came to the defense of every other Jew. Our celebration of Purim reflects this unity. We do not celebrate individually. We have a collective celebration with a public reading of the story, a large festive feast, the distribution of charity, and generous gifts to friends.

What is true for one religious group is true for every religious group. Catholics, for example, were for many centuries guilty of the gravest crimes against humanity, all in the name of their version of Christianity. Eventually they were compelled to recognize that if inquisitor torturers and killers were Catholics who were committing atrocities in the name of Catholicism, all other Catholics could legitimately be identified as inquisitor torturers and killers, even those who had never set foot in a torture room. Contemporary Christianity can fairly be labeled a peaceful religion, as nowadays there are no Christians of any denomination who kill or torture for their faith.

The Islamic religion is often touted by Muslims and non-Muslims alike as a religion of peace. But while there may be a huge number of Muslims who are entirely peaceful, conducting blameless non-violent lives — and that is certainly true! — if there is a Muslim or Muslims in any part of the world who murder innocents in the name of Islam, then every Muslim in every other part of the world belongs to a religion that kills innocent people. It is as simple as that.

Islamic leaders along with apologists for radical Islam must urgently grasp this truth. And, to be clear, moral relativism is certainly not the way forward, whether it comes from a US president or from anyone else. Moderate Islamic leaders need to be encouraged to speak up and be the voices of their faith, while radical Islamists must be marginalized out of existence. No more excuses. If Islam is indeed a religion of peace, let there be no violent Islamist left who can ever claim that violent behavior is part of their religion.

REAL COMMUNITY IS ASPIRATIONAL NOT SOCIAL

first published March 13, 2014

I recently read something that I found absolutely incredible. Exactly ten years ago, on February 4, 2004, a nerdy 19-year-old Harvard sophomore called Mark Zuckerberg launched the social networking website Facebook from his college dorm room.

Now, to be clear, I didn't find this fact incredible because of the one-and-a-quarter billion active users on the website every month — and don't get me wrong, that number is beyond remarkable! No, I found it incredible because it dawned on me how unthinkable it is that just ten years ago no one in the world had ever heard of Facebook.

Not everyone uses Facebook, and it is certainly the case that many people who do use it, even regularly, could survive quite happily without it. But what is so striking is that Facebook has become such an entrenched part of the fabric of contemporary life, it seems impossible that only ten years ago it was just a college geek's hobby no one had ever heard of.

One could come up with countless theories as to why the Facebook idea took off, while so many other internet ideas did not, including other social networking sites. Every theory might be right, or some of them, or none of them. That is not the point.

What the discussion demonstrates is that it is possible for an idea to take such deep root in society that life without it cannot even be conceived.

And Facebook is not like a car, or a phone, or a computer. It is an idea, a concept. It uses technology and clever software to harness people's natural desire to communicate with each other as part of a group. These groups have become what we refer to today as "online communities," with thousands of individuals connected to thousands of others, who identify with and follow each other's social lives, despite great geographic distances.

None of this is new. The concept of a community made up of individuals from disparate locations who remain connected at all times was pioneered — by Jews! And it didn't happen recently. As far back as the Persian period of Jewish history, some two-and-a-half thousand years ago, the antihero of *Megillat Esther*, Haman, warned King Aḥashverosh about a community of people who stayed in constant touch with each other, and yet they were "scattered and dispersed among the nations." Aḥashverosh found this concept so frightening — a widely distributed group of people fiercely loyal to each other rather than to the king — that he agreed for all of them to be exterminated in an act of genocide.

Interestingly, the sages of the Talmud believed that this holocaust against the Jews could easily have succeeded. The reason for this negative prognosis is encoded in the story itself. If one transposes the word "God" for every time the word "king" is mentioned in *Megillat Esther*, then Haman's appeal to Aḥashverosh takes on a whole new meaning. Haman says to Aḥashverosh (Esther 3:8):

וְדָתֵיהֶם שֹׁנוֹת מִכָּל עָם וְאֶת דָּתֵי הַמֶּלֶךְ אֵינָם עֹשִׂים

Their laws are different from all other nations, and they do not keep the king's laws.

The word "king" in this verse is usually understood to be referring to Aḥashverosh; Haman was telling Aḥashverosh that the Jews were disloyal, hoping to get him to agree to his plan.

But if "king" means "God" then the message of this verse is quite different. According to this alternative reading, the Jewish nation's vulnerability lay in the fact that they had abandoned their faith as "they do not keep the King's — i.e., God's — laws."

The Jews might have had strong community values and they were certainly very devoted to each other, but that was never going to be enough to sustain them. Nor would it ever be enough just to keep the faith to the exclusion of robust community values — as various sects of extremely devout Jews would find out later on in Jewish history. The key to Jewish survival is faith in God combined with unity and community.

According to some pundits — and I am by no means suggesting they are right — Facebook may ultimately be doomed. In another ten years, or so, we are told, people may barely remember that Facebook existed. If that happens, it will be because the bonds that tie Facebook friends together are not bound up with anything more profound than the thrill of finding some long-lost acquaintance online.

If a community is to be enduring and meaningful, it must be greater than the sum of its social networking parts. It must aspire, both individually and collectively, to higher ideals and to spiritual growth, not just friendship for its own sake.

In ancient Persia, it was the religious reawakening of the Jews that assured their survival. And it was their bonds with each other that ensured this revival was widespread and real. For us, too, it is not enough to be a community of friends.

We must aspire to grow in our faith and in the practice of our faith, so that we become a link in the chain that has connected a people scattered and dispersed both geographically and over millennia, and that we will continue to do so long after Facebook is no longer a thing.

PESACH

VANQUISHING KHNUM THE RAM GOD

first published April 7, 2022

For as long as there have been historians and archaeologists, ancient Egypt has been an object of fascinated study and research. During the earliest era of human history, Egyptian influence and culture dominated the developed world, with its complex perception of the human experience and its sophisticated approach to every aspect of human existence.

And yet, unlike the cultures of subsequent world powers, such as those of the Greeks and the Romans, the impact of ancient Egypt on the world that ensued after its dramatic decline was minimal in real terms, with numerous features of its all-encompassing worldview abandoned entirely, in favor of new ideas that were precursors of many aspects of the world with which we are familiar in the twenty-first century.

The dominant view of historians is that it was an economic decline that precipitated the collapse of the Egyptian Empire. Egypt's earliest pharaohs presided over a wealthy kingdom, and built temples, palaces, and pyramids. But Egypt's prosperity was entirely contingent on the Nile River, which provided bountiful water to a country that is essentially a desert. All it needed was a few years of drought, amplified by military invasions and a range of bitter internal disputes, and the results were widespread ruin and irreversible decline.

But even if this explains why Egypt lost its status as a superpower, it does not explain why ancient Egypt's approach to life and death, and to so many other aspects of the human condition, were completely discarded and replaced by the civilizations that followed on after it. From the sixth century BCE onward Egypt was governed by a succession of foreign powers. But although these rulers left Egyptian culture largely intact, the ideas and ideals that this culture represented lost their grip, and eventually they vanished completely.

One possibility which might explain the ultimate complete collapse of Egyptian ideas and ideals is the determined approach of Judaism to replace the religion and culture of their former masters with a system that was the absolute antithesis of everything that Egypt represented.

A remarkable example of this phenomenon is recorded as the very first instruction given to the nascent Jewish nation in anticipation of their impending redemption (Ex. 12:3): "Speak to the community of Israel and say that on the tenth of this month each of them shall take a lamb for their father's house, one lamb per household."

The medieval commentator Rashi cites a Midrash which explains the reason for the Pesach lamb and, in particular, why on this first occasion it had to be kept in their homes for four days before it was sacrificed. The ancient Hebrews, says Rashi, had lived in Egypt for centuries and they were completely steeped in idolatry. Consequently, the use of a lamb as a sacrifice to God and as the initiation rite of the Jewish people was no accident — it was a deliberate first step, intended to wean the descendants of Abraham, Isaac, and Jacob off Egyptian paganism specifically because the sheep was a prominent Egyptian deity.

The deity in question was Khnum, usually depicted in hieroglyphics as a ram with horizontal twisting horns. Khnum was Egypt's most dominant god before the rise of the sun god Ra. Khnum was considered the god of fertility and procreation and was also associated with water and the River Nile.

Sometimes Khnum was represented as a man with a ram's head, and Khnum was also believed to have created the first human beings from clay, like a potter. All of this was why Khnum — embodied by the lamb taken into their homes by the Israelites — had to be slaughtered, if the Jewish people were to emerge from Egypt the country, and Egypt the mindset.

And not only did the Jewish nation need to sacrifice this venerated symbol of Egyptian prosperity, but they were also instructed to set aside their sacrificial lamb four days before the designated date of sacrifice. At first glance, this four-day requirement seems somewhat superfluous. By the time the Jews were instructed to prepare the lamb for sacrifice and for its meat to be consumed at the first-ever Seder Night, they had all observed their Egyptian enslavers go through nine devastating plagues that were wrought by God as part of the countdown to salvation.

Surely they no longer needed to be weaned off idolatry as God had made Himself amply known via these miracles and wonders.

So why the need to vanquish Khnum by preparing the lamb four days in advance?

According to Rabbi Henoch Leibowitz (1918–2008), the specific requirement to prepare the lamb four days before the fourteenth of Nissan was a consequence of the human weakness for bad habits. Of course, the Jews believed in God, but they had nonetheless got into the bad habit of idol worship even as they declared their fealty to God. And when something is deeply ingrained in a person, it is almost impossible to remove it.

Despite the evidence of God in front of their eyes, the idea that Khnum was fake or that Khnum could be sacrificed to God was not something the Jews could simply adopt from one moment to the next. Their belief in idols lingered on, and it needed to be worn down over a period of time. It was for this reason that the lamb was taken into their homes a few days before.

Even today, thousands of years after the Egyptian empire has disappeared and is no longer a material or spiritual threat to the Jewish faith, we are still instructed to spend time preparing for Pesach, the festival designated as a time to commemorate our rescue from the dangers posed by this anti-God culture.

None of us are safe from bad habits, even if we believe in God. Certain aspects of our lives are the antithesis God-belief, even if it is unwitting. Pesach, and in particular the days leading up to Pesach — when we get ourselves ready for this annual celebration of our most seminal moment — acts as a reminder that all of us need to be weaned off any bad habit that distracts us from our primary directive: a close and meaningful relationship with God.

We all have a Khnum hovering somewhere in the background. Pesach offers us the opportunity to embrace the only alternative to Khnum's destructive force, so that we can all experience our own personal redemption.

WHY OPTIMISM WORKS

first published March 24, 2021

Countless studies have explored the usefulness of optimism as a psychological phenomenon, and the consensus is that optimists have a higher quality of life compared to pessimists.

Being optimistic significantly affects both your mental health and your physical well-being — for several measurable reasons. Optimists tend to lead a healthier lifestyle; they are ready and able to adapt in difficult situations; and they are always more flexible than pessimists, because they are able to embrace problem-solving as a solution and they handle negative information constructively.

Just to prove the point, here's a great rabbi story for you. It may be anecdotal, but it sums up the concept beautifully.

Someone comes to meet a local community rabbi to discuss whether it would be a good idea for him and his family to move into the rabbi's neighborhood.

"I've heard that the people here are lovely, that there are good schools, and that the community is really thriving. In fact, everyone I speak to has told me that you have a very welcoming community, and that the people here are very hospitable. I just want to hear from you whether this impression is correct and if you think it's a good idea for me to come and live here with my family."

The rabbi unhesitatingly nods his head, and says: "Absolutely, I think you'll do very well."

Soon afterwards another guy walks in to see the rabbi, with the same inquiry. He's been thinking of moving into the neighborhood, he says, but had recently been having second thoughts.

"I've heard that the people in your community are not so friendly, in fact they're very cliquey. I've also heard that there's not much interest in advanced Jewish learning, and that your community is quite satisfied with what they already know. So now I'm thinking that maybe it's not such a good idea for me to join this community. What do you think, rabbi?"

Again, the rabbi unhesitatingly nods his head: "You're absolutely right, I think it would be a mistake for you to move into our community."

The rabbi's wife overhears both conversations and wonders why her husband would give such conflicting responses. Both visitors had the same exact question — "Should we move into this neighborhood?" And yet the rabbi's response to each of them was the polar opposite of the other; it seemed as if he was just validating whatever they said.

Bewildered, she marches into her husband's study: "What is going on? Why are you so inconsistent?"

"It's simple," he tells her. "Both of them could move into this neighborhood, but the experience will be totally different for each of them. The first guy who came to see me is full of optimism, fully committed to making the move work; his aspirations are unfailingly optimistic and upbeat. And I don't need to tell you, there are plenty of lovely people in our community who are equally optimistic and aspirational, and they are also hospitable. Let's face it, these are the people to whom this guy and his family will gravitate, and as a result everything will work out."

"But the second guy couldn't be more different — his whole vibe is negative. And guess what? His negativity will accompany him every step of the way. The nice people will try at first and quickly be rebuffed for no good reason, while the unpleasant, non-aspirational people will become his obsessive focus, proof that his pessimistic predictions were spot-on. His gloomy outlook will destroy any chance of success before he's even gets to first base."

Commenting on the final narrative of the Exodus story, Rashi explains that God ordered the Jewish people to take the Pesach lamb into their homes four days before it needed to be killed so that they would do a mitzvah which would enable the redemption process to proceed. Or, as God put it, "The time to fulfill the promise I made to Abraham has arrived, and the Jewish people must do something in order to earn the promised redemption."

Rabbi Ahron Leib Steinman (1914–2017) poses an obvious question. If redemption from Egyptian slavery had already been promised by God to Abraham — which meant it would happen whether or not the Jewish people deserved it — why was it necessary for them to do this mitzvah to "earn the promised redemption"? Surely God was going to keep His promise either way.

Rabbi Steinman's answer is very revealing, and solidly based on the "optimism is the way to success" idea. If the Israelites were freed from slavery but were not simultaneously invested in the realization of the new nationhood endeavor, their move from slavery to freedom would be doomed before it had even begun.

God wanted to see a demonstration of their buy-in, their optimism, their enthusiasm, and their willingness to take risks, so that He knew that when the redemption kicked in, it would be bound to succeed. By insisting that they should take in the lamb — an Egyptian deity — in full view of their tormentors, and then to slaughter it and paint their doorposts with its blood, all done with the optimistic outlook that it would facilitate their redemption from slavery, God was ensuring that the promised redemption wouldn't collapse shortly after it happened.

And how right He was. Well over three millennia later we still sit down each year at Seder Night, reliving that pivotal moment in our history, as enthusiastic and as optimistic now as our ancestors were then, ready to succeed and to build on every success — even when the odds are stacked against us.

If ever the optimism route needed proof of its efficacy, the Exodus story and Seder Night are undoubtedly its greatest advocates.

WHEN THE LUBAVITCHER REBBE SELF-QUARANTINED FOR SEDER

first published March 29, 2020

I wrote this article during the early stages of the COVID-19 pandemic, when strict lockdown restrictions meant that many people would be holding their seders in isolation. The article received wide attention, appearing in numerous media outlets and distributed via countless WhatsApp groups. It acted as a source of inspiration for many thousands for whom the thought of Pesach seder without family was weighing heavily on their hearts and minds.

One of the issues that has come up again and again over the past couple of weeks is the fact that people will be on their own for the Seder this year, or their Seder will be drastically reduced in numbers, with children or parents elsewhere, as they are at home in isolation because of COVID. Some people will literally be by themselves, solitary, with no one to do the Seder with at all.

"How can we do Seder by ourselves?" they ask me. "Doesn't the Pesach Seder need to be done with family and guests?"

In response to this troubling situation and the concerns it has thrown up, I would like to share an extraordinary conversation I had about eighteen months ago. I was in New York, and a friend of mine messaged me that his daughter had become engaged. I messaged him that I would attend the engagement party, and that night I drove to Monsey to celebrate the simcha.

At the party, I bumped into a friend of mine, Rabbi YY Jacobson, a well-known inspirational speaker on the East Coast. I knew that Rabbi Jacobson grew up on Montgomery Street in Crown Heights, in the heart of the Chabad community, just a few blocks away from the home of the late Lubavitcher Rebbe, Rabbi Menachem Mendel Schneerson (1902–1994).

There is an aspect of the late Lubavitcher Rebbe's life that I feel is often overlooked, and we got to talking about it. The Lubavitcher Rebbe was incredibly down-to-earth, and, together with his late wife Rebbetzin Chaya Mushka (1901–1988), the Rebbe led a very simple life. Indeed, as hard as it may be to believe, their life together was very private.

Rabbi Jacobson often tells stories about the Rebbe when he speaks to audiences, so I asked him if he ever focuses on this particular aspect of the Rebbe's greatness. Namely that the Lubavitcher Rebbe had no airs and graces, nor was he interested in the pomp and ceremony that is often the hallmark of other Hasidic leaders and their "courts".

"For example," I asked Rabbi Jacobson, "do you ever tell audiences that in their sixty years of marriage, the Rebbe and his wife ate every Shabbes meal together on their own? No guests, no attendants, no public spectacle — just a married couple eating together — bringing the food in, eating, clearing the table, doing the washing up. A man who had literally tens of thousands of people at his beck and call! What a powerful lesson!"

Rabbi Jacobson paused for a moment, and then he smiled. "I've got one better for you," he said. "A few weeks ago, I led a workshop for single mothers, and at the end of the session, I took questions from the women and encouraged them to ask any question that was on their mind. One of the ladies put her hand up, and this is what she asked me…it's a crazy story."

"A few months ago," she said, "it was Pesach. The thing is, my ex-husband and I went through a very difficult breakup. After years in court over our kids, we finally settled on a shared custody arrangement, which means that we alternate Jewish holidays. This past Pesach it was my turn — my children were coming to me for Seder, and I was so excited. I changed over my home for Pesach and prepared everything beautifully; it was going to be just me and the kids."

"I was so happy about them being with me, that I told everyone: my family, my friends, my neighbors. Then, one hour before yom tov, I got a phone call from my ex-husband — for some reason, the kids were not going to be coming. I almost fainted from shock and heartache. I was also so ashamed. I guess I could have called my parents, or I could have called my neighbors — and gone to them for the Seder. But how could I actually do that? I had told everyone my kids were coming! The truth is, I did not have the energy to even be with anyone. I felt completely and totally numb — dry and lifeless."

"So, I did the Seder by myself. On my own. It was the worst and most bitter Seder I have ever had. I just sat there crying the whole way through. Weeping. It wasn't Pesach. It was Tisha B'Av. I did not have to eat maror. I — my entire life! — was maror. Yes,

I went through the Haggadah and ate the matzah; but the entire Seder took me 25 minutes."

"Rabbi Jacobson, did I do the right thing? Did I fulfil my Seder obligation? Was it even called a Seder? Because it did not feel like a proper Pesach."

Rabbi Jacobson told me — and believe me, as a public speaker, I know exactly what he means — sometimes your most inspirational moments in a speech or a public presentation are not prepared in advance. They are a gift from God. You can prepare for hours. And then inspiration drops into your lap. Right then and there, when faced by this divorced woman, Rabbi YY Jacobson had such a moment.

"Lady," he said, "in 1988 the Lubavitcher Rebbe's wife died, and he was left on his own, as they sadly had no children. She passed away in February, and two months later was Pesach. Every year the Rebbe and his Rebbetzin had Seder together, but this year he was on his own, totally by himself. Who would the Rebbe conduct the Pesach Seder with?"

"I recall that a young boy, Ari Halberstam — who was later tragically gunned down on Brooklyn Bridge, in 1994 — approached the Rebbe after Maariv on the first night of Pesach and, on behalf of his mother, invited the Rebbe to his home for Seder. Ari's family lived at 706 Eastern Parkway, just one block away from "770". But the Rebbe just smiled at Ari and shook his head. "Thank you so much," he replied, "but I have already prepared to have the Seder on my own."

"I was a yeshiva student at the time," continued Rabbi Jacobson, "so I am a first-hand witness to this story. In fact, the

Rebbe's longstanding assistant Rabbi Leibel Groner offered to stay with the Rebbe, but the Rebbe sent him home to have Seder with his wife and children."

"And so, the great Lubavitcher Rebbe — the man who inspired countless people around the world for their Seders, who personally undertook to provide a meaningful Pesach Seder for Israeli Army personnel who were on duty on the first night of Pesach via his shluchim in Eretz Yisrael — had the Seder on his own. Not one other person was present. As the Talmud says: If you are on your own, you ask yourself the 'Ma Nishtana' questions, and then you answer them to yourself."

"A few of us yeshiva boys did not go home that night; we waited outside in the street opposite the Rebbe's house — and after a couple of hours, the Rebbe opened the door to welcome Eliyahu Hanavi and recite Shefokh Ḥamatkha. He walked outside holding a candle and his Haggadah, said the prayer, gave us a wave, and then went back inside to finish the Seder — by himself."

"My dear lady," said Rabbi Jacobson, "if it was good enough for the Lubavitcher Rebbe to have the Seder on his own, trust me, your Seder was perfect!"

"The Rebbe could have had his Seder with 100 people, 1,000 people, or 10,000 people. He personally arranged for all the army Seders in Israel to be sponsored. He was responsible for hundreds of thousands of people celebrating Pesach on Seder Night, from Kathmandu to Alaska, and from San Francisco to New Zealand. But at the end of the day, he went and did the Seder on his own. He didn't need anyone else for him to be close to God. He didn't need adulation. He didn't need validation. He sat alone and relived the Exodus from Egypt."

"I was only 15 at the time," concluded Rabbi Jacobson, "but even at that age I felt sad that the Rebbe had nobody to be with for the Seder. Why did he not invite even one person to be with him? But today, after hearing your story, I may have discovered the answer — and it is just a personal feeling. As a true Jewish leader, the Rebbe wished to empower all those souls who would ever need to do their Seder alone. He wanted them to know that their solitary Pesach Seder was powerful, meaningful, and real. Jewish history and the Divine presence would dwell at their Seder just as it does at a Seder that has many people there."

Over the past couple of weeks, as the coronavirus crisis has unfolded across the world, and the reality of our isolated situations has become ever more evident — this incredible and very moving story about the Lubavitcher Rebbe has been at the forefront of my mind.

This year, so many people — probably more people than at any other time in Jewish history — will be having the Seder on their own or without their families. All our Seders will be diminished, and anxiety will be hovering in the air. And all of us will be thinking to ourselves, "Is this really a proper Seder?"

I think Rabbi Jacobson's story about the Lubavitcher Rebbe in 1988 answers that question, and it eases any doubts we may have about our impending "depleted" experience. After all, as Rabbi Jacobson said, "If it was good enough for the Lubavitcher Rebbe to have the Seder on his own, trust me, your Seder is going to be just perfect!"

GROUNDHOG DAY AND THE JEWISH EXPERIENCE

first published April 28, 2019

You may recall the 1993 movie *Groundhog Day*, starring Bill Murray and Andie MacDowell. The premise of the movie is simple. Murray is Phil Connors, a TV weatherman assigned to cover an annual Groundhog Day event. Somehow, though, he finds himself caught up in a time loop, reliving the same day over and over again.

The main thrust of the movie is an examination of what someone might do if they had the opportunity to correct their mistakes and missteps, and turn their life into a perfectly polished product, a fully finished article with no flaws.

It has been calculated that Murray's character repeated Groundhog Day 12,395 times during the movie, although we only get to see 38 of those days on-screen. Just to put that into perspective, 12,395 days is two weeks short of 34 years. During that time Phil Connors evolves from a selfish, self-centered narcissist into a kind, thoughtful person who can fluently recite French poetry and play piano, while saving people's lives and acting selflessly.

And while the fact that no aspect of the day can change until he has somehow redeemed himself is presented to us as a curse, the predictability of each day from dawn to nightfall is actually his salvation. He knows exactly what is going to happen every minute of the day, with every detail fixed in a familiar montage of moving parts. The only variable is his reaction to those details and events. They will happen regardless of his response, while his attitude towards them and how he responds to them is up to him.

Every year at Pesach we experience the Jewish religion's version of *Groundhog Day*. We call it "Seder Night" — and it is the annual event that commemorates the founding of the Jewish nation. Just like Groundhog Day in the eponymous movie, the timetable on Seder Night is governed by a prescriptive schedule, unchanged for over a millennium.

The original Seder script was finalized during the Second Temple period, and the script we use closely follows the version created at that time. But the actual text we use — what we call the "Haggadah" — was only completed just over 1,000 years ago, and the oldest example can be found in the siddur of Rabbeinu Saadia Gaon (882–942).

Every year we sit down to the Seder — we begin with Kiddush, then the Seder leader washes his hands without a blessing, we all eat a vegetable dipped in salt water, we split the middle matzah — and this goes on in hundreds of thousands of homes across the world as it has done for more than 1,000 years — all using the exact same formula. Millions of seders in every fathomable location and setting.

But just as no two Groundhog Days in the movie were ever the same, no two Seders have ever been exactly the same. Every aspect at every Seder has followed the formula set out in the Haggadah, and we all use the exact same Haggadah, and yet—every Seder is different.

In the Diaspora we have two Seders over two nights, one night after the other, but remarkably, even though we are in the same place, with the same people, reading the same script, and eating the same foods — each Seder is different.

Our challenge is to use the familiar Seder accompaniments and guidelines and nonetheless turn it into a unique Seder experience that improves every year. The familiar pattern can become a platform for a better and more meaningful experience, so that at our Pesach Seder Groundhog Day we improve, and improve — until we get it perfect. And even then, we can still take it to the next level.

And actually, this idea is a perfect microcosm of our Jewish faith identity. The Torah is a flawless book, a gift from God to His Chosen People, the ultimate vehicle for self-improvement and for carrying out God's mission. It is immutable. It is unchangeable. And even so, when Moses was transported to the Beit Midrash of Rabbi Akiba (Menahot 29b), he finds himself unable to understand even one word of the Torah discussion that is going on there. Crestfallen, he needs to be reassured by God that the Torah taught by Rabbi Akiba is the same Torah that he received at Mount Sinai.

In the early twentieth century, Rabbi Hayyim Soloveitchik (1853–1918) published his seminal work on Maimonides' *Mishneh Torah*, *Hiddushei Rabbeinu Hayyim HaLevi al HaRambam*, in which he reconciled a range of contradictory passages. I have a feeling that if Maimonides would read Rabbi Soloveitchik's work he would struggle to recognize his words in Rabbi Soloveitchik's novel explanations.

But in the same way that God reassured Moses that Rabbi Akiba's Torah was the same Torah as he had received at Sinai, Rabbi Soloveitchik's explanations of *Mishneh Torah* are a product of Maimonides' work, whether he would understand that or not. And it does not end there. Maimonides' *Mishneh Torah* was a rearrangement of the Talmud, which was, in turn, a work produced by the Talmudic sages to unpack the Torah, so that it could be practiced and preserved as history unfolded.

That is the wonder of Judaism — it is Groundhog Day. It is the same, and yet it is different. Judaism is a system that allows us to hone and refine the Torah, while at the same time preserve it and cherish it as our authentic heritage and tradition.

There is a wonderful Midrash that explores a remote facet of the Exodus odyssey. When the Jewish people departed Egypt, they took whatever they had for the journey: some scraps of unleavened bread, a few animals for transportation, and the clothes on their back. Miraculously the clothes they wore when they left Egypt never wore out, lasting them throughout their years in the wilderness. The shrouds we use when burying those who die are modeled on these original Jewish clothes.

What a wonderful metaphor for Judaism. The clothes we were wearing when we became a nation are the eternal vestments of our identity — never wearing out, reminding us of who we are and where we come from. And ultimately, they accompany us on our final journey. We wrap ourselves in our Groundhog Day, and at the same time we live out our individual lives.

Egyptian culture was the exact opposite. They mummified their dead. They were experts at preserving remains. Because in their mind all that mattered was ossifying the past. There was no development and no growth. Even as the culture thrived, it was already destined for oblivion.

Which brings me to Yizkor, the memorial service we recite on the last day of festivals and on Yom Kippur. Yizkor is not about the deaths of the people we loved. Our loved ones are not dead if they are the clothes that we wear as we go through life after they are gone. And if we wear those clothes — our parents, our grandparents — as life unfolds, not only do they never wear out, but they improve.

It is entirely possible that if our parents could see us five years, ten years, or fifty years after they died, they would be like Moses sitting at the back of Rabbi Akiba's Beit Midrash, or Maimonides reading Rabbi Soloveitchik's book. And yet we could tell them — we are your Groundhog Day, and we have taken that script, that model, and have improved on it and perfected it, so that we can pass on these clothes to the next generation, and they too can wear the clothes that will never wear out.

Yizkor is not a morbid moment. It is our moment to revisit the Seders we had with our parents, and they had with theirs. We are not expected to remember that they died. Rather, Yizkor is a time to remember how they lived, so that we can emulate their faith and their goodness.

In March 1955, Albert Einstein was asked to eulogize his closest friend, Swiss engineer Michele Besso. Shortly afterwards, he wrote a letter to the Besso family to express his sorrow, but at the same time to convey his sense of closeness to his dear departed friend, which had barely diminished.

"Now he has departed from this strange world a little ahead of me," Einstein wrote. "But that means nothing. People like us, who believe in physics, know that the distinction between past, present, and future is only a stubbornly persistent illusion."

How very inspiring, and how very true.

A PESACH LESSON FROM ENTEBBE

first published April 17, 2019

A couple of weeks ago, former airline pilot Michel Bacos died in France at the age of 94. Although Bacos had been retired for many years, his extraordinary courage in the summer of 1976 was fondly remembered across the world after his passing.

Michel Bacos was celebrated as a hero after he refused to abandon his Jewish passengers when a gang of Palestinian and German terrorists hijacked his plane, Air France Flight 139, on its way from Israel to Paris via Athens. The plane was diverted to Libya, and then flew to Entebbe, Uganda, where the non-Jewish passengers were released, while Jewish passengers were locked up under armed guard in the transit hall of an abandoned former terminal building.

Offered the chance to join the hostages who were being freed, Bacos refused to leave his passengers behind, and convinced his crew to do the same. "There was no way we were going to leave them," he recalled later, "we were staying with the passengers until the end."

In real time this seemed like a suicidal decision, particularly as the PFLP and *Revolutionäre Zellen* terrorists who had seized the plane and kidnapped the passengers were known for their utter ruthlessness. In addition, Israel had an established policy of never negotiating with terrorists.

Riots broke out outside Prime Minister Yitzḥak Rabin's house in Jerusalem, as it dawned on the families of hostages that a negotiated solution was not on the cards, and the deadline after which their relatives would be butchered was drawing ever closer. What both the families and Bacos did not know was that Israel was about to embark on one of the most audacious rescue missions in history — a mission that would result in the death of all the hijackers, and the dramatic rescue of almost all the hostages, with just a handful of casualties.

Tragically, the fatalities included Yoni Netanyahu (1946–1976), commanding officer of the elite commandos who carried out the mission. His brother Benjamin would later become Prime Minister of Israel.

Sara Guter Davidson was one of the 100-plus Jewish hostages held captive in Entebbe that fateful week. Caught up in the nightmare together with her husband Uzi and their two teenage sons, she kept a diary throughout the ordeal. As the days unfolded and tension increased, her sense that death loomed increased. On July 3, 1976, exactly one week after the hijackers had forcibly taken control of the plane, Davidson went to sleep knowing that the first hostage executions were scheduled to begin the following day.

An hour later she awoke to the sound of gunfire, and immediately feared the worst. She spread herself out over her 13-year-old son to protect him from bullets and prayed that it would all be over quickly. But a moment later Davidson heard Hebrew and looked up to see Israeli commandos ushering them to safety.

Bullets whizzed past as they shuffled out of the terminal towards a waiting Hercules aircraft that had appeared out of nowhere to whisk them away to safety. It was a miraculous moment, one that she and her fellow hostages had never dreamed would happen.

Although Davidson has never been back to Entebbe, this February, for the first time since 1976, an Israeli plane carrying tourists landed at Uganda's Entebbe Airport. Over 250 Israelis arrived for the three-day trip, and the first place they visited was the site of the terminal building where the Jewish hostages were held and later rescued.

Itzik Gerber, the Israeli pilot who flew the group to Uganda, was very taken by the moment. "On July 5, 1976, I was 10, and like all the Israelis I woke up in the morning and heard about the daring operation that was carried out in Entebbe to free the hostages," he told reporters. "If an angel had come and whispered in my ear that ... 42 years later I would land at Entebbe as a pilot, I would have laughed out loud."

Three years ago, Prime Minister Netanyahu visited Entebbe for the fortieth anniversary of the ambitious operation. Yoni's death was a pivotal moment in his brother's life, forcing him to reconsider his chosen career path in business, and motivating him to focus on a career for Israel. Choking back tears, he told those who had gathered for the anniversary event that he was "moved to be standing here as the prime minister of Israel in this place."

Coming full circle is not a chance afforded to everyone, and many people who go through harrowing experiences understandably shy away from reliving those moments in the places they occurred. But just as the mythical phoenix rises from the ashes, the greatest incubator for positive growth is somehow reliving the very experience that once threatened to destroy you.

On Pesach we are subjected to a strange directive: relive the Exodus, be a slave in Egypt, eat the bread of affliction, and dip bitter herbs into a cement-like mixture to remind you of the years of bitter slavery when your ancestors were forced to construct edifices for their Egyptian overlords. And at the same time, we are expected to drink four cups of wine to celebrate our freedom, and to eat the feast of a lifetime to commemorate our salvation in the face of destruction.

בְּכָל דּוֹר וָדוֹר חַיָּב אָדָם לִרְאוֹת אֶת עַצְמוֹ כְּאִלּוּ הוּא יָצָא מִמִּצְרַיִם — "In every generation each person must visualize themselves as if they went out of Egypt." This instruction, recorded in the Pesach Haggadah, is not simply an exercise in experiential education — it is a mandated process of coming full circle, so that we can truly maximize the formative experience represented by the Exodus.

You can talk about it all you want, but unless you've personally experienced it, and regularly reinforced it by revisiting that moment in as vivid a way as possible, the value of this seminal moment will be lost over time, and certainly over generations.

Jewish tradition does not demand that we visit Egypt annually to benefit from this phenomenon; rather we are expected to recreate ancient Egypt in our homes each year to ensure that the "full circle" experience continues to impact our Jewish identity and reinforces the powerful relationship we have with God that began in Egypt. And what is so incredible is that this process has worked — each one of us is living testament to its success.

A PRAYER FOR EATING CHOMETZ

first published April 16, 2019

I n 1943, Rabbi Aharon Davids was the highly revered and much-admired Chief Rabbi of Rotterdam when the Nazis deported his entire community to the Westerbork concentration camp in Holland. Within a matter of months, in early 1944, all of Rotterdam's Jews were taken from Westerbork to Bergen-Belsen.

Conditions in Westerbork had been very difficult, but at least religious observance had been somewhat possible, helping to preserve the dignity of the Jews, and also their will to live. But when they arrived at Bergen-Belsen, families were divided, and their meager possessions were confiscated. Within a short time, the killings began, and deadly diseases became rampant. Each day, more people were killed or died. Spirits sank, and despair set in.

With Pesach approaching, Rabbi Davids realized that he had to rally his family and community — while they still remained alive, even as they mourned those who had already died or had been killed. Obviously, this was not going to be an ordinary Pesach. It would be impossible for them not to eat ḥametz during the week of Pesach, as their tiny daily ration of bread was crucial to their survival. And — there would be no matzah and no haggadahs.

But Rabbi Davids knew that it was not just important for him and everyone else to have a Seder, it was crucial. And so, on the first night of Pesach, Rabbi Davids gathered everyone together in a group, and they sat down for a "seder."

The rabbi recited as much of the haggadah as he could from memory. When he reached the point when one is supposed to make a blessing over the matzah, he took a piece of bread in his hand and said, in a voice cracking with emotion:

Avinu Shebashamayim, our Father in Heaven:
You know and are fully aware that we want to carry
out the commandment to eat matzah, and that we

don't want to eat ḥametz on the festival of Pesach. But regrettably, we are prevented from doing what we want because of the oppression and deadly danger in which we find ourselves.

Nevertheless, we are ready to perform Your commandments, and we know that You commanded us "You shall do them — and live by them" (Lev. 18:5) and not die by them. And we also stand ready to perform Your commandment: "Take care of yourselves and keep your souls alive." (Deut. 4:9)

Therefore, our prayer to You is this: Keep us alive, sustain us and redeem us speedily, so that we may observe Your statutes, carry out Your will, and serve You wholeheartedly. Amen.

And as soon as he finished this unusual prayer, Rabbi Davids made the prescribed blessing for bread and ate his tiny piece — and everyone else in his group did the same. It was a very moving moment. Through flowing tears and with the heaviest of hearts, Rabbi Davids and his family, together with their congregation, observed Pesach that year in Bergen-Belsen — by eating bread.

Tragically, Rabbi Davids and his son Eli died in Bergen-Belsen, shortly before it was liberated by the Allies. But his wife, Erika, and their daughters survived. In 1947, Erika Davids, together with her daughters, immigrated to the Land of Israel. Each year until her passing in 1997, her family would repeat the prayer Rabbi Davids had said at the Seder in Bergen-Belsen, reading from a scrap of paper on which this extraordinary declaration of faith was recorded immediately after their liberation. Even today, the

Davids family continues with this poignant tradition, a testament of faith amidst the hell that was the Holocaust.

Remarkably, Rabbi Davids knew that doing the Seder properly that year was not going to be possible. Nevertheless, with unimaginable courage, he began the Seder anyway. And it was a Seder never to be forgotten, a Seder that lives on in his family — and for all of us.

בְּכָל דּוֹר וָדוֹר עוֹמְדִים עָלֵינוּ לְכַלּוֹתֵנוּ וְהַקָּדוֹשׁ בָּרוּךְ הוּא מַצִּילֵנוּ מִיָּדָם — "In every generation they rise up to destroy us; but God rescues us from their hands."

> *Rabbi Davids's mother was Rosa Dunner, first cousin to Rabbi Dunner's great-grandfather, Baruch Chaim Dunner (who was murdered at Auschwitz in 1944). Rosa Dunner was the daughter of Rabbi Josef Hirsch Dunner (1833–1911), the Chief Rabbi of Holland.*

BACKS TO THE WALL

first published December 24, 2018

As the row over President Trump's border wall gathers pace, with thousands of Central Americans camped in Tijuana on the Mexico-United States border, and the president holed up in the White House over the holidays in the midst of a government shutdown, the media has gone into an absolute frenzy.

From the moment Donald Trump declared his candidacy in June 2015, he made building a wall spanning the entire southern border of the United States a central promise of his presidential campaign. At the end of his candidacy announcement speech, he pledged to "build a great, great wall on our southern border," adding that he would get Mexico pay for it.

On January 17, 2017, immediately after becoming president, Trump signed Executive Order 13767, "to secure the southern border of the United States through the immediate construction of a physical wall on the southern border."

Of course, Mexico had no intention of paying for a $22 billion border wall, and neither did Congress. Which has meant that the border wall has so far remained nothing more than a meaningless electioneering slogan. But with problems mounting for the beleaguered president, and his support base refusing to accept any capitulation on this contentious issue, Trump is digging in his heels, refusing to approve the government budget until it includes a $5.7 billion spending bill to fund the wall.

The face-off has resulted in a partial government shutdown, affecting hundreds of thousands of workers across nine federal agencies, and although a range of compromises have been discussed, so far, they have all been summarily rejected by the president. And as we head towards a Democratic majority in the House of Representatives, hopes for a "great, great wall on our southern border" are fading fast.

What strikes me most about this entire issue is that the conversation is all about the wall, and on the rights and wrongs of building a border-spanning barrier between the United States and Mexico. The benefits or otherwise of immigrants coming to the United States — a subject that is in desperate need of an honest national debate — has receded into the background, or disappeared completely, as politicians and pundits clamber over themselves to vilify the president's intransigence, or alternatively to hail his heroic stand.

What have we become if we allow ourselves to forget that this controversy is not simply about a wall? Because what it is actually about is people. And I am not just referring to the illegal immigrants already in the United States, nor to those making the effort to get into the country. It is not solely about them — because ultimately it is also about us.

Everyone in the United States is affected by this issue. Not merely in terms of the economic benefits of dynamic legal immigration weighed up against the negative impact of unfettered illegal immigration — truthfully, that is something us noneconomists will probably never properly understand. No. What I am referring to is how this issue affects us in terms of who we have become as people when immigration has evolved into nothing more than a political football, a talking point, an ideological badge.

The Exodus story in the Torah begins with a fly-on-the-wall report of a conversation between Pharaoh and his courtiers regarding the dangers of the growing Israelite community in Egypt. Concerned by the ludicrous idea that the Israelites were a fifth column, and that they would align themselves with Egypt's enemies in the event of a regional war, posing a security danger to Egypt, Pharaoh and his advisors proposed a draconian course of action to ensure that this outcome would never materialize.

When reading Haggadah at the Pesach seder, we recall this moment by introducing it with a verse from the Torah (Deut. 26:6). In recalling the leadup to the Exodus story forty years after the events occurred, Moses tells the nation that when Pharaoh strategized with his advisors, it demonstrated the ultimate wickedness of the Egyptian regime. As Moses puts it: וַיָּרֵעוּ אֹתָנוּ הַמִּצְרִים — "The Egyptians dealt with us in a malevolent manner."

At first glance, it appears rather puzzling that Pharaoh's closed-door strategizing is presented to us as his most malicious act against the Israelite minority in Egypt. After all, he went on to enslave them and wantonly mistreat them, and he also perpetrated mass genocide, murdering their male babies. Surely this was far worse. In any event, why would we fault Pharaoh for being concerned about his nation's security?

However, upon closer analysis, the real issue with Pharaoh's solution was not the solution; rather it was his misidentification of the problem. There was never actually a threat from the Israelites living in Egypt, as they were never going to undermine his kingdom. But once Pharaoh and those around him had decided that the threat did exist, this imagined "threat" became the source of everything that unfolded subsequently. Had the Israelites truly been enemies of Egypt, the campaign to neutralize them might have been justified. But they were not enemies at all — and mislabeling them as such was Pharaoh's greatest act of malice.

Ironically, the Achilles heel of any public policy is very often the problem it is trying to solve. Once the problem is identified, any discussion will revolve around the relative merits of possible solutions. But what if the problem being addressed is not the real problem? It follows that any debate over potential solutions is misguided. After all, even when one is certain about a problem, finding the right solution can be a challenge.

The debate over the proposed border wall and how it should be paid for concerns a controversial solution to the wrong problem. The United States is a country noted for its economic opportunities, understandably attractive to economic migrants. A recent Pew Study reported more than 10 million illegal immigrants are already resident in the United States, with almost 8 million of them in the workforce, and two-thirds of them having lived in the US for more than 10 years.

It is not the immigrants who are the problem, rather it is the lack of a workable and coherent immigration policy. The time has come for politicians to stop fuming over a wall that is nothing more than a distraction — and which will never solve the real problem — and instead they should start looking for solutions that will.

PHARAOH AND HIS PICTURE OF DORIAN GRAY

first published March 28, 2018

Earlier this month, Oscar Wilde's iconic novel, *The Picture of Dorian Gray*, opened as a play adaptation at a theater in Chicago. The new production — which sets the story in 1970s New York instead of 1890s London — has been universally slated by critics, for its "flawed" script and "sluggish" cast. But most disappointing of all is its self-defeating depiction of the eponymous picture, about which I will say more in a moment.

To have ruined this acclaimed masterpiece is quite an achievement. Perhaps Paul Edwards, to whom we owe this new stage adaptation, was unwittingly influenced by one of the book's most famous lines: "To be popular, one must be a mediocrity." After all, *Dorian Gray* is a literary work that transcends time and place, and Wilde's razor-sharp prose is as fresh today as when it was written.

Dorian Gray first appeared in the July 1890 edition of *Lippincott's Monthly Magazine*, a semi-annual literary journal published in Philadelphia. The premise of the story is quite simple. Dorian Gray, the book's main character, is a hedonistic, handsome young man pursuing all the pleasures of life. Early on, Gray's full-length likeness is painted by a famous artist. Enamored by how he appears in the portrait, Gray makes a wish for his exterior perfection to remain unaffected by the debauched lifestyle he leads, and for the portrait image to age and wither instead.

His wish is granted, and the novel goes on to chart Gray's libertine, selfish existence, with each passing episode resulting in further deterioration to his likeness in the painting, as it coldly records each of Gray's sins in vivid visual detail. In the dramatic climax, Gray attempts to destroy the painting, resulting in his own grisly death.

This compelling novella has been adapted dozens of times for both film and stage. The evolving portrait is always central to the drama, held up as a living reflection of Gray's self-destructive decadence. In 1943, noted artist Ivan Albright was commissioned to paint Gray's decaying image for the 1945 movie of *Dorian Gray* that later won an Academy Award. Albright's painting, which can still be seen in the Art Institute of Chicago, stunningly depicts the degenerating decrepitude of Gray, and is shocking in its vileness (see illustration).

Which makes the decision to confine the picture's changes to Gray's psychotic mind in the Chicago play, with the image itself remaining static throughout the performance, all the more surprising. The entire story hinges on the contrast between picture and reality; without this contrast the narrative is lacking in both depth and dimension.

Ironically, when the story first appeared, Wilde was compelled to defend it against charges of immorality. But as he pointed out, this was a story with a powerful moral: "Dorian Gray, having led a life of mere sensation and pleasure, tries to kill conscience, and at that moment kills himself."

In any event, this was hardly an original storyline. As Wilde himself noted, *Dorian Gray*'s central premise was "an idea that is old in the history of literature, but to which I have given new form." This was a reference to the medieval German legend of Johann Georg Faust, who makes a pact with the devil in exchange for a life of pleasure but is ultimately bound for eternal servitude and oblivion.

Although, as it happens, the real origin of this storyline is not the legend of Faust; rather, it can be found in the spectacular nation-forming narrative at the dawn of Jewish history. One of the great puzzles of the Exodus narrative is the Israelites' descent from relative freedom into hopeless slavery. Why was it necessary for them to suffer the misery of enslavement before they could experience Divine redemption?

Another enigmatic aspect of the story is Pharaoh's refusal to acknowledge his nation's impending demise in the face of overwhelming evidence they were up against a force they could never overcome.

Ancient Egypt was a culture obsessed with materialism. To ancient Egyptians, a full-on materialistic life was not just the ultimate goal, it was the only goal. Even in death, their physical bodies were preserved, and then adorned with the best that the material world had to offer, surrounded by a range of material accessories. The afterlife's only value was as a continuation of the life lived in a material setting.

So that they could appreciate the futility of this outlook before becoming God's chosen nation, the Israelites had to come face to face with everything that could be wrong with humanity, in order to ascend to the lofty spiritual heights of the Sinai revelation. The nascent Jewish nation, in their slow descent from invited and revered guests of Pharaoh towards their wretched fate as despised slaves, evoke the deteriorating picture of Dorian Gray, while Pharaoh is Dorian, determined to celebrate and perpetuate his self-perceived omnipotence and invincibility.

In his refusal to acknowledge Egypt's fading powers, Pharaoh was setting himself up for the disastrous climax at the Red Sea, when instead of destroying the painting, the damage he had brought upon himself, and his nation, crystallized in Egypt's devastating demise.

Rabbi Judah Loew (1520–1609), the rabbinic luminary known as the "Maharal of Prague," notes that the ten plagues of the Exodus story increased progressively in their severity. He interprets this as an ever-intensifying message to the stubborn

Pharaoh: Unless he heeded the call from God, he was propelling his nation over the abyss one sure step at a time.

And while Pharaoh's Dorian Gray portrait was in plain sight for all to see, we all have our own Dorian Gray portrait hidden somewhere. We can either pay it attention or hide it away in the attic — as Gray does in Wilde's novel — and pretend at our peril that life is normal.

The Torah is generally dismissed by non-believers as an irrational anachronism, with the argument that society has progressed beyond its outdated morals and messages. But is that really the case? To quote none other than Oscar Wilde himself: "The books that the world calls immoral are books that show the world its own shame."

SEDER NIGHT — YOU ARE WHAT YOU DO

first published March 22, 2018

W e live in an age where every single one of life's challenges that can affect our moods and disposition is handled by either psychology or psychiatry. Or, to put it another way: if therapy won't help, medication certainly will. Often it is a combination of both. Which leads one to wonder — what was the world like before the advent of clinical psychology?

It wasn't so long ago. The father of modern psychology was a kindly German doctor, Wilhelm Maximilian Wundt (1832–1920), who launched the Institute for Experimental Psychology at the University of Leipzig in 1879, becoming the first person to refer to himself as a psychologist.

Wundt's main innovation was the separation of psychology from philosophy, which had dominated all study of human behavior for thousands of years. His primary revolution was the introduction of a scientific analysis of human behavior and the workings of the mind via objective measurement and controlled studies, as opposed to scholarly observation and opinion, unsupported by empirical evidence.

That psychology emanated from philosophy is not as surprising as it might at first seem. Although Wundt trained as a medical doctor and taught physiology, he considered himself a philosopher first, and his two professorial chairs — in Zurich and Leipzig — were both in philosophy.

And while turning psychology into its own discipline was Wundt's idea, the study of human behavior and character stretches back to ancient Greece. Indeed, it is worth remembering that in this regard, Greek philosophy was concerned with defining moral virtue in human behavior, as opposed to the modern obsession with personality types and gaining closure.

Aristotle (384–322 BCE) was the first one to initiate a formal study of moral virtues, the yardstick by which humans can judge themselves. According to Aristotle, no person is born righteous or malicious. He defined virtue as the central point between excess and deficiency, an idea later employed by Maimonides. Most importantly, he said that all behavior is learned, and then established through habituation.

The American writer and historian, Will Durant (1885–1981), in his excellent survey work, *The Story of Philosophy*, summarized Aristotle's view as follows: "We are what we repeatedly do. Excellence… is not an act, but a habit." In other words, a person will only become what they aspire to be by actively doing whatever is needed, and then by doing it repeatedly, so that it becomes a second nature. Aspirations that are not accompanied by relevant actions are hollow, and possibly destructive.

Any study of successful people amply demonstrates this idea. In a recent interview for *Fortune* magazine, PayPal CEO Dan Schulman declared that he owed all his incredible success to his father — "his hero"— who told him: "Son, you are what you do, not what you say — that's what defines you as a person."

One of the great puzzles of the Haggadah text that we read on Seder Night is the exchange between the "father" and his "wise son", who asks him: מָה הָעֵדוֹת וְהַחֻקִּים וְהַמִּשְׁפָּטִים אֲשֶׁר צִוָּה ה' אֱלֹקֵינוּ אֶתְכֶם — "What are the testimonies, decrees, and ordinances that God commanded you [to do]?" The father responds by describing the laws of the Pesach offering, and specifically the prohibition against eating dessert after the Afikoman.

The father's answer is hardly the comprehensive response one would have expected it to be. Which must mean that we have misunderstood the question he was being asked. Because, as it turns out, the wise son's query is really far more fundamental. While the Exodus story is undoubtedly the foundational narrative of our people and our faith, the wise son is puzzled by the fact that there is such an abundance of complex duties and obligations to commemorate it. Surely a couple of symbolic customs would suffice. Why the need for all of the many "testimonies, decrees, and ordinances"?

The author of *Sefer HaḤinukh* — a medieval work that lists and elucidates all of the Torah's 613 commandments — appears to be addressing this exact question in his explanation of the prohibition against breaking a bone when eating the Pesach offering. On Seder Night we need to feel like kings and princes, says the *Sefer HaḤinukh*, and kings and princes don't break bones when they eat their meat. Consequently, so that we feel like kings and princes, the Torah commands us to emulate royal behavior by not breaking any bones while we eat the Pesach offering.

The *Sefer HaHinukh* goes on to use this as a platform to explain the multiple commandments relating to Seder Night:

Do not think the number of commandments relating to the Exodus is excessive, and that one or two rituals would suffice for our children and grandchildren to remember the historical events of the redemption from Egypt. To think this is utterly misguided…as man is influenced by his actions.

If we drink plenty of wine, lean back as we eat, do not break bones, and generally behave like kings and princes — then, guess what? We become kings and princes. And the more we behave this way, the more that feeling of freedom will linger.

It is for this exact reason that we do not eat dessert after the Pesach offering. We want the taste of freedom to remain in our mouths for as long as possible, and for the actions relating to God's redemption to become habituated. When we perform these mandated commandments again and again, and let the taste linger, we become different people, meaning that we become better people.

And if you think to yourself, as many people do, "It's not me to do those things, I can't fake it!" — that's just a copout.

In his 1962 novel, *Mother Night*, the atheist novelist Kurt Vonnegut (1922–2007) wrote, "We are what we pretend to be, so we must be careful about what we pretend to be." I suspect Vonnegut understood the power of habituated actions, which ultimately evolve to become who we truly are.

Meanwhile, doing nothing at all will inevitably result in being nothing at all. Or, as Carl Jung (1875–1961) put it, "You are what you do, not what you say you'll do." How right he was. And actually, I think that would make a great slogan for Seder Night.

THE SECRET OF JEWISH ENDURANCE

first published January 19, 2018

T his article was written shortly after the arrest of David and Louise Turpin, a California couple who held their 13 children — aged 2 to 29 years old — captive, in prison-like conditions. After one of their children managed to escape and alert the police, the Turpins were arrested. They were charged and tried for 14 felony counts of abuse and cruelty, and later sentenced to life imprisonment.

The arrest of David and Louise Turpin in Perris, California, earlier this week was immediately followed by details of one of the most disturbing news stories in quite some time.

The authorities described the alleged abuse carried out by the couple against their 13 children, over a period of several years — abuse that defies rational explanation and societal norms. The emaciated, undernourished children, were apparently held captive in shackles at their home, punished with beatings, and prevented from engaging with the outside world.

Remarkably, the 17-year-old daughter who alerted authorities to the abuse had been planning to escape with her siblings for over two years, before finally plucking up the courage to bolt. To get out, she jumped through a window together with one of her siblings — but even at that stage, her sibling was too frightened to go through with the plan and returned home.

Although news reports of murder and violence are ubiquitous — often featuring family members — we are not used to seeing the family structure itself used as the weapon to destroy lives. This is undoubtedly the most disturbing aspect of the Turpin story — it was the normal family structure that was used to terrorize the children. Parental authority, group dynamics, and reward and punishment, were all exploited to create an environment of fear and dependency that prevented the children from developing into healthy members of society.

In 2002, a study that compared 50 years of research papers looking into the routines and rituals of family life, concluded that it was the fundamental aspects of inter-generational dynamics that were "important to the health and well-being of today's families trying to meet the busy demands of juggling work and home."

It added that "family routines and rituals are powerful organizers of family life that offer stability during times of stress and transition." Bedtime stories, silly names for each other, inside jokes, daily or weekly meals together — all of these things make the mundane aspects of life special, and they also make the special things more memorable.

And later in life, when the earlier generation has gone, we pass down these treasured habits and routines to our own children and grandchildren, developing a home that bonds disparate family members together even when they are far apart. Moreover, we rely on these memories and dynamics as an invaluable resource in times of crisis.

The first directive given to the Israelites as a nation, was the instruction by God to acquire a lamb for the night of redemption from Egypt (Ex. 12:21): מִשְׁכוּ וּקְחוּ לָכֶם צֹאן לְמִשְׁפְּחֹתֵיכֶם וְשַׁחֲטוּ הַפָּסַח — "Take for yourselves a sheep for your families and slaughter the Pesach offering."

The reference to "your families" seems somewhat superfluous in the context of this commandment. Nevertheless, it represents possibly the greatest miracle of all — truly greater than all the wondrous plagues and the splitting of the Red Sea combined: namely, the creation of a nation that has endured for thousands of years. A people that had been downtrodden and enslaved for generations — totally dehumanized and humiliated — were brought together and elevated to the heights of chosen nationhood, and this was all done via the medium of family togetherness.

The Pesach offering was not an individual responsibility; rather it was a family ritual, bringing each family unit together for a joint project that would be unique and special for them as a group, setting the tone for the future, and establishing the family at the heart of Jewish life for all time. Throughout our turbulent history, and to this day, Pesach is celebrated together as a family — with every family coming together annually, each with its own traditions and customs to commemorate the origins of our identity.

A 2013 Pew Study reported that 70% of American Jews participated in a Seder, compared with just 53% who observe Yom Kippur. That number includes 40% of unaffiliated Jews, for whom the Seder is probably the only Jewish ritual they observe each year.

While the dreadful Turpin story represents the aberration of a family unit gone horribly wrong, we are all far too familiar with the fragmentation of our society over the past few decades. Family units are no longer valued as a priority, and the breakdown of family life is common.

Western civilization celebrates individuality and independence, but these values often come at the expense of family unity and cohesiveness, with families torn apart as the individuals within them pursue their own aspirations. And while Judaism is not opposed to individuality per-se, the importance of family, and the nurturing a solid sense of family identity, must always be at the forefront of who we are.

This idea stretches beyond the family, and into community as well. Each community is a large extended family, united by its shared experiences and unique makeup, strengthened by its bonds, and representing a unit that is ultimately greater than the sum of its parts.

The miracle of Jewish endurance has been the success of family and community, resources that not only ensure our ability to function in regular life, but also guarantee our resilience in crisis. This critical factor has seen our people outsurvive numerous civilizations and empires, starting over 3,300 years ago — when we departed Egypt, and left Egyptian civilization trailing in our wake. It is a lesson we must remember and celebrate — which is why Seder Night is such an important part of Jewish life and will remain so for every generation into the future.

REVOLUTIONS MUST COME IN PAIRS

first published April 20, 2017

It is in an axiom of the American national narrative that in 1776, citizens of the thirteen colonies of the Union declared themselves independent of Great Britain, freeing themselves from the control of the British monarch, George III, and his government of pompous, autocratic aristocrats. The Revolutionary War that accompanied the formal severance of ties with Great Britain resulted in tens of thousands of deaths, and both sides in the conflict spent huge sums of money to secure victory.

Ultimately, when the dust had finally settled, it was the American patriots who had won the day, partly due to French military support, but principally as a result of the widespread revulsion across the colonies for British arrogance, and the blatant insensitivity to the needs and concerns of the colonists they sought to control.

But although this narrative is the one that is widely embraced, it actually fails to take into account a powerful truth that undercuts it completely, namely the emergence during the 1780s of a powerful group of legislators, known as the Federalists, who sought to reunite the United States with Great Britain, and to ditch republican democracy in favor of a monarchical system, or at least a system far more similar to the one they had just repulsed than the one represented in the lofty ideals of the Declaration of Independence.

At the head of the Federalist group was Alexander Hamilton (1755–1804), the first Secretary of the Treasury, who counted John Adams (1735–1826) among his many avid supporters, while George Washington (1732–1799) — who remained largely aloof from partisan politics — was also broadly sympathetic to the Federalist cause.

Opposition to the Federalists was led by Thomas Jefferson (1743–1826), the brilliant Virginia-born polymath who single-handedly wrote the 1776 Declaration of Independence, and who was utterly devoted to the republican cause. Believing that the future of universal freedom depended on a system which allowed everyone to have a voice, not just a bunch of self-important legislators and rich people, he refused to bow to Federalist pressure, even after the republican-inspired French revolution turned sour and produced the infamous Reign of Terror, casting plausible doubt upon the very new "democracy-for-all" experiment.

The pivotal moment for America came after the presidential election of 1800, when Jefferson beat Adams for the presidency, but tied with Aaron Burr (1756–1836), his choice for vice-president. According to the peculiar constitutional rules that were then in place this meant that either of them could be named president. The Federalists preferred Burr over Jefferson, their avowed enemy, and did everything in their power to ensure that Burr secured the top job. Ultimately, Jefferson prevailed, in what became known as the "Revolution of 1800."

What makes this revolution far more remarkable than the one in 1776 was not that Jefferson beat Adams in a bitterly fought election, nor that he unpredictably prevailed against the Federalists and their British patrons. Rather it is the fact that this is one of the most prominent examples in recorded history when power passed from one group to another without anyone being killed or imprisoned, despite the great mutual enmity between the parties involved, and the profound disagreements that characterized their ideologies.

There is no doubt that the year 1800 was the year true democracy, and the benefits it offered to ordinary individuals, was born. Moreover, this second American Revolution strikes me as an extremely important, if overlooked, historical example of the phenomenon of one momentous transformative event needing to be followed by another in order for the first to be truly consequential.

Our own history as Jews began with exactly this sequence, with the Exodus from Egypt of a slave nation into freedom, followed seven weeks later by the revelation at Mount Sinai, and the gift of God's Torah for the nascent Jewish nation. The first "revolution" only became meaningful once the ex-slaves had internalized their freedom from human oppression and their direct involvement with God, both individually and collectively.

Once identified, this dual-revolution phenomenon is both observable and obvious throughout history. Nevertheless, it seems curious, to say the least. Why are first revolutions never enough to force a permanent break with the past? Why would American colonists, who had suffered under the yoke of British tyranny and misrule, ever have contemplated a return to anything remotely connected to British governance? Why would Jews emerging out of a Red Sea that had miraculously split to save their lives, and that had also drowned their oppressors, not immediately be ready to receive the Torah? In short, why does one need a second epiphany to perpetuate the first?

It is often the case that the ecstatic emotions which accompany a transformation from one reality to another are dampened and overshadowed by the challenges emanating directly from the overwhelming success of that transformation. The elusive pot of gold at the end of the rainbow doesn't glitter quite as brightly when it is encountered close-up. Suddenly, the abandoned material comforts of Egypt (or Great Britain) seem rather more attractive than they did before the celebrated moment of redemption.

It is only once this anticlimax has been experienced, and then overcome, that the true revolution can take place, shattering the psychological bonds with the past once and for all. And, as it turns out, the second revolution is just the final act of the first.

Which is why we count out the days between Pesach and Shavuot, the festival that commemorates receiving the Torah. This period, referred to as sefirat ha'omer, is akin to the intermediate days of the Pesach and Sukkot festivals, as we recall in real time the period that separated the first revolution and the second.

And this might also be a reason why the period between Pesach and Shavuot has traditionally been considered a challenging time, as we struggle to find our feet in the midst of our newfound freedom and liberty. Although, as long as we stay focused on the consummation of the initial redemption through the Mount Sinai revelation, we can be sure to shake off the shackles of Egyptian slavery, so that our Pesach freedom brings us into God's Shavuot embrace. Because revolutions always come in pairs.

GENOCIDAL INTENTIONS IN EVERY GENERATION

first published April 9, 2017

Probably the most challenging aspect of Holocaust history for Jews is the issue of Jewish collaboration. It would somehow be easier to deal with the Holocaust if it was just about heinous genocidal crimes carried out by evil Nazis against the hapless Jewish population of Europe. The idea that Jews cooperated with their mortal enemies and had a hand in the murder of their brethren is abhorrent, and patently antithetical to the Jewish ethics we proudly uphold and proclaim as the backbone of our longevity as a people.

Sadly, what people are willing to do to survive is not always honorable, and the Holocaust era was certainly no exception.

Anna van Dijk (1905–1948) was a Dutch Jewess who helped the Nazis track down hidden Jews in Amsterdam after 1943, in exchange for her life. Her collaboration probably resulted in the death of as many as 700 Jews, including her own brother and his family. She was executed for war crimes in 1948.

Chaim Rumkowski (1877–1944) was a Polish Jew appointed by the Nazis in 1939 to head the Jewish council in Lodz ghetto. He eagerly cooperated with his overseers, turning the ghetto into a ruthlessly run labor camp, providing the Nazis with lists of the young and elderly, or anyone he believed would not contribute to the productivity of the ghetto. Everyone on such a list was sent to their deaths, and he knew it. According to at least one account, fellow Jews beat Rumkowski to death when he eventually arrived at Auschwitz in 1944, shortly after the ghetto was liquidated.

These two are just a couple of examples of the dark side of the Holocaust narrative, a side we would all prefer not to dwell on. Rather we prefer to focus on the countless stories of selfless heroism, as well as the utter helplessness of those caught up in the Nazi death machine.

People like Anna van Dijk and Chaim Rumkowski undoubtedly rationalized their collaboration by telling themselves that any Jew who died as a result of their cooperation with the Nazis would probably have died anyway. In any event, collaboration by a handful of individuals is hardly a collective indictment against the Jews of Europe, the vast majority of whom refused to engage with the Nazis at any level.

The issue seemingly becomes rather more complex when one addresses the issue of Jewish organizational collaboration with the Nazis, and in particular the formal agreement in August 1933 between the Zionist leadership and the newly formed Nazi government. Known as the "Ha'avara Agreement," it enabled German Jews to immigrate to Mandatory Palestine and export their possessions and other German goods there, which was both economically and politically advantageous to Nazi Germany, as it undermined the growing movement advocating a total boycott of German exports.

Although Hitler was not directly involved in any of the negotiations, he most certainly approved the final agreement, which resulted in the immigration of 60,000 Jews from Germany to Palestine — among them my great-grandparents and three of their children. The Ha'avara Agreement was considered extremely controversial as soon as it was signed, which was long before the Nazis began to murder Jews in concentration camps. It would later be used, along with other examples of official Zionist cooperation with Nazi authorities, as proof that the Zionist movement had lost its moral compass in its zeal to create a Jewish state.

But this harsh verdict is deeply flawed for a number of reasons — principally because hindsight is not a valid basis for condemnation. Over many centuries Jews negotiated with all kinds of vile despots and evil murderers to ensure the security of Jewish communities, and to secure Jewish survival. That Nazi Germany was an adversary that would ultimately seek the elimination of world Jewry was not evident in 1933, and notwithstanding contemporary opposition, the Ha'avara Agreement simply modeled an established Jewish approach to existential threats.

This being the case, what are we to make of former London Mayor Ken Livingstone's claim that his incendiary statement regarding this topic is innocent and objective historical fact?

Just to remind you, this is what he said:

> **When Hitler won his election in 1932 his policy then was that Jews should be moved to Israel [sic]...he was supporting Zionism.**

Earlier this week Livingstone was suspended from the UK Labour Party for a year — although remarkably he was not expelled — after his remarks were found to be antisemitic, thereby damaging the reputation of the party.

Livingstone, like so many other antisemites and racists, is convinced that he is not guilty of any prejudice, and that those who are offended by what he said just don't have his grasp of the facts. After all, he argues, even Jews have told him he's right — as if the subjective views of some random Jewish woman he bumped into on a bus is evidence of his innocence.

Unfortunately, this episode has had unavoidable repercussions. Suddenly it is legitimate to synonymize Israel with Nazis in polite conversation, and it results in nothing more than a rap on the knuckles and a flurry of op-ed pieces.

Part of the Haggadah liturgy recited on Seder Night is the song that begins with the words וְהִיא שֶׁעָמְדָה לַאֲבוֹתֵינוּ וְלָנוּ — "It is only this [covenant with God] that has stood firmly for our ancestors and for us. It wasn't just one enemy that rose up against us to wipe us out, but in every generation there are those who want to wipe us out — and God saved us from their hands."

I have always been struck by the words "one enemy," and the notion that it is the "covenant" and "God" that have been our salvation. We Jews usually see our enemies as easily identifiable villains — all of them violent brutes, like the Cossacks, the Nazis, or Islamic terrorists — but that's actually a mistake. We are deluding ourselves. Enemies are not monolithic; they come in all shapes and sizes.

Sometimes, as with Livingstone and those like him, they appear in the form of public figures who cite "historical facts" while claiming to be our friends. Or they can appear as defenders of Palestinian rights who support a two-state solution. But whatever their appearance, and whatever they say and do, it is important to realize that we can only defend ourselves by our loyalty to the covenant, and by our faith in God. In every generation, this has been the secret of our survival, and so it will remain until the Messiah arrives. May it happen speedily, and in our days.

EXPOSING THE ANTITHESIS OF JUDAISM

first published April 3, 2015

In anticipation of Pesach this year, I resolved to explore the concepts of slavery and freedom. Personally, I have always struggled to find contemporary models to help me comprehend the transition from slavery to freedom so that I can experience them both during the "Jewish origins and identity crash course" that drives our annual Seder Night.

One could argue that it has never been possible to experience them both. In times gone by, when Jews were confined to ghettoes or worse, it would have been easy to tap into the slavery aspect on Seder Night, but what about freedom? Perhaps it was possible in aspirational terms, but certainly not in any practical sense. And once one is freed from the chains of bondage, while it may be possible to recall difficult years of persecution through reminisces and narrative, when one is free, one is free, and no amount of storytelling can change that reality.

I think if we truly want to discharge our Seder Night obligations, we need to move away from the conventional mechanisms for generating the two conflicting mindsets of slavery and freedom, and instead move towards a more cerebral approach. Our starting point is generally this: We know what slavery is — the absence of liberty — which means that we must understand what freedom is — if someone is liberated, they are free.

Actually, it is far from being that simple. The eighteenth-century French political theorist, Charles-Louis de Secondat (1689–1755), better known as "Montesquieu," wrote:

A nation may lose its liberties in a day and not miss them for a century.

These powerful words may be the best springboard for a Seder Night discussion that have ever been written. Are any of us really free? Or is our "freedom" merely an illusion?

The inclusion of Montesquieu in our Exodus discussions is particularly relevant this year. A few months ago, a political crisis erupted in Israel that provoked furious reactions around the world. The crisis was triggered by Prime Minister Binyamin Netanyahu's backing for a Knesset bill referred to as the "Jewish Nation State Law."

This bill represented an attempt to resolve the tension between Israel's dual Jewish and democratic character, enshrined in the 1948 Declaration of Independence. The proposed law declared Jewishness the default identity of the state in any instance, legal or legislative, in which the state's Jewishness and its democratic aspirations clash.

What, or who, defines Jewishness is another discussion, but the idea that Jewishness should trump democracy was widely seen as racist, even by Jews. Moreover, Netanyahu was labeled a xenophobe intent on undermining the democratic foundation of the Middle East's only democracy.

I never fail to be amazed at how poorly informed people are about both the ideals and the mechanics of democracy. Unfortunately, space limitations do not allow me to say everything I should on this topic, but at the very least let me help you understand that the arguments for and against the Jewish Nation State Law are based on a far broader argument about the nature of true democracy, sourced in the political philosophy of Montesquieu, and his bête noire, Jean-Jacques Rousseau (1712–1778).

Montesquieu believed that different national groups need very different constitutions so as to take into account their particular historical narratives. Trying to create a constitution that erases one or multiple national narratives is deeply flawed, in the same way as it would be flawed to pretend that another person's child is as important to you as your own. It is self-evident that people want what is best for someone else's child, but if that aspiration comes into conflict with aspirations for your own child, the needs of your own child will — and should! — always come first.

Meanwhile, Rousseau was an advocate of something widely known as a "state of its citizens," which proposes that once a particular territory has been defined as a state, all its citizens must enter into a constitutional agreement to forego any national, tribal, religious, or other identifying considerations, in order to become equal citizens of that state.

This idealized-but-flawed vision of democracy was the one adapted and adopted by Georg Wilhelm Friedrich Hegel (1770–1831) and Karl Marx (1818–1883), leading to the political system we know as Communism, which ultimately resulted in widespread oppression and suppression of identity.

Despite the rejection of Rousseau's theories by some of the greatest political thinkers of the twentieth century, his dystopian vision of true democracy has seen a resurgence over the past half century, advocated by many on the left as the only true representation of democratic values.

Theodore Herzl, in his monumental tract *The Jewish State*, scathingly attacked Rousseau, dismissing his ideas as utterly unworkable, and incompatible with human nature. Instead, he aligned himself closely with Montesquieu.

Similarly, the founding fathers of the United States revered Montesquieu, whose opinions on government and politics are quoted by America's founders more often than any other source besides for the Bible.

And, just to be clear, Judaism utterly rejects Rousseau's ideas. There is no such thing as a one-size-fits-all society. It is only when you are secure in your own identity that you will treat others who are not like you with respect and dignity. The Egyptians — and every other group of antisemites throughout history — hated Jews for not being like them. They believed that society would only function properly if everyone bought into a homogenized identity.

God took us out of Egypt to demonstrate how wrong they were. A unique national and religious identity can still enshrine respect for all others — and such a nation is bound to be a light unto all the nations.

The Nazis advocated a homogenized identity that was intolerant of any other. So did the Soviet Union. So do ISIS and Iran. And so, it seems, does the United Nations. Apparently, Israel and the Jews have no right to assert their own identity while respecting the rights of non-Jews.

The democratic world has been bullied into a Rousseau-oriented dictatorship that will inevitably result in the loss of our liberties — or maybe we have already lost them, and it will take a century for us to realize. Now, there is something that is surely worth contemplating at the Seder.

EDUCATION IS NOT ONCE A YEAR

first published January 27, 2015

Τ his article contains the text of a speech that I gave at Lincoln Square Synagogue for the New York launch of the "70-for-70" project on January 27, 2015, in the presence of Rabbi Lord Jonathan Sacks (1948–2020).

On January 27, 1945, the Soviet Red Army arrived at the entrance of Auschwitz, where the dreadful words Arbeit Macht Frei — "work sets you free" — adorned the gates of hell, and they liberated it from Nazi control.

No amount of work could free the inmates of Auschwitz. They were humiliated and mistreated, tortured and murdered. Jews from every corner of Europe, along with gypsies, homosexuals, undesirables, and the mentally and physically handicapped — every kind of human that Nazi ideology deemed unworthy of dignity or life — were murdered in the inhuman hell of Auschwitz. An inhuman hell conceived of and run by humans, whose humanity and compassion had evaporated in a frenzy of prejudice and propaganda.

But why do we remember this moment specifically on January 27th?

In the Torah portions we read in synagogues at this time of year we recall the first liberation of the Jews. The portions begin by recalling the evil perpetrated against the ancient Hebrews in Egypt. Then they recall the despair of the ordinary Jew and even of the leadership. Moses and Aaron even doubted that the mission to free their brethren would ever succeed.

After this, we read of the extraordinary miracles that led up to and followed the redemption. We recall that the Exodus was a precursor to our standing at the foot of Mount Sinai just seven weeks later, as we declared in unison נַעֲשֶׂה וְנִשְׁמַע — "we shall do, and we shall heed."

We have an annual anniversary to commemorate that moment of liberation. It is called Pesach. On Pesach we relive the experiences of Egypt, and the exhilaration of the Exodus. And yet this is still not enough. The Torah demands that we remind ourselves each and every day of the miraculous redemption from Egypt, a seminal moment that resulted in our formation into a national entity that has endured for almost three and a half thousand years.

My late father would recall that as a young man he worked alongside a remarkable Holocaust survivor called Simcha Bunim Unsdorfer. This scion of rabbinic leadership in Slovakia survived various concentration camps and later moved to England, where he worked for the Jewish community until his untimely death in the late 1960s.

My father remembered that he would often arrive at the office to find Mr. Unsdorfer had locked himself in his room. Eventually Mr. Unsdorfer would emerge, and my father would query his self-imposed seclusion.

"Why are you so upset today?" he would ask.

Mr. Unsdorfer would look at him quizzically.

"Today?" he would respond, with a glint in his eye. "Today, in 1944, Mr. Chaim Gross, the president of the community, was dragged away by the Nazis and shot and killed in full public view." Or alternatively, "Today, in 1945, in Auschwitz, my childhood friend Moshe Katz died from malnutrition." Or perhaps it would be, "Today, my cousin, his wife and his children, were all gassed and cremated, moments after arriving at the concentration camp."

The list of tragic anniversaries didn't end. Which was why for Mr. Unsdorfer, there was no "today." There was every day.

On January 27th we commemorate one very specific moment. The moment that the nightmare was over. Just as on Pesach we commemorate our Exodus.

But what of the millions who suffered and died before that moment? How do we commemorate them? The Torah instructs us to remind ourselves on a daily basis that we were slaves in Egypt and that eventually God redeemed us. It is not good enough to do that once a year. That's something we must do every day.

For me, a child and grandchild of Holocaust survivors, there is no once a year. There is only every day. Every day I wake up and think to myself — so many died, including so many members of my own family — and yet my parents and grandparents survived.

How will today justify their survival? What will I do today to ensure that there is less evil and more good in the world? What will I do today to bring someone closer to God?

That urgency is not once a year. That urgency is every day, and that is the message of

זֵכֶר לִיצִיאַת מִצְרַיִם — "a reminder of the Exodus from Egypt."

In an article for the UK's *Daily Telegraph* newspaper, Rabbi Lord Sacks recollected how he advocated strongly for the Holocaust to be formally remembered in the UK when the idea was first proposed in the 1990s. He reminded the Prime Minister at the time, Tony Blair, that despite the fact that the Holocaust happened relatively recently, its lessons had not been learnt, and Jews were still being targeted.

That was then, and now it is worse. As Lord Sacks wrote: "Anti-Semitism is rife in the Arab and Muslim world. Jews have been accused of everything: controlling America, dominating Europe, manipulating the economy, running the media, perpetrating 9/11 and all subsequent terrorist attacks, creating AIDS, Ebola, the 2004 tsunami, and global warming."

Without constant reminders of how this happens as a result of prejudice and hatred, distortion and bigotry, antisemitism will increase, as the Holocaust becomes just another tragic brutal episode in history, like the Crusades, or the Napoleonic Wars.

There is too much at stake. The State of Israel was created by the UN in the wake of the horrors of the Holocaust. It was not the Holocaust that prompted it. But it was the Holocaust which forced the world to realize that Jew-hatred was too strong to allow the Jews to remain without their own country.

Nevertheless, as the horrors of the Nazi genocide have receded into history, attitudes to Israel have shifted. Israel is in grave danger. And while it may be protected by a strong army, even the strongest army is weak without robust education to underpin it.

Pesach is certainly dramatic, a concentrated moment of memory — but the important lessons of education are never just once a year. Education has to be every day. Because our very survival depends on it.

THE HERO WHO FOUGHT FOR SOVIET JEWRY

first published April 10, 2014

Yesterday, we lost a genuine Jewish hero. Jacob Birnbaum, who passed away at the age of 87, rose to prominence during the 1960s after he founded an organization called the Student Struggle for Soviet Jewry — or SSSJ, as it was known.

Birnbaum was not a communal grandee, or a remote figure at the head of a polished organization that supported good work. He was a grass-roots activist who made a real difference.

The timing, in some way, couldn't be more poignant. When we sit down to the Seder, we say, as part of the recitation of the Haggadah: בְּכָל דּוֹר וָדוֹר חַיָּב אָדָם לִרְאוֹת אֶת עַצְמוֹ כְּאִלּוּ הוּא יָצָא מִמִּצְרַיִם — "In every generation each person must visualize themselves as if they went out of Egypt."

There are numerous interpretations and understandings of how one might fulfill this obligation. But Jacob Birnbaum offers us one of the most compelling.

SSSJ began as a result of Birnbaum's vehement conviction that Soviet Jewry could not be allowed to suffer the same fate as Jews who had fallen under the shadow of Nazi Germany, of whom he had been one — although luckily, he and his family had escaped their native Hamburg, and settled in England shortly before World War II.

Birnbaum's modus operandi was simple. Living in Washington Heights, in the vicinity of Yeshiva University, he would visit the YU dormitories every evening, night after night, and knock on students' doors to cajole them, and convince them, and energize them, and enable them, and organize them, to become foot soldiers in his campaign to bring the plight of Soviet Jewry to the attention of the world, and principally to the attention of those in power. It is fair to say that he single-handedly forced the Soviet Jewry agenda onto the desks of congressmen, senators, diplomats and even presidents.

Most famously he coined the phrase "Let My People Go!" as the rallying call of the struggle for Soviet Jewry.

The commemoration of the Exodus from Egypt, we are told, must be deeply personal. A ritualized retelling of the narrative that does not penetrate one's inner core, that does not animate a person to do something that echoes the epic events of our ancient history, is a waste of time, and ultimately an abrogation of one's Jewish duty.

I imagine that Jacob Birnbaum, sitting down at his Seder in 1964, and reading of the ancient Jewish victory in Egypt, thought to himself: "What is the point of celebrating the freedom of the Jews of Egypt, if there are Jews today who are still enslaved?" Not content with his own freedom, he sought the freedom of every Jew, and particularly those whom he knew were being terrorized and prevented from emigrating to the West, or to Israel, by the Soviet authorities.

It is certainly no accident that the first public meeting over which Birnbaum presided, at Columbia University, took place in 1964 just a couple of weeks after Pesach.

"Let My People Go!" was the phrase that Moses repeated to Pharaoh as he sought freedom for his nation; and "Let My People Go!" was the phrase Birnbaum adopted to push for the redemption of Soviet Jewry.

When we remember Birnbaum, we should not just remember him as an extraordinary hero — although he certainly was that. Instead, let us remember that he was, like you and me, an ordinary Jew, inspired and motivated by the message of Pesach to ensure that each and every generation of Jews will have the same ability as the Jews of the Exodus to be proud of their identity, and to practice their religion without hindrance, and without being fearful for their lives or their livelihood.

PESACH AND JONATHAN POLLARD

first published April 10, 2014

He is surely the most infamous spy of modern times. Jonathan Pollard, who spied for Israel during the 1980s while he worked at US Naval Intelligence, was convicted in 1987, and sentenced to life imprisonment. Time after time his case has come up and calls for clemency have gathered pace over the years — even among those who loathe the fact that Israel used a US-born Jew to spy on its closest ally.

Pollard himself is not an endearing victim — he is no Andrei Sakharov or Natan Sharansky. Nevertheless, a consensus has built up over the years that he has paid his price, and that no purpose is served by his continued incarceration.

This week, in a desperate attempt to prevent the collapse of the Middle East Peace Process, the White House announced that plans for Pollard's release were underway, as part of a broad range of items on the table to ensure the survival of the current talks.

Of course, we only know what we are told — and we are told only what they want us to hear. We certainly cannot be sure that Pollard will be imminently released, nor even if the Israelis have agreed to include his potential release as part of the negotiations between them and the Palestinians.

To be perfectly frank, it was not the statement regarding Pollard's release itself that interested me. What really drew my attention were a number of statements made when news of Pollard's possible release emerged.

Josh Marshall, of *Talking Points Memo*, a blog site that the *New York Times* refers to as "one of the most popular and respected sites" in the blogosphere, wrote: "Let me just say it: No, no, no, *no!*" The *New York Times* itself editorialized that this was a "desperation move" on the part of the US, and "a bad idea." Opinion formers and peace lovers all seem to concur that the release of this solitary prisoner, even if it could potentially save the peace process, would be a terrible idea.

The frightening aspect of this is that none of the people who are lining up to condemn Pollard's potential release raised their voices or lifted their pens when Israel not only promised but carried out the release of hundreds of Palestinian prisoners — murderers and terrorists — even as the current peace talks have been ongoing.

In fact, over the weekend, when Israel decided to cancel the fourth — yes, fourth! — release of prisoners, as it became evident that the Palestinians had no interest in fulfilling their own promises, these same opinion formers condemned Israel for causing the breakdown of the negotiations!

On Pesach, we are obligated to retell the story of the Exodus from Egypt, an event that took place many thousands of years ago. Not only must we retell the story, but we must actually tell it in such a way that it becomes relevant to us. As we say each year at the Pesach Seder: בְּכָל דּוֹר וָדוֹר חַיָּב אָדָם לִרְאוֹת אֶת עַצְמוֹ כְּאִלּוּ הוּא יָצָא מִמִּצְרַיִם

— "In every generation each person must visualize themselves as if they went out of Egypt."

But it is easier said than done. How exactly can we relate to our ancestors at the dawn of Jewish history? It seems that in order for us to understand who we are as Jews, we must understand the hypocrisy of ancient Egypt, and of its leader. While projecting himself as a deity, Pharaoh knew that he was nothing of the sort. He demanded justice for himself and his people but refused to offer justice or respite to those he was oppressing. He conceded at the end, but it turned out to be a purely tactical move; as soon as he had the chance, he attempted the genocide of the nascent Jewish nation.

Our Exodus from Egypt represents a break with ideals that look and sound good, but in the end are used as window-dressing, and then manipulated to suit the ugly prejudices of those who promote them. And we can apply that idea today with the same force as we have applied it at each and every point in our history. We were redeemed from slavery in Egypt so that we can identify right from wrong and live our lives by the ideals of the Torah.

No one can teach the Jewish people about human rights, nor can they tell us anything about morality and fairness. Those who remain silent while murderers are released by the hundreds, and then raise their voices when the release of a harmless former spy is proposed as a lifesaving measure, have absolutely nothing to teach us Jews. Indeed, it is the story of our Exodus, retold and refreshed every Pesach for thousands of years, which enables us to understand that.

Jonathan Pollard was released on November 20, 2015, a year and a half after this article was first published. He now lives in Israel.

SHAVUOT

MESSAGE FROM A DESERT

first published June 2, 2022

I recently discovered some interesting facts about deserts. The first fact is probably the most astounding one of all — did you know that deserts cover about one-fifth of Earth's land area? And here's another astounding fact: considering that the word "desert" is derived from the fact that deserts are thought of as vast, "deserted", empty spaces, it was a shock to discover that deserts across the world are inhabited by around 1 billion people, amounting to one-eighth of the Earth's population.

According to National Geographic, a desert is best defined as an area that consistently receives low annual precipitation — namely, no more than 10 inches (25 centimeters) of rain a year, and often much less. Deserts are usually thought of as "very hot", but although it is true that some deserts are extremely hot, with temperatures that can exceed 130°F (54°C) — such as the Sahara Desert in North Africa — there are also vast deserts that have very cold climates, the best-known being Antarctic and the Arctic ice cap.

Astonishingly — although perhaps not such a surprise, with what we now know about the dramatic effects of climate change

— the deserts of today were not always deserts in the past. For example, in prehistoric times, the Sahara Desert enjoyed a mild, moist climate, and there is even archaeological evidence of human settlement, including art, burial locations, and manufactured implements. But now, in the very same parts of the Sahara that were once full of humans, fauna, and flora, you will find windswept, sun-parched sand dunes — areas incapable of supporting life. Although, as it turns out — that is not quite true.

Most deserts are not quite as uninhabited and as lifeless as they seem. In fact, they are home to a range of very specialized plants and animals, all of which have adapted to life in extreme conditions. And being so precisely calibrated for life in such a harsh environment, the slightest change can spell disaster for these creatures and organisms.

One curious example is the Mohave tui chub, a fish originally native to the Mojave River that runs through the San Bernardino Mountains in California. This once vigorous waterway running through the arid Mojave Desert region was drastically diminished by the damming of its headwaters and reductions to the river's underflow, which, in turn, resulted in the decline of the Mohave tui chub species.

The final nail in the coffin came in the 1930s, when non-native arroyo chub fish were illegally introduced into the Mojave River by anglers as baitfish. The arroyo chub was much more suited to the now much warmer and much shallower habitat conditions in the river and as a result quickly spread through the river, ultimately replacing the native Mohave tui chubs via competition and hybridization.

And if it weren't for the eccentric radio evangelist and self-proclaimed physician, Curtis Howe Springer (1896–1985), the Mohave tui chubs might have disappeared for good. In 1944, with the encouragement of his fiancée Helen, Springer purchased an old abandoned military outpost at Soda Springs, California, where he built a fake hot-springs resort at the now renamed town of Zzyzx — so named so that Springer's "mineral springs resort" would always be "the last word" in health.

Springer was convicted in 1974, and eventually imprisoned, for squatting on federal land and making the false claim that his health foods would cure everything "from sore toes to cancer." Following his conviction, the former resort was given by the Federal government to the administrators of California State University, who converted the area into a research station called the Desert Studies Center, and then introduced the Mohave tui chub into Lake Tuendae, an artificial pond excavated by Springer in the mid-1950s.

The fourth book of the Torah is known as "Bamidbar," which means "in the desert" — a reference to first verse of the book: וַיְדַבֵּר ה' אֶל מֹשֶׁה בְּמִדְבַּר סִינַי — "God spoke to Moses in the Sinai Desert." The commentaries offer a range of explanations for this unusual mention of a geographic location, with the consensus among them being that during the entire first year after the Torah was given, all instructions from God to Moses were given on Mount Sinai, whereas once the Tabernacle temple was constructed, and over the next almost forty years, God's communications with Moses occurred in the Tent of Meeting, wherever it was located in the Sinai Desert.

But while this very literal understanding of the "desert" reference offers a practical explanation for the inclusion of the geographic location in the opening verse, it does not explain why the Torah's foundational instruction had to occur in a desert environment rather than in the Land of Israel. A clue to the answer can be found in the Talmud (Eruvin 54a), which offers an explanation for a verse later on in Bamidbar (Num. 21:18): וּמִמִּדְבָּר מַתָּנָה — "and from Midbar (desert) to Matana (gift)." The Talmud informs us that this verse contains a profound lesson: If someone humbles themselves like a desert, then their Torah study will endure and be given to them as a gift. But if not, says the Talmud, their Torah will not endure.

In numerous places, Jewish traditional sources compare Torah to life-nourishing water — without which we would perish from thirst. But nowhere is this analogy more resonant than in a desert, which is where water is so scarce — so much so, that the slightest change in the availability of water can alter our prospects or doom us into oblivion.

The Torah, which is the binding constitutional document of the Jewish people, is a spiritual water source. Utilized properly and treated as a precious resource not to be tampered with, the Torah can be a never-ending source of life. But if there is the slightest change, the impact on us can and will be devastating.

Unlike the rather lucky Mohave tui chub, those who find themselves in a precariously water-reduced environment won't have a weird savior like Curtis Howe Springer to rescue them from extinction.

And remarkably, the Talmud is clear on this point, in its commentary on a verse in Ḥabakkuk (1:14) that describes how

God "made mankind like the fish of the sea." Why are human beings compared to fish, asks the Talmud? Simple, it explains — just as fish cannot survive without water, people who separate themselves from the words of Torah and from doing mitzvahs are similarly fated.

Which is precisely the powerful message of Bamidbar, the book of the Torah that is fittingly begun on the Shabbat before Shavuot, the festival anniversary of God giving us the Torah so many thousands of years ago.

A SOCRATIC PARADOX AT SINAI

first published May 27, 2020

Socrates, the father of Greek philosophy, is reported by Plato to have declared: "If I know one thing, it is that I know nothing." This absurd statement is often referred to as the Socratic Paradox but would more correctly be defined as an oxymoron — a self-refuting statement.

In fact, Socrates reveled in making such confounding statements, and he also enjoyed making his disciples feel uncomfortable by challenging anything and everything they said with clever refutations and pithy rebuffs. He single-handedly turned incisive rational thinking and logical argument into a sport — but with this most famous of his quotes, he readily admitted that it was all just a front. Ultimately, he knew nothing — or as he might have put it, had he lived in the twenty-first century, he was constantly at the beginning of a new learning curve.

It has always struck me that the Socratic Paradox has a parallel in Jewish tradition. The Talmud (Shabbat 88a) records the dramatic moment when the Jewish nation received the Torah at Mount Sinai: "Rabbi Simai said, when the Jewish nation declared נַעֲשֶׂה — "we shall do," before saying וְנִשְׁמַע — "we shall listen," 600,000 heavenly angels came down to every member of the Jewish nation and crowned each of them with two crowns, one of them to correspond with "we shall do," and the other with "we shall listen."

There is no greater paradox in Jewish history than this blind acceptance of Torah whilst at the same time declaring that it needs to be understood, albeit only once the Jews had already agreed to be bound by its requirements and restrictions. After all, if they were ready to honor their "we shall do" declaration whatever lay ahead for them, why was there any need to later seek an understanding of the Torah by saying "we shall listen"? What would be the point?

Jewish tradition informs us that Torah is the ultimate expression of God's will on Earth. In reality, as Maimonides makes clear, God and His will are entirely inseparable, which means that if God is infinite, the Torah must also be infinite. A human being possesses limited intellect; consequently, had the nation initially said, "we shall listen" before saying "we shall do," this would have indicated that they wanted to make a decision about their commitment to Torah based on what would have been by definition limited comprehension — as if it was possible for them to cogently opine on God's infinite wisdom, and only then to accept it.

By saying "we shall do" before saying "we shall listen," the Jewish nation indicated their unconditional acceptance of God's Torah, acknowledging their own inability to ever truly comprehend it fully.

The question this forces us to ponder is where exactly the Jewish nation had acquired their ability to do this?

Rabbi Meir Shapiro (1887–1933), the legendary founder of the prewar Ḥakhmei Lublin yeshiva, suggests that this incredible national characteristic originated with our patriarch Abraham. When God assured Abraham that he would be the father of a great nation, He told him to go outside and "look toward the heavens and count the stars." Without thinking twice, Abraham went out and began counting the stars. The verse continues with God asking Abraham (Gen. 15:5): "Are you able to count them? So shall be your offspring."

What was going through Abraham's mind as he attempted to count the stars? Surely he knew it would be totally impossible for a human being to count all the stars in the sky. But the answer is simple — that is just who Abraham was. If God asks you to do something, you do it — because God is God, so if He asks you to do something, you do it. Similarly, when the Jewish nation was told that they were about to receive the Torah at Mount Sinai, they immediately indicated that they were ready to receive it without going through a prolonged process of consideration and reflection to see if it all made sense.

That is what the verse means when it says: "so shall be your offspring" — God was telling Abraham: your descendants will also possess this trait of devoted loyalty, and when they are about to receive the Torah they will declare "we shall do" before saying "we shall listen."

The sheer magnitude of the Torah at every level means that if we are only willing to accept it if we grasp it intellectually, our intellectual limitations will prevent us from ever understanding it, and therefore we will never accept it. It is only by knowing that we know nothing that we can ever begin to know anything at all. In other words, "we shall do" must come before "we shall listen."

Meanwhile, the even greater paradox is this: If we are willing and ready to accept God's Torah without first understanding everything, then we just might merit to understand it — at least at some level. And I think that is a paradox truly worthy of Socrates himself, or, as he might have said, "naaseh ve'nishma!"

THE TRIUMPHANT MESSAGE OF NAOMI
IN THE BOOK OF RUTH

first published May 17, 2018

For many Holocaust survivors, Shavuot was their first festival after liberation from concentration camp. One of the first people to encounter the emaciated survivors was a man called Rabbi Herschel Schacter (1917–2013), a young Brooklyn-born chaplain attached to General Patton's Third Army. There is a famous photograph of Rabbi Schacter conducting services for hundreds of Jews in Buchenwald — and this photograph was probably taken on the first night of Shavuot.

One of the survivors who was there in Buchenwald was Isaac Leo Kram (1921–2013). He later wrote about his experiences, and recalled what Rabbi Schacter had told them that night:

> [There will be] those who say, "I have suffered so much as a Jew until now, from now on I will cut myself off from my nation and from my religion!" ... [but] do not despair and do not be quick to leave your people. Your personal fate is testimony to the fact that no person in the world can destroy our people. For thousands of years, they have pursued us, in every generation they stand up against us to destroy us, and, nevertheless, we are alive! Believe in

the eternity of our people! Place your hope in the eternity of the Jewish people — "the Eternal One of Israel does not lie." (I Samuel 15:29)

Reading those words in a week during which the world's most powerful nation formally recognized Jerusalem as the capital of the Jewish State, while at the same time the terrorist group Hamas tried to overrun Israel by breaching the Gaza border so that a multitude of Palestinian murderers could run amok, I was struck by the fact that this counterintuitively optimistic streak is found at the heart of the Megillah we traditionally read during Shavuot.

The Book of Ruth is a confusing biblical text. Its inner meaning is obscured by the seemingly parochial nature of the storyline. Moreover, the Book of Ruth hardly seems like a dramatic tale of triumph in the face of adversity, like its counterpart, Esther. Nor is it a poetic or theological masterpiece, as are the parallel scriptural texts, Song of Songs and Ecclesiastes.

Besides, after reading through its four short chapters, one finds oneself wondering whether its lead character, Ruth, is demure and submissive, merely following her mother-in-law's lead, or whether she is calculating and precocious, pushing all norms and boundaries to get what she wants. And what are we to make of her romantic conquest, Boaz? Or of the fact that this unlikely couple are the antecedents of the Royal House of David?

These, and various other puzzles, have preoccupied commentaries for millennia. The mere existence of the Book of Ruth as a separate narrative text in the Hebrew scriptures is a clear indicator of its centrality in the emergence of the Davidic monarchy, itself a primary component of Jewish identity, both in historical and contemporary terms. Getting to the core of who

Ruth and Boaz were appears to be crucial if we are to truly understand the concept of a messianic redeemer.

But rather than focus on the personalities of Ruth and Boaz, I would instead like to focus on a central character in the narrative who often gets overlooked, but whose role cannot be overemphasized. I speak, of course, of Naomi — the impoverished widow of Elimelekh, who returns home to Bethlehem after losing her husband and sons, only to discover that her late husband's home and farmlands are no longer hers, as a result of the death of all the male members of her family.

The only thing Naomi has left are painful memories, and although she can count on the support of her devoted daughter-in-law, Ruth, this is tempered by the fact that Ruth is an outsider with little if any hope of ever becoming anyone's wife and building a family and a future.

For all intents and purposes, Naomi is a woman whose life is over. And truthfully, Naomi seems to be acutely aware of her plight, evident from her response to those who greet her by name as she arrives back in Bethlehem (Ruth 1:20): אַל תִּקְרֶאנָה לִי נָעֳמִי קְרֶאןָ לִי מָרָא כִּי הֵמַר שַׁדַּי לִי מְאֹד — "do not call me Naomi (pleasant), call me Mara (bitter), for God has made my lot very bitter."

And yet, despite this miserable proclamation, Naomi never gives up, instead setting for herself impossible aspirations. Although her daughter-in-law is from the despised Moabite nation, Naomi wants her to marry Elimelekh's nephew, Boaz, a wealthy landowner from the uppermost echelons of society. With quiet determination, Naomi sets the stage for this improbable "shidduch," so that her misfortune can be reversed, and the hopelessness of her life replaced by success and meaningful hope for the future.

Confusingly, while her optimism and confidence seem utterly misplaced, her victory, when it occurs, seems almost inconsequential, certainly by comparison with stories like the one contained in the Book of Esther. In reality, though, the results of Naomi's efforts are no less triumphant than the spectacular victory against Haman and his genocidal intentions.

The message conveyed by Naomi is that no matter how bleak one's personal situation, set your sights high, and then go for it. Not only can you succeed beyond your wildest dreams, but it is these kinds of triumphs that will result in a Royal House of David. This was what Rabbi Schacter meant when he spoke about the eternity of the Jewish people — and how right he was.

Anyone who survived the horrors of the Holocaust could easily have allowed their bitterness and destitution to swallow them up and then disappeared without trace. But instead, they set their sights high, building new Jewish communities, schools, and institutions — and even more remarkably, a Jewish country, Israel, that with all its flaws is the equivalent of a Royal House of David, itself not without flaws, but which nonetheless became a powerhouse of Jewish identity, synonymous with both our proud history, and with the ultimate redemption of mankind.

MESSAGE AND MEDIA IN THE AGE OF DONALD TRUMP

first published February 1, 2018

Earlier this week, I came across a remarkable article in the *New York Times* written by their media correspondent, Michael Grynbaum. Using an interview with former White House supremo Steve Bannon as a hook, Grynbaum focused on the role and fortunes of the news media in the era of President Donald Trump.

"It's the first McLuhanesque presidency," was Bannon's startling opening line when he sat down with Grynbaum. Marshall McLuhan (1911–1980) was the notorious postwar Canadian professor who coined the phrase "the media is the message" in 1964, and then went on to become a media celebrity in his own right. Grynbaum reminded us that McLuhan believed we would one day all live in "a media-saturated era where reality is less important than its representation."

While trying to work your head around that concept, it is worth noting that in January 2016 *The New Yorker* ran an article in which it breezily predicted the demise of the social medium, Twitter. Stock in the company took a dive, but a year later, in February 2017, *Fortune* magazine reported that Twitter users had grown by almost 25 million people in the previous year, i.e., by almost 10%.

The share price immediately began to climb, and since February 2016 the share price has almost doubled. Twitter use has also continued to rise. So how did Twitter pull it off? Simple, it didn't. According to *Fortune* the resurgence of Twitter is due to one factor, and one factor only — Donald Trump.

McLuhan himself could not have made this up. The president's notorious tweets have brought in a whole new generation of Twitter users, as well as reawakening dormant users, the result of people realizing that only on Twitter could one encounter @realDonaldTrump.

And Twitter is just the tip of the iceberg. Newspapers that struggled to stay afloat have suddenly been given a new lease of life. Journalism, widely held to be a dying profession, has seen its fortunes revived, and a resurgence of serious investigative journalism has replaced the kind of trashy, superficial "scoops" we all imagined had become the new reality.

Intriguingly, this revival is being generated by the very media that benefits from its own success. The story, you might say, has become the story. Or, as Grynbaum put it, "a story's 'buzz' [is] variously defined by the number of retweets, Facebook likes or panicked text messages from White House aides that it generates."

This phenomenon has had its own knock-on effect — political reporting has morphed "from 1,000-word stories into stand-alone nuggets designed to set Twitter aflame." Trump, who eschews formal press conferences, and frequently attacks the big news organizations in his quirky tweets, has nonetheless taken to using White House photo-ops — always attended by dozens of reporters — "to spar with reporters off-the-cuff, sometimes for nearly an hour at a time."

Another person who has seized the moment is Jim VandeHei, co-founder of *Politico*, who last year launched a news website called Axios that publishes stories of 250 words or less about Washington politics, all of them containing deliberately designed soundbites for social media.

Just consider this — the President Trump we "know" is not actually a person, he's a media story, a soundbite, a tweet, a post. Trump gets it, Bannon gets it, and the media gets it.

"When [Trump] says you'll miss me when I'm gone, and your ratings will go through the floor, he's absolutely correct — that's McLuhan talking through Trump," said Bannon.

The big question is — do we get it? And the answer to that is, we only get it if we understand the power of a message. And although I don't buy into some of McLuhan's wackier theories about media — such as the weird idea that it depends on which senses are engaged by a given medium as to whether the resulting impression will be visual or acoustic — I do fully concur with his view that the power or effect of any message is completely dependent on the method of its presentation, and the impression it makes on those who receive it.

Actually, McLuhan didn't come up with this — rather, its origins can be found in an unusual directive associated with the revelation at Mount Sinai. In the leadup to God giving the Torah to His Chosen Nation, He instructed Moses to prepare the nation for this seminal moment. "If they uphold the covenant," said God, "and faithfully fulfil the words of the Torah, they will be my treasured people."

Instead of ending it there, God added a further piece that is both cryptic and unique. "Tell them," He said to Moses (Ex. 19:6): וְאַתֶּם תִּהְיוּ לִי מַמְלֶכֶת כֹּהֲנִים וְגוֹי קָדוֹשׁ — "be for me a kingdom of priests, and a holy nation." This instruction seems to be over and above the one to uphold the covenant and to remain faithful to God.

The phrase "kingdom of priests" is not found anywhere else in Hebrew Scripture, and although the concept of aspiring to holiness does appear elsewhere (for example, see Lev. 19:2), it must be contextualized in terms of the preceding injunction if we are to understand both of them properly, or at all.

The sixteenth century Italian Bible commentator, Rabbi Obadiah Sforno, was acutely aware of this anomaly, and proffered an enlightening explanation that echoes our earlier theme. Being a "kingdom of priests" — namely, a self-assured nation that is not only pious in its behavior, but pious in its appearance; and a "holy nation," immortal in who they are, and in their endurance with that identity, is the key to being God's chosen and treasured people.

It is not enough to observe the law and believe in God. While that is certainly the foundation, it has no impact nor any lasting value if it makes no impression. Priests must be visible in their priesthood by being cloaked in their priestly vestments. Which means that while the media may not be the message, the message will never amount to anything if there is no media.

LIKE ONE MAN, WITH ONE HEART

first published June 9, 2016

One of my favorite Midrashic narratives describes God's attempt to find a nation willing to accept His Torah (Sifrei Devarim 343). The narrative depicts the nascent Jewish nation's willingness to embrace the Torah, and then juxtaposes their enthusiasm with the reaction of various other nations who refused the Torah on the basis that it included elements they deemed intolerable.

God approaches the descendants of Ishmael and asks them if they want the Torah.

"What does it contain?" they inquire.

"Do not steal," God replies.

"In that case," they respond, "it is not for us."

The descendants of Esau similarly reject the Torah, because it prohibits murder, while the descendants of Ammon and Moab, nations whose origins are rooted in an incestuous liaison between Lot and his two daughters, rebuff the Torah because it disallows incest.

The narrative concludes with God offering the Torah to the Jews, who make no inquiries as to its content, declaring in unison נַעֲשֶׂה וְנִשְׁמַע — "we will do whatever it tells us to do, and we will listen to whatever it says."

The Midrashic account is obviously fanciful and the interactions between God and these nations are hardly likely to have taken place in the way the Midrash describes them. Clearly the idea behind this narrative is message orientated, and the message appears to be the Jewish nation's unconditional willingness to abide by the Torah, in contrast to the other nations cited in the story.

The problem with this being the only message is that it fails to acknowledge the unfairness of God's exchanges with those other nations. After all, if God's first and only demand was that these nations must renounce their favorite sin, surely He was setting them up to say no. Why didn't He tell them that the Torah contained the laws of Shabbat and festivals, or that it contained the laws concerning sacrifices, or honoring one's parents? These might have been mitzvot they could have embraced immediately, and then, in the fullness of time, their observance of these less objectionable parts of the Torah might have led them to abandon their cherished sin.

It is also worth reflecting that God confronted each nation with their Achilles heel, driving them into an Orwellian "Room 101" before they had even had the chance to see what else the Torah offered. Would the Jews have fared any better in the same situation? It is all very well to say that we declared our allegiance to the Torah without demanding to know its content, but over the weeks and months that followed we failed God and His Torah on countless occasions. If anything, those other nations should be commended for having been far more honest in their response to God. By rejecting the Torah, they had demonstrated a greater self-awareness than the Jewish nation.

Rabbi Chaim Yaakov Goldvicht (1924–1994), rosh yeshiva of Yeshivat Kerem BeYavneh, suggests that the response of the Jews to God's inquiry demonstrated they had conquered their greatest weakness of all — an almost instinctive lack of unity and mutual respect. When they declared in unison "we will do and we will listen," they demonstrated their ability to rise above the sum of their parts by putting aside their differences and becoming one nation in the service of God.

This idea is hinted at elsewhere in the story of Mount Sinai: In anticipation of the Sinai revelation, the Torah first says of the Jews that "they came to Sinai, they camped in the desert" — all in the plural. But once the Jews arrived at Mount Sinai, they are referred to in the singular. Rashi quotes a Midrash stating that at Mount Sinai the nation was "like one man, with one heart."

But although Rabbi Goldvicht's thesis is compelling, it still leaves an open question. If the nations of Ishmael, Esau, Ammon, and Moab each collectively rejected the Torah, surely their unity for this purpose is equally laudable?

The solution to this conundrum lies in the difference between unity that is based on selfishness, and unity that is based on empathy for others.

One of the definitive characteristics of sociopaths and psychopaths is their lack of empathy. They have little or no ability to understand and share the feelings of others, which results in behavior that is risky or harmful to others, as they are not inhibited by guilt, fear, anxiety, self-doubt, or remorse. The unity of the nations that rejected the Torah was based purely on selfishness and self-interest — each nation was a collection of psychopaths and sociopaths acting not as a singular unit, but as a unit of multiple individuals motivated by common interest.

But ultimately there is no such thing as common interest for a psychopath, only mass individual self-interest. God needed to know if these nations could let go of the parts of their national culture that would eventually lead to a complete breakdown of their societies. But the answer was an unequivocal "no!" — and God knew then that these nations were all doomed to spiritual oblivion.

The Jewish nation was different. Uppermost in every mind was a desire to help others and to be there for each other, even if this meant their individual lives would suffer. If God assured them that the Torah was good for the nation as a whole, even if as individuals they might end up struggling with all of its many rules, and even if they were unable to match up to its requirements, they instinctively knew what they had to do.

Sadly, they failed to uphold this ideal from time to time — and quite frequently to start with! — but overall, and over millennia, our success as a nation has stemmed from this one overriding trait: the individual desire of each and every one of us to concern ourselves for the welfare of others at our own cost, so that our nation as a whole can thrive and prosper, and be true to our original declaration of "naaseh ve'nishma!"

HOW WE TREAT EACH OTHER MUST COME FIRST

first published May 28, 2015

A few weeks ago, our community hosted the chief rabbi of Efrat, Rabbi Shlomo Riskin. My own connection with Rabbi Riskin goes back many years, long before I moved to Los Angeles.

I first met Rabbi Riskin in 1998, when he was invited to London to speak at Encounter, an annual outreach conference launched a couple of years earlier with a very specific agenda — to eclipse the pluralistic and ever expanding Limmud outreach phenomenon by showcasing the broad spectrum of Orthodox outreach alternatives in a setting that did not compromise the principles of Orthodox outreach professionals.

But suddenly, and without any warning, Rabbi Riskin was uninvited a week before the conference. Evidently, some of his more controversial opinions had surfaced — opinions the conference organizers considered too radical, and they no longer felt that he was an appropriate guest speaker.

Up until then I had been a vocal and active supporter of Encounter, particularly because the most effective Jewish outreach organizations and activists hail from the strictly Orthodox world (Chabad, Aish, Ohr Somayach, just to name a few), and yet they were being deliberately marginalized by Limmud's pluralistic organizers, who were openly hostile to Orthodox outreach organizations because of the halakhic red lines their field workers refused to cross.

Limmud's hostility was strictly passive aggressive: participation at their flagship winter conference required crossing exactly those red lines, and the committee running Limmud had made clear they were not interested in finding workable compromise solutions. So, having set up Encounter in response to Limmud's insensitivity, inflexibility and intolerance, the irony was that Encounter's organizers were now displaying exactly the same insensitivity, inflexibility, and intolerance, when Rabbi Riskin's participation at their own conference became an issue.

Although I had never met Rabbi Riskin, I reached out to him and asked if he would accept a Shabbat invitation to my shul, the Saatchi Synagogue. We advertised a keynote address, using a photo of Rabbi Riskin with a photo-shopped image of masking tape superimposed over his mouth under the headline "Gagged!"

Rabbi Riskin chose to speak about "daat Torah" — a Hebrew phrase that describes the concept of senior rabbinic authority being of the oracle of Jewish life, a guiding principle within the strictly orthodox community.

At a packed Saturday night event, Rabbi Riskin passionately described how "daat Torah" was a modern concept, justifiably created by a terrified Orthodox leadership in the nineteenth century, to prevent their communities from disintegrating in the face of mounting assimilation and the alluring appeal of Reform Judaism.

But the notion that any rabbi's views are infallible, and that no dissenting view is allowed, is anathema to normative Judaism, argued Rabbi Riskin, and moreover, turning it into a bedrock of faith would mean that most of the Talmud would need to be deleted, as well as the thousands of recorded rabbinic opinions that had not found their way into mainstream halakhic practice for one reason or another.

Earlier this week, I recalled this whole astonishing episode, when it was reported that the Israeli rabbinate had decided not to renew Rabbi Riskin's tenure as chief rabbi of Efrat, apparently because his moderate views on conversion standards, among other things, do not accord with theirs.

Before I get to that, let me make two things clear. First of all, I do not concur on every issue with Rabbi Riskin. Although he is a scholar and a thinker, and tackles issues with deep sensitivity, he occasionally leans towards progressive solutions that make perfect sense from a social perspective but find themselves on thin ice in terms of halakhic tradition.

Nevertheless, Rabbi Riskin's opinions cannot and must not be dismissed, nor can they be trivialized. He is absolutely and unquestionably committed to traditional Orthodoxy, no less so than Israel's two chief rabbis and their subordinates. You can agree with him or disagree with him — but Rabbi Riskin's voice comes from within the camp, not from beyond it.

Secondly, it is neither my place nor my intention to interfere with the employment practices of Israel's rabbinate. They employ many hundreds of rabbis, and possibly thousands of people, and as I do not participate in their processes, it would be inappropriate for me to weigh in on whether a popular rabbi should be forced to retire or allowed to stay on beyond his retirement age.

Having said that, I do wish to express my utter disgust at the flagrant public humiliation of a distinguished public servant and religious leader — a man who is not only fully committed to Torah, but to the widest possible perpetuation and dissemination of Torah. A man who has worked day and night for decades to keep Torah institutions alive, giving up precious time with his family, and his own Torah study, so that he could help provide support for institutions which have produced outstanding scholars and rabbis, proud Jews and committed religious Zionists.

How dare anyone summarily disrespect him on the basis of their own view that his calls for greater inclusiveness are an offense to Judaism? How dare they?

On Shavuot we recall the luḥot — the two stone tablets inscribed with the Decalogue. Each one of the two tablets was inscribed with five commandments: the first five were those between man and God, while the other five — those between man and his fellow man — were on the second.

What is curious is that if these stone tablets were identical in size, as one assumes they were, then the letters engraved on the first tablet would have to have been much smaller than those on the second, as the first five commandments are much wordier.

Perhaps this was deliberate. Perhaps when it comes to commandments between man and God, God is quite happy not to have them projected as screaming headlines. But when it comes to the laws between man and fellow man, God wants us to get the message loud and clear — **"DON'T STEAL!"** — **"DON'T MURDER!"** — **"NO IMMORALITY!"**

Our relationship with God is meaningless if we have no respect for our fellow man. It is really that simple.

THREE WEEKS AND TISHA BE'AV

A POWERFUL LESSON FROM HISTORY

first published July 13, 2021

One of the most startling narratives of the Talmud concerns Rabbi Yoḥanan ben Zakkai, the rabbinic leader of Jerusalem's Jews during the devastating Roman siege of Jerusalem — a siege that ultimately resulted in the destruction of the Jerusalem Temple in 70 CE.

Rabbi Yoḥanan ben Zakkai attempted to bring the extremist "zealot" faction under control, pleading with them to reach a compromise with the Roman enemy so that they would survive, and the Temple would remain standing, but they summarily rejected his appeals.

Amidst ever-worsening circumstances for Jerusalem's inhabitants, much of it precipitated by the zealots, who were determined to force a military confrontation, and with no realistically attainable respite on the horizon, Rabbi Yoḥanan ben Zakkai sought advice on how to escape the city from his nephew Abba Sikra, who led one of the insurgent factions.

Just as an aside, I have always found it bewildering that Rabbi Yoḥanan ben Zakkai, the paradigm of levelheaded leadership, had a nephew who was irretrievably ensconced at the center of one of the most violent militias of Jewish history.

Abba Sikra claimed that he was unable to pacify his compatriots, but nonetheless, he was willing to help his uncle commit an act of treachery and advised him to feign illness and "die" so that he could exit the city gates inside a coffin. He even went as far as protecting his uncle from having his body impaled by swords on the way out of the city by telling his fellow brigands how terrible it would look to the Romans if they mutilated the body of their own revered leader.

Abba Sikra's fate after his duplicity remains unrecorded, but we are informed that his very-much-alive uncle emerged from the coffin and quickly gained an audience with Vespasian, supreme commander of the Roman army.

Rabbi Yoḥanan ben Zakkai began the meeting by addressing Vespasian as the Emperor of Rome, a position to which Vespasian had not yet been appointed. Even as Vespasian expressed surprise, a messenger arrived informing the general of his elevation to the leadership of Rome's vast empire. Suitably impressed with the great rabbi's prophetic powers, Vespasian granted him three wishes — and it is fair to say that the realization of two of them utterly changed the course of Jewish history.

Grasping that it would be pointless to ask Vespasian to spare Jerusalem and its inhabitants after they had conducted a multiyear bloody war against the forces of Rome, Rabbi Yoḥanan ben Zakkai instead asked that the leadership family of Rabban Gamliel, a descendant of the great Hillel, be given their lives and freedom, and that the coastal city of Yavneh (Jamnia) be established as a center of rabbinic Judaism, so that the Jewish faith would survive the inevitable imminent catastrophe of the destruction of its central shrine.

This practical foresight ensured Jewish continuity and provided a workable solution for the future, demonstrating that Rabbi Yoḥanan ben Zakkai's wisdom was equally matched by his precognition of the looming tragedy — a tragedy he had so valiantly attempted, but failed, to avert.

All these details are remarkable enough in-and-of-themselves, but undoubtedly the most extraordinary aspect of the whole story is that Rabbi Yoḥanan ben Zakkai had concluded that his own community — the very community he had grown up in and led for years — had sunk into an abyss of wanton self-destruction. And while he was powerless to ameliorate the situation of those trapped by the zealot leadership's intransigence, including his own nephew, he realized that at the very least he could preserve the values and traditions of his beloved heritage by finding a compromise that would dovetail with the realities of the time so that any survivors would have a future — and that is what he bravely did.

Drawing parallels from history to help us understand or resolve current crises is always a fraught path, prone to whimsical wishful thinking. But at the same time the study of history is pointless if we don't take on board that *plus ça change, plus c'est la même chose* — namely, that the human condition doesn't change, and that history has a tendency to repeat itself — even if never entirely identically.

My point is this: Once again, as in ancient history, the Jews of Israel who most visibly and by their lifestyle represent the strictest application of our faith have painted themselves into a knotty corner. And when faced with increasing threats to their Israeli-government funded status quo — as was the case last week when incoming Israeli Finance Minister, Avigdor Liberman, ended yeshiva and kollel learners' childcare subsidies — instead of looking for a compromise, the Haredi sector always seems to double down.

In this latest situation, United Torah Judaism's party leader Moshe Gafni called Liberman an "evil man," while the Shas party leader Aryeh Deri described Liberman's decision as "wicked."

For many years the Haredi political parties have been government kingmakers — crucial to the cobbling together of fragile right-leaning coalitions, even though strictly speaking they do not support the Zionist enterprise, nor do they wish to be officially identified with the State of Israel. And while in the early years of the state they were a beleaguered minority, struggling to reestablish themselves after the Holocaust while battling the hostility of secular Zionists, today, with well over a million Haredim in Israel, they represent 12.6% of the total population of Israel. In 2009, Haredim under the age of 20 represented 16.3% of that population demographic — 29% in terms of Israel's Jewish demographic — and that was 12 years ago!

Although wholesale non-participation in the civic activities of the State of Israel may have made sense for the Haredi community during those early years, today it is leading inexorably towards an economic drain on Israel that could affect Israel's overall success — and Haredim are included in that success. It is also causing incredible resentment among Israel's non-Ḥaredi citizens and may ultimately be the foundation of future security issues if Ḥaredim continue to grow in numbers whilst collectively rejecting army service.

If there's one lesson we should learn from the destruction of the Beit Hamikdash almost 2,000 years ago, and the revealing story of Rabbi Yoḥanan ben Zakkai, it is that Jerusalem and the Temple's destruction might have been avoided if the zealots had seen things differently and acted reasonably. And imagine this: Our Temple could still be standing today if the squabbling and inflexible faithful — who all no doubt believed fervently that what they were doing was for God's glory and the greater good — would have understood that the sands had unalterably shifted.

While Rabbi Yoḥanan ben Zakkai was ensuring the future of the very Judaism they assumed they were protecting, this group was simultaneously guilty of wanton self-annihilation which resulted in their Temple — our Temple! — burning and crumbling to the ground.

And just to be clear — the State of Israel is not a Roman military siege intent on subduing Ḥaredim, or worse. On the contrary, all the non-Ḥaredi leaders and citizens of Israel I have ever met over the years seem fully prepared to do what they need to do to accommodate their Ḥaredi brothers and sisters, as long as they actively participate in the incredible miracle of renewed Jewish control in the Promised Land.

Truthfully, it is not too late to turn the tide and to ensure the thriving existence of Ḥaredim as full partners in the State of Israel, so that they avoid the extraordinary pain and pointless struggles they seem destined to face. All that is needed for that to happen is for those within the Ḥaredi system who yearn to remove the shackles imposed on them by others to accept the example set by the Temple-era rabbinic luminary, Rabbi Yoḥanan ben Zakkai, so that they don't get trapped like Abba Sikra, who felt unable to stand up to his fellow zealots.

Tragically, nobody listened to Rabbi Yoḥanan ben Zakkai then, and it turned out a disaster for them. But if people heed his wisdom today the outcome could be different. I pray that those who cherish Rabbi Yohanan ben Zakkai's memory and legacy follow his path, and in that merit, may the Temple be rebuilt, speedily and in our days. Amen.

THE UGLY SCOURGE OF HATRED

first published August 8, 2019

At 3:00 a.m. this morning, Dvir Sorek, a yeshiva student from Ofra, was found stabbed to death close to Efrat in Gush Etzion. Dvir was just 19 years old. His murderers — who have not yet been found — are presumed to be Arabs who kidnapped their victim at random, and then stabbed him multiple times until he was dead. Their motive — a pathological hatred of Jews.

Heartbreakingly, this horrific tragedy is the second terrorist murder to affect the Sorek family. Nineteen years ago, Dvir's grandfather, Rabbi Binyamin Herling, was murdered by Arabs who opened fire on a group of Israelis on a Ḥol Hamoed Sukkot trip to Mount Ebal, near Nablus.

Dvir's grieving father described him as "a kid with light in his eyes," and added that "whoever didn't know him missed out — he always helped the less fortunate around him who were in need of a friend."

There is something about murderers motivated by hatred that stops everyone in their tracks. They are somehow more heinous, if that is possible, than murderers motivated by greed or personal animosity. The thought that one human being can randomly kill another human being simply because of their religion or race is almost beyond comprehension.

The preservation of human life as a moral objective is enshrined as the highest ideal of civilization, and even a soldier at war, or someone who kills in self-defense, is subject to the rule of law, and certainly to a moral code. The killing of an innocent person because of something they represent in a warped worldview is the absolute height of depravity, the twisted result of human intellect gone awry.

Which is why the Holocaust is considered the most monstrous crime in human history. The industrialized scale of the Nazi killing-machine was fueled purely by hatred for Jews — who posed absolutely no threat to the Germans, or to anyone else for that matter. It stands out as the ultimate example of the moral depravity of those who kill for hate.

Ultimately, love always prevails over hate, and haters are left behind. Earlier this week, Holocaust survivor Shoshana Ovitz turned 104 years old. She survived Auschwitz having seen her mother being led to the gas chambers and having lost most of her family.

After being liberated in 1945, she married Dov, another survivor, whose first wife and four daughters were also murdered by the Nazis. They moved to Haifa, where Dov became a poultry butcher and Shoshana worked as a seamstress.

Shoshana had one request from her family as a gift for her 104th birthday — that all of them gather at the Kotel for a family photo. Remarkably, after overcoming a host of logistical issues, the family somehow pulled it off. Over 400 of her descendants came to Jerusalem and posed together, as Shoshana sat among them beaming, surrounded by her children, grandchildren, and great-grandchildren.

Some of them wept, overwhelmed by what they were experiencing, while the youngest descendants ran in and out of the family group, squealing with joy. It was a triumph of love, the ultimate victory against the hatred Shoshana experienced in Auschwitz, at the hands of those who murdered her family, her community, and so many millions of her fellow Jews.

The Talmud (Yoma 9b) records that the first Jerusalem Temple was destroyed as a result of the prevalence of paganism, immorality and murder among the Jews of ancient Israel, while the Second Temple's destruction was due to the widespread phenomenon of "senseless hatred."

The Talmud's conclusion is that such hatred is equivalent to the three cardinal sins of Judaism. And even though the people who lived during the Second Temple period were engaged in Torah study, observed mitzvot, and engaged in numerous acts of kindness, the Talmud says that they were ultimately undermined by the rot of hatred. The message is that haters are bound for oblivion, while those who love will prevail.

It always strikes me that the period in the Jewish calendar known as "The Three Weeks," between the Fast of Tammuz and the Fast of Av, runs counter to Judaism's fixation with joy and the celebration of life. Why are we commemorating death and destruction so many thousands of years after they occurred? Aside from anything else, it is difficult to emotionally connect with a tragedy that happened so long ago, however appalling it was, and however central it is to Jewish identity.

The Jerusalem Talmud (JT Yoma 5a) proposes that "any generation in which the Temple is not rebuilt is considered as having destroyed it." This critique appears overly harsh if it is not put into context. What the Jerusalem Talmud is actually saying is that unless the causes of the Temple's destruction are properly addressed, the destructive cycle will simply continue, which means that the Temple's absence is not an event that took place in the distant past — it is happening here and now, and we are the destruction's protagonists.

According to Rabbi Abraham Isaac Kook (1865–1935), the fact that our Temple was destroyed, and the Jewish nation dispersed because of hatred means that the Temple can only be rebuilt, and our people reunited in the land if they disavow hatred and promote love. Both among ourselves and for the world, the Jewish nation must be ambassadors of love, calling out hatred and its ugly consequences, and trying to ensure that hate is identified as the underlying cause for so much pain and suffering.

If we succeed, our generation can be the one that rebuilds the Temple. And surely, that is a worthy goal.

(Shoshana Ovitz passed away on February 7, 2021, at the age of 105.)

THE JEWISH STATE MUST REMAIN JEWISH

first published July 19, 2018

The world has reacted with outrage to the legislation passed this week in Israel that defines the country as the nation-state of the Jewish people. The law — which has been labeled by almost every media report as "controversial" — legislates Israel as the historic home of the Jewish people with a united Jerusalem as its capital and proclaims the Jewish people to "have an exclusive right to national self-determination" in Israel.

"No mention of equality or minority rights" thundered CNN on its website, while the *New York Times* referred to the law as "contentious," noting that its critics believed it to be "discriminatory, racist and a blow to democracy."

Notwithstanding this hostility, and the hysterical reaction from Arab legislators in Israel's Knesset, along with the overeager condemnations by American Jewish organizations such as the Union for Reform Judaism, J-Street, and the AJC, the facts are rather less exciting. Even the *New York Times* admitted that "the law is largely symbolic and declarative."

Since 1948, Israel's Declaration of Independence has been superseded by a series of "basic laws" passed by the Knesset, which can only be repealed by a supermajority Knesset vote, as opposed to a simple majority vote or a Supreme Court ruling. These laws are in lieu of a constitution, and in combination are considered the de facto constitution of the State of Israel.

The thorniest issue of Israel's identity has always been its Jewish character. The delicate, sometimes clumsy balance between a "Jewish" state and the preservation of equal rights for all its citizens has often been used as proof that Israel is inherently undemocratic, and that it favors Jews over non-Jews.

Until this week, attempts to regularize the day-to-day realities of life for the Jewish and non-Jewish citizens of Israel through legislation was purposely delayed, so as to prevent the backlash we have seen erupt over the past few days.

But let's get one thing straight — this new law changes nothing. Israel was originally set up as a country where Jews could live without fear that the government or population would target them for their Jewish faith or ethnic origins. This objective was envisaged by Israel's ideological father, Theodore Herzl (1860–1904), as well as by his many heirs.

In every period of history there have been countries who turned against their Jewish citizens, and the Jews have suffered everything from institutionalized discrimination to genocide, and all that lies in between. By establishing Israel as a country that has our backs, Jews simply reacted to the fact that no country had ever consistently protected our rights.

Although non-Jewish citizens of Israel have equal rights to Jewish citizens in terms of justice and economic or other benefits, those rights cannot ever include the possibility — however remote — that they might change the dynamic of the world's only

"Jewish" state so that its Jewish character, which is the only safety net we have, is undermined — or worse!

What I find staggering, and incredibly hypocritical, is that the same people who lobby for a free Tibet, or for Native Americans, or indeed for Palestinian rights, are the very same ones who are so critical of Jewish rights in our ancestral homeland, the Promised Land of Israel.

And unlike the so-called Jewish organizations jumping over themselves to demonstrate their faux-democratic credentials, I am proud to say that I back this law wholeheartedly, without equivocation — and particularly during the days leading up to the Fast of Av, when we commemorate the tragic end of Jewish hegemony over our own country at the hands of the Babylonians and the Romans.

The Haftarah, the selection from the Prophets, which is read on each of the three Shabbatot between the Fast of Tammuz and the Fast of Av, reflect the mood of this period in our calendar — a time of mourning for the destruction of our Temples in Jerusalem and the final removal of Jewish control over our national affairs.

On the Shabbat prior to the Fast of Av we read the first chapter of the book of Isaiah. Intriguingly, the prophet mentions Sodom and Gomorrah twice, although the second reference appears to contradict the first.

"Had God not left us a remnant, we would be like Sodom, we would resemble Gomorrah," Isaiah begins (1: 9), referencing the complete destruction of these two cities during the patriarch Abraham's lifetime (Gen. 19). Fortunately, God did not consider the Jews to be like those two wicked cities, Isaiah quotes the nation as saying, otherwise the Jewish nation would have been utterly obliterated.

And yet, in the very next verse, Isaiah refers to the Jewish nation as "rulers of Sodom" and "people of Gomorrah."

The Talmud quotes Rabbi Yosei, who says, "Never open one's mouth to Satan" — in other words, one should never speak of one's own demise, as this might very well create circumstances in which the demise occurs. We derive this principle from these same two verses in Isaiah. The first infers that the nation believed they deserved to be destroyed like Sodom and Gomorrah, and by the time we get to the second, Isaiah addresses them as Sodom and Gomorrah.

The Talmud explains that by comparing themselves to those evil cities, the Jews gave the prophet an opening to endorse that comparison. The Talmud wants to convey how crucial it is for us to stand up for ourselves, by telling us how we can affect reality by how we project our image. When we diminish our identity and don't fight for our rights, we can be sure that our enemies will be in full agreement.

Those who succumb to the pressure on Israel to "democratize" by criticizing Israel's decision to enshrine the primacy of Jewish identity into the fabric of Israel's constitution, are guilty of pushing Israel into setting itself up for its demise.

There are so many who have fought so valiantly for Israel on every possible stage and in every possible setting over such an extended period of time — the least we can do is protect our country from the insidious fate our enemies dream of, by formalizing our right to be in control of our own land in perpetuity.

EVIL IS NEVER BANAL

first published August 11, 2016

The annual mandated period of mourning for the destruction of two Jerusalem Temples thousands of years ago does not match up with the idea of Judaism as an optimistic faith, full of joy and positivity.

Every year, as we enter the three-week mourning phase, I struggle with this inconsistency — on the one hand trying to stay true to the Jewish "be happy" primary directive, while on the other trying to honor the memory of tragedies in our past.

This year I resolved to delve deeper into it all by looking at how those who have suffered calamity in their lives revisit those experiences as part of the process of catharsis and rehabilitation.

In the course of my research, I came across an extraordinary series of YouTube videos. Posted five years ago by Yad Vashem, the 138 separate video clips show the full, unedited trial proceedings of Adolf Eichmann (1906–1962), the Nazi bureaucrat who organized and ran the logistics for Nazi Germany's "Final Solution." Long before the Second World War began, Eichmann was appointed to head what was known as the "Jewish Desk" at the "Sicherheitsdienst" (SD), the security services arm of the notorious SS.

Initially responsible for fomenting violence and economic pressure against the Jews so that they would emigrate voluntarily, he later took charge of concentrating Jews into ghettos in various major cities in Poland, with a loose plan to relocate them into "reservations" in the far eastern regions of Russia, or possibly overseas, after the Nazis had conquered the Soviet Union.

Ultimately, as we all know, the Nazis decided to implement the infamous "Final Solution," which mandated the elimination by murder of every Jew living under Nazi jurisdiction.

Eichmann proved to be an extremely diligent and talented organizer, relentless in his zeal to see the task done. Tragically, he was extremely successful, and he personally ensured the annihilation of European Jewry with the death of six million Jews — a number that remains as astounding today as it was when it first became known, not least because it encompassed at least forty percent of all the known Jews who were alive when the war began.

After the surrender of Nazi Germany in 1945, Eichmann somehow evaded capture by the Allies and then disappeared from sight. Initially he lived in Austria under an assumed identity, later moving to Argentina. In May 1960, a team of Israeli secret agents captured him in Buenos Aires, and he was brought to Israel to stand trial.

The trial began in April 1961 and was adjourned for the judges' verdict exactly 55 years ago this week, on August 14, 1961. In December 1961, Eichmann was sentenced to death for war crimes, and he was executed on June 1, 1962 — the only man that the State of Israel has ever executed in its history.

This past week I sat and watched several hours of the trial, trying to get a sense of the atmosphere in the courtroom and of the conduct of those who were present. The film quality is remarkably good, and the sound is very clear. Besides the fact that it is in black and white, the film record of the trial could easily have been shot much more recently than 1961. That being said, I have rarely sat through such harrowing footage in my life.

The charges against Eichmann, read out during the course of the first session, is the stuff of nightmares. But far more harrowing are the detailed testimonies of the over one hundred witnesses who testified, all of them Holocaust survivors from different spheres of wartime Nazi influence, excerpts of which I watched with horror and a constant lump in my throat.

What I found more disturbing than anything else was Eichmann himself. Political theorist Hannah Arendt (1906–1975), who attended the trial as a journalist, famously responded to his demeanor by coming up with the idea of "the banality of evil." She meant that ordinary people could perpetrate great evil in the belief that what they are doing is not evil at all, rather that it is perfectly acceptable and totally in keeping with normal human behavior.

Watching the film clips, one can see why Arendt believed this assessment of Eichmann to be true. He has the look of a middle ranking administrator — deferential, courteous, and even in moments of irritability, contained and restrained. He looks like the type of man you would comfortably trust to take care of your affairs, and yet he stood at the helm of one of history's greatest crimes.

But Hannah Arendt got it completely wrong. Whilst in hiding in Argentina, Eichmann told a sympathetic Dutch journalist that as the war was ending, he called in his men and informed them he would gladly "jump into my grave in the knowledge that five million enemies of the Reich have died like animals." This is not the statement of a phlegmatic middle manager; it is the raw animus of a sociopath with no humanity or concern for the fate of those he has harmed.

I had always wondered what the purpose of the Eichmann trial actually was. My impression, now that I have seen it on film, is that the trial often bordered on clumsy in its execution, and in any event the guilty verdict was surely a foregone conclusion. In which case, why didn't the Israeli agents simply kill Eichmann in Argentina, and take photos of his corpse for later publication?

The answer became evident the more I watched. Unless one is aware of what one has lost and how, there will never be any chance of rebuilding, nor of true renewal. More importantly, the gravest danger posed by evil is the fact that it can come in the form of an Eichmann, who looks and seems innocuous.

And it is exactly for this reason that we commemorate Tisha Be'Av each year and recall the loss of our Jerusalem Temple for the three weeks that lead up to this tragic anniversary — to remind ourselves that we must know what we've lost in order to yearn for it, and moreover, so that we can internalize the fact that not everything evil is self-evidently so.

THE ENDURANCE OF CAUSELESS HATRED

first published August 8, 2014

With the ceasefire that was abruptly agreed to earlier this week, the world has finally turned its attention away from Israel and Gaza — at least for the moment — and is now focused on other things. A double tropical storm in Hawaii. An outbreak of the deadly Ebola virus. Oh, and an attack by the Iraqi air force on a Sharia court controlled by ISIS, in which 60 people died, many of them civilians.

Did you miss that story? Did you also miss the story about 40,000 Yazidi refugees fleeing their villages on Mount Sijar in northeastern Iraq, to escape certain death at the hands of bloodthirsty ISIS militants? Apparently, Yazidis practice a religion that melds Christianity with Islam and ancient Zoroastrianism. In any event, according to ISIS their religious faith makes them heretics who must choose death or conversion, if they are unlucky enough to fall into ISIS hands.

The reason you are missing all this stuff is because the media barely reports it, and there are no emergency UN Security Council sessions to call for an immediate ceasefire. The US government and other Western governments are largely silent on these issues, and — remarkably! — there have been no demonstrations anywhere calling for the downfall of ISIS.

What seems particularly jarring about all this, is that the civilians under threat, or who are dying, seem remarkably similar to the ones in Gaza, who found themselves caught in the crossfire between Israel and Hamas. How are we to understand this hypocrisy?

In fact, the most arresting aspect of these past weeks was that the animosity against Israel inexplicably expanded to include all Jews. Earlier this week school children on a bus in Australia were accosted by thugs threatening to slit their throats. Last week, mobs in Paris ransacked the Jewish area howling "death to the Jews!", and *Newsweek* ran an article titled "Exodus: Why Europe's Jews Are Fleeing Once Again."

And so, it goes on. How is it possible that the world is entirely blind to its own double standards, and how can it be that all Jews are being scapegoated and vilified for Israel's actions in Gaza? Can you imagine what would happen if a Muslim was attacked for the ISIS treatment of Yazidis? The very same demonstrators who attack Jewish property would utterly condemn an attack against a Muslim as a misguided protest against ISIS.

Meanwhile, whereas the Israel-Gaza situation has the IDF legitimately protecting Israel against murderers who are intent on killing them, ISIS is clearly a vicious radical Islamic group with a lust for murder. Why the double standards?

On Tisha Be'Av, we all sit on the floor and hear Eikha (Lamentations) being chanted — five chapters of mourning that describe the devastation which accompanied the destruction of the Jerusalem Temple.

The Hebrew name for the Book of Lamentations is אֵיכָה, which means "how?" — not "lamentations." This, the true title, indicates that the entire episode of the Temple's destruction, notwithstanding our sins and misdemeanors as a nation, is completely inexplicable. The suffering of the Jews in ancient Israel seems totally out of proportion to any wrongdoing on their part. The message of "how?" is this: How can the excessive mistreatment of the Jews at that time, and since, by the nations of the world, ever be explained?

The Talmud observes that the Second Temple was destroyed as a result of a causeless internecine hatred that permeated the Jewish nation at that time. The Talmud gives us some narrative examples of the prevalent hatred, but never goes into the exact details of its definition, nor does it offer advice for how we can avoid falling into the same trap. And yet, we must conquer and reverse causeless hatred if we are to get our Temple back. In which case, we need to understand exactly what this causeless hatred is.

I believe that causeless hatred can best be defined as a hatred that is out of all proportion to the reason that prompted it. It is a hatred that includes things and people that have nothing to do with its cause. It is hatred that transcends group affiliation. These are the hallmarks of the kind of hatred that caused our Temple's devastating destruction, and these, ironically enough, are the hallmarks of the world's most enduring hatred — antisemitism — a revulsion against Jews that is out of proportion to anything any Jew may have ever said or done.

If any other group does the things that Jews are accused of doing, they will never become the subjects of such animosity. Moreover, antisemitism is directed against all Jews, even if it was only one Jew, or a particular cluster of Jews, who stimulated the reaction.

The weirdest element of antisemitism is the broadness of its tent. Radical Muslims stand alongside extremist Catholics and progressive atheists, while White Supremacists align themselves with vicious fascists. How that dynamic works for all of these groups I have absolutely no idea, but it helps us understand the malicious power of causeless hatred and how hard it is to conquer.

The only antidote to causeless hatred is causeless love. Based on the evidence, it is clear that this means we must show warmth and tolerance to people well beyond our immediate group, in a way that is disproportionate to any logic.

With the world's reaction to the Gaza War this past summer, we have just been given a reminder of the negative effect of causeless hatred. Within our own wider Jewish community, it should prompt us to bury our differences, and to learn to love and respect one another.

Causeless love has to be our primary goal. Failure is not an option. Our future literally depends on it.

GILAD, EYAL & NAFTALI: THE LEGACY OF ZION AND JERUSALEM

first published July 31, 2014

On July 30, 2014, I addressed a packed event at the Saban Theater in Beverly Hills. This event marked the end of the 30-day mourning period for the three teenagers — Gilad Shaer, Eyal Yifraḥ, and Naftali Frenkel — who had been kidnapped and brutally murdered in Israel a few weeks earlier.

As I put together my remarks before the event, I reflected on the fact that the kidnap and frantic two weeks of searching until the bodies were discovered had already receded into the past. So much had happened since then. We had all been so distracted by the events unfolding in Israel and Gaza, that the horror we all felt for those two weeks had been entirely overwhelmed by our absorbed concern for Israel under threat, and IDF soldiers at war.

But I feel very strongly that we must never forget what happened to those beautiful boys, and for that reason I would like to share the remarks I made that emotional night.

This is what I said:

> **We are currently in the midst of three weeks of mourning, a period in the Jewish calendar during which we mourn the destruction of our Temple, the holy sanctuary which was the center of Jewish**

religious life for hundreds of years, and whose destruction almost spelt the end of the Jewish nation, and of the Jewish faith.

And tonight, we are here to reflect on the horrific loss of 3 young boys — Gilad Shaer, Eyal Yifraḥ, and Naftali Frenkel — holy souls, whose kidnap and murder horrified all of us. We have a confluence of mourning.

This mourning is further augmented by the dreadful situation that has unfolded in Israel over these past weeks since the boys were killed. Rockets raining down on our brethren, aimed at the indiscriminate slaughter of Israeli civilians. A daily toll of dead IDF soldiers deployed to root out the threat from the Gaza Strip. The pain is unbearable.

I want to focus on this confluence. It is reflected in the blessing we say when visiting mourners during a Shiva: הַמָּקוֹם יְנַחֵם אֶתְכֶם בְּתוֹךְ שְׁאַר אֲבֵלֵי צִיוֹן וִירוּשָׁלַיִם — "May God comfort you among the mourners of Zion and Jerusalem."

It seems strange to offer this as a comforting line as we leave mourners who have just lost their loved one. When someone has lost a father, a mother, a brother, a sister, a child — why would they care about Zion and Jerusalem?

The answer is simple. We are only Jews because of the legacy of Zion and Jerusalem. No Jew is a Jew if he rejects the essence of Judaism as represented by the holiest shrine of our faith. The site of our Temple represents our relationship with God, our relationship with the Torah, and our relationship with the piece of land — the tiny piece of land — that is a portal to God Himself.

When a Jew dies, we mourn his or her loss, but we are comforted in the knowledge that our tradition continues, that our love for God, for our faith, for our Holy Land, and for our people, continues, even as one link in that chain is taken from us. That is why we bring up Zion and Jerusalem as a source of comfort when we mourn for an individual Jew.

Gilad Shaer, Eyal Yifrah, and Naftali Frenkel — your names will forever be etched in our memories. You reminded us that although we have returned back to our Promised Land, and we have seen how Jewish life and Jewish pride has increased and thrived as never before over the past 2,000 years, the quest for Zion and Jerusalem is far from over.

Your families need comfort, but we too are mourners — together we all mourn — and that is a great comfort.

Families Shaer, Yifrah, and Frenkel — we mourn with you.

We mourn for Gilad. We mourn for Eyal. We mourn for Naftali.

And we mourn for Zion and Jerusalem.

On Tisha Be'Av we will remind ourselves that the struggle is far from over. Even as we sit and pray for the reinstatement of our Temple, our brethren in Israel and the holy soldiers in Gaza and beyond find themselves in the crosshairs of evil beasts — beasts who would delight in not just the death of every Jew and in the destruction of Israel, God forbid, but also in the death of the dream and the message of Zion and Jerusalem.

I don't want to end on such a sour note, so let me add one more thing.

Our greatest monarch, the extraordinary King David, wrote in Tehillim, (Ps. 30), and we recite it each morning: הָפַכְתָּ מִסְפְּדִי לְמָחוֹל לִי פִּתַּחְתָּ שַׂקִּי וַתְּאַזְּרֵנִי שִׂמְחָה — "You turned my mourning into dancing; you removed my sackcloth and clothed me with joy."

Even as we mourn Gilad, Eyal, and Naftali, we must acknowledge the extraordinary unity that has resulted from them having been taken from us.

This unity has continued these past weeks, and long may it continue. The boys are surely dancing as they watch us — old and young, religious and secular, left and right — coming together as one united group of Jews, to remember them, and to dedicate ourselves to the future of Judaism and to the continuity and safety of Jewish life.

My friends, we will continue. We will prevail. And as a united force, we are invincible. May their

memory be a blessing, and may God bless us, and all
of Israel. Amen.

APPENDIX

YOM HA'ATZMAUT

MARK TWAIN VISITS THE HOLY LAND

---

first published April 19, 2018

In 1867, a young man called Samuel Langhorne Clemens set sail from New York, bound for Europe, Africa, and the Middle East. Clemens is better known by his pen name, Mark Twain, although in 1867 he was still just an obscure journalist who had somehow convinced a California newspaper to fund this spectacular trip abroad, in exchange for regular updates from different stops on his journey.

Twain's two most famous books, *Tom Sawyer* and *Huckleberry Finn*, were still many years away, and much rested on the success of his travelogue. As it turned out, the five-month cruise was a gamechanger, and the resulting book, *The Innocents Abroad* (1869), sold 70,000 copies in its first year, and was Twain's bestselling book during his lifetime.

Twain carefully constructed his reports to reflect the reactions of an average layperson visiting exotic lands far away from home, and specifically a person who would not allow preconceptions and mythology to overwhelm the reality of what he saw. The result was refreshing, and highly unusual for the nineteenth century.

Lake Como in Italy was nice, Twain said, but Lake Tahoe back home in the United States, was much nicer. And Mount Vesuvius was unimpressive when compared to the Kilauea volcano in Hawaii. Although Twain was enthralled by the grandeur of Milan, Venice, Florence, and Rome, he was disgusted by the vast economic gap between rich and poor in Italy, particularly as it was evident that all available resources had been invested in architecture and edifices, instead of the impoverished population.

The most important leg of the journey for Twain and his fellow passengers was their visit to the Holy Land, then known as Palestine, at the time a minor outpost within the Syrian province of the Ottoman Empire.

Most of the tourists on Twain's trip were devout Christians on their first pilgrimage to the land of the Bible, and Twain, who was brought up Presbyterian, was undoubtedly swept up by the excitement and anticipation of reaching the Promised Land, spurred on by his distaste for almost everywhere else he had visited along the way. But just about every myth and expectation was dashed by the reality Twain confronted when he arrived.

"The word Palestine always brought to my mind a vague suggestion of a country as large as the United States," he began, "I do not know why, but such was the case. I suppose it was because I could not conceive of a small country having so large a history."

Unlike the grandiose palaces and churches Twain had encountered in Europe, along with the teeming cities and towns of Turkey and Syria, the land of the Bible was not just a jarring contrast, it was incomprehensible in light of the rich history with which it was associated. Western civilization owed itself to countless centuries of events that had occurred in this exact geographic location, and yet it was a veritable wasteland, whose inhabitants — of all faiths and cultures — were primitive and unsophisticated.

> **Palestine sits in sackcloth and ashes. Over it broods the spell of a curse that has withered its fields and fettered its energies.**

Twain described in vivid, unfiltered detail the squalor and desolation he witnessed in every place he visited across the country, and his description of Jerusalem, once the crown of Judea, is particularly disturbing.

> **Renowned Jerusalem itself, the stateliest name in history, has lost all its ancient grandeur, and [has] become a pauper village; the riches of Solomon are no longer there to compel the admiration of visiting Oriental queens; the wonderful temple, which was the pride and the glory of Israel, is gone.**

The state of Jerusalem's inhabitants only underscored just how much this once glorious city had sunk into decline.

> **It seems to me that all the races and colors and tongues of the earth must be represented among the fourteen thousand souls that dwell in Jerusalem. Rags, wretchedness, poverty and dirt...abound.**

Twain was particularly struck by how barren the country was, and how few people there were. As he traveled through the Jezreel Valley he noted, "there is not a solitary village throughout its whole extent — not for thirty miles in either direction…. [and] one may ride ten miles hereabouts and not see ten human beings."

With hindsight, this was hardly surprising. The population of Palestine in the 1860s was 350,000 — compare that to today's 8.5 million.

Twain's conclusion was that the Land of Israel was a bitter disappointment. It is "desolate and unlovely," he wrote, although "why should it be otherwise? Can the curse of the Deity beautify a land? Palestine is no more of this work-day world. It is sacred [only] to poetry and tradition; it is dream-land."

Twain's final analysis was that the Holy Land was a fantasy for religious dreamers looking for ghosts in a cemetery that was trapped in eternal damnation.

But how wrong he was. Approximately 2,600 years ago, the prophet Ezekiel prophesized (Ez. 36:8): וְאַתֶּם הָרֵי יִשְׂרָאֵל עַנְפְּכֶם תִּתֵּנוּ וּפֶרְיְכֶם תִּשְׂאוּ לְעַמִּי יִשְׂרָאֵל כִּי קֵרְבוּ לָבוֹא — "But you, mountains of Israel, will produce branches and fruit for my people Israel, for they will soon come home."

According to the Talmud (Sanhedrin 98a) "there is no greater sign of the redemption than [the fulfillment of] this [verse]."

The Holocaust martyr, Rabbi Yissaḥar Shlomo Teichtal (1885–1945), in his seminal work *Eim Habanim Semeikha*, writes that the desolation of the Land of Israel is an essential component of that prophecy, a precursor to the flourishing renewal of the land in Messianic times.

Seventy years after the creation of the State of Israel, we have all personally witnessed the fulfilment of that prophecy, and as we contrast the highly developed, prosperous country with the dreadful place described by Mark Twain, and even with the struggling Israel that marked most of its formative years, let us all be acutely aware that the fulfilment of Ezekiel's prophecy was highlighted by the Talmud as the greatest sign of imminent Messianic redemption.

THE ḤASIDIC REBBE WHO CAN INSPIRE US ALL

first published May 2, 2017

Earlier today, the last surviving great-great-great-grandson of the illustrious nineteenth-century Ḥasidic leader, Rabbi Yisrael of Ruzhyn, died at the age of 94. Rabbi Yisrael Shalom Yosef Friedman Ben-Shalom was an unassuming and fairly anonymous man who lived in Gilo, Jerusalem, for the last few years of his life. Known as the "Pashkaner Rebbe", he was an enigma — although even the word "enigma" does not quite do his story proper justice.

It is no coincidence that this unusual rabbi died on the fifth day of the month of Iyar — the Jewish calendar anniversary of Israel's Declaration of Independence in 1948. Not only was he a lifelong dedicated and devoted Zionist, but in contrast to every other Ḥasidic rabbi of his pedigree, Rabbi Friedman Ben-Shalom treated Yom Ha'atzmaut (Israel Independence Day) as a religious festival and recited the Hallel prayer with a blessing as part of his Yom Ha'atzmaut morning prayers.

Rabbi Friedman Ben-Shalom was descended from the most aristocratic Ḥasidic dynasty of all — Ruzhyn-Sadigur — whose founder, the aforementioned Rabbi Yisrael, was himself a scion — the great-grandson of Rabbi Dov Baer, the Maggid of Mezeritch, leading disciple of the founder of Hasidism, Rabbi Yisrael Baal Shem Tov.

It was through the Maggid of Mezeritch's single-handed efforts that the teachings of Rabbi Yisrael Baal Shem Tov were organized, propagated, and popularized. From his "court" in Mezeritch, and despite mounting opposition from critics of Ḥasidism within the Jewish mainstream, Rabbi Dov Baer turned his small parochial group of followers into a powerful movement within Jewish life, and it is as a result of his efforts that the Ḥasidic movement endured.

So, who was his descendant Rabbi Yisrael Shalom Yosef Friedman Ben-Shalom, and how did this anachronistic personality evolve out of the background from which he emerged?

Rabbi Friedman Ben-Shalom was born in Bohush, Rumania in 1923. Both his mother and father were descendants of Rabbi Yisrael of Ruzhyn, and his mother's father, Rabbi Menachem Mendel, the acclaimed Rebbe of Bohush, was also his father's first cousin.

At the tender age of nine, Rabbi Friedman Ben-Shalom's mother died, and he was brought up in his grandfather's house, where at first he was taught Torah by an elderly Bohush Ḥasid who had tutored Ruzhyn family members for generations, after which he began private studies with his revered grandfather, to whom he became a devoted disciple.

In the late nineteenth century and early twentieth century, the Ruzhyn Ḥasidic leaders were already notorious for their enthusiastic support for the resettlement of Jews in the Land of Israel — unlike many of their Ḥasidic leader counterparts — and a number of them openly supported the Zionist movement after it was launched in 1896, a factor that set them apart from almost every other Ḥasidic leader in early twentieth-century Europe.

The Bohush dynasty was no different than other branches of the Ruzhyn sect, and the young Rabbi Friedman Ben-Shalom was raised in an environment broadly sympathetic with Zionist aspirations for a Jewish National Home in Palestine that would be internationally recognized as an independent Jewish State.

It was probably this that inspired Rabbi Friedman Ben-Shalom to join the secular Zionist youth movement "Hashomer Hatzair" as a counselor, coupled with his family's belief that religious Jews had to proactively engage with non-religious Jews in order to draw them closer to Judaism.

Nevertheless, it is hard to overstate the incongruity of the scion of such a distinguished Ḥasidic dynasty who had in no way abandoned his roots, aligning himself with a militantly secular Zionist organization that openly disparaged old-world Judaism, in favor of a Jewish "national" identity that rejected the ancient system of Jewish laws and customs.

During the Holocaust years, Rabbi Friedman Ben-Shalom escaped to Bucharest, Rumania, where he lived together with his immediate family. It was there, in 1944, that he met his distant relative, the Vizhnitzer Rebbe, Rabbi Chaim Meir Hager, also a descendant of Rabbi Yisrael of Ruzhyn, who passed through Bucharest as part of a miraculous journey that thwarted determined Nazi attempts to kill him.

As a result of this encounter, Rabbi Friedman Ben-Shalom also met Zipporah, the Vizhnitzer Rebbe's youngest daughter, whom he married in 1946, very shortly after they had both managed to smuggle themselves illegally into Palestine. Their parents and family were not at the wedding, which was performed perfunctorily by a Yemenite rabbi who happened to be on hand at the time.

In June 1948, the young couple joined together with a group of Rumanian and Bulgarian Holocaust-survivor immigrants who had founded a secular kibbutz called Reshafim in the Bet She'an valley, and they remained there for 18 years. During this period, the Friedman Ben-Shalom's religious observance was confined to their home, while any religious celebrations — such as the bar mitzvahs of their sons — were transported to Tel Aviv, where Rabbi Friedman Ben-Shalom's father now lived, in close proximity to his brother, Rabbi Yitzḥak Friedman, who had become the new Rebbe of Bohush.

In the late 1960s, the Friedman Ben-Shalom family moved to a religious kibbutz called Sa'ad. They also spent time in Marseilles, France, as emissaries for the Jewish Agency. Keen to broaden his knowledge, Rabbi Friedman Ben-Shalom enrolled at Tel Aviv University's Jewish History department, where he completed a Ph.D. on the subject of "Beit Shammai's political influence in first century Judea."

During the 1970s, after the passing of his father-in-law, the Vizhnitzer Rebbe — who, following the founding of the state, had become a leading voice in the strictly Orthodox non-Zionist faction, Agudat Israel — the Friedman Ben-Shalom family started to spend more time with the strictly Orthodox community, and to associate more closely with their prestigious Ḥasidic relatives.

In light of their familiarity and association with secular Israelis, Rabbi Friedman Ben-Shalom and his family acted as a bridge between secular Israeli society and the insular Ḥasidic world, diverse communities that were divided by a gulf of mistrust and antipathy — on both sides of the fence.

When he eventually retired from his role as an educator, Rabbi Friedman Ben-Shalom and his wife moved to Jerusalem to be close to their son Hoshea Ben-Shalom, who had set up an "urban kibbutz" called Beit Yisrael in the Jerusalem neighborhood of Gilo.

Remarkably, besides for being an ordained rabbi and a spiritual mentor to thousands, Hoshea Ben-Shalom is also the Chief Reserve Officer of the IDF. Indeed, all the Friedman Ben-Shalom children are remarkable — deeply committed Jews as well as extremely accomplished in contemporary terms — bright, charismatic, inspired, inspiring, and proactive in their mission to find common ground between the Jewish past and the Jewish present, between the glory of Ḥasidism and the miracle of the State of Israel.

But their inspiration was undoubtedly their remarkable father, along with their esteemed mother Zipporah, who is a sister of the Vizhnitzer Rebbe (Monsey, NY),* as well as aunt to the Vizhnitzer Rebbe (Bnei Brak), the Satmar Rebbe (Monroe, NY), the Belzer Rebbe (Jerusalem), and the Skver Rebbe (New Square, NY).

In his last few years, Rabbi Friedman Ben-Shalom finally evolved into a full time "rebbe", with his own "court" and hundreds of followers — and was known as the Pashkaner Rebbe of the Ruzhyn Dynasty. He attracted countless Jews from every walk of life into his orbit — each one of them moved by his authenticity, and by his genuine love for every kind of Jew.

Anyone who encountered the Pashkaner Rebbe immediately understood that here was a man who embodied a uniquely modern Jewish narrative — a prince of Ḥasidic royalty, a master of Jewish history, a soldier of Jewish destiny, and a proud Zionist who had worked the land, and helped to build the State, preparing it for the Messianic age from the ground up, and from the Heavens down.

The Pashkaner Rebbe was a Ḥasidic leader whose life story can truly be an inspiration to us all.

הרב ישראל שלום יוסף פרידמן זצוק"ל, אדמו"ר מפאשקאן זי"ע ועכי"א

תהא נשמתו צרורה בצרור החיים

The Vizhnitz-Monsey Rebbe, Rabbi Mordechai "Mottel" Hager, passed away March 16, 2018. Zipporah Friedman Ben-Shalom passed away June 4, 2019.

"IF YOU WILL IT, IT IS NO DREAM"

first published May 1, 2014

It was Friday afternoon, on May 14, 1948, when David Ben Gurion, leader of the Jewish Agency and veteran Zionist activist, declared the independence of a new Jewish State, called Medinat Yisrael.

Jews in the new state, and around the world, weary from the recent devastating destruction of the Holocaust, and many years of Arab terrorism and aggression against Jews in Palestine, could hardly believe their good fortune — finally, after 2,000 years, a broken nation was finally in possession of its national homeland. Jews were finally free to practice their faith unhindered, and without restrictions.

Incredibly, after many turbulent years, Israel is a thriving, vibrant country, full of color and texture — the center of Jewish life in all its many forms. That wasn't the case even in 1948. At that time there were still many more Jews living outside of Israel than in the nascent state itself. The country was an economic disaster, ravaged by war and heavily under industrialized. Slowly but surely, decade after difficult decade, Israel has evolved into the go-to place for every kind of Jew, and into an economic success story that is marveled and admired by the entire world.

Of course, none of this happened in a vacuum. In 1896, Theodore Herzl wrote in his seminal pamphlet, *The Jewish State*: "The Jews who will it, shall achieve their State. For them it is no dream." This short quote summarized his entire approach to the Zionist endeavor that he was proposing.

The underlying theme was simple. While every Jew in Herzl's day who was active in the service of the Jewish community agreed that their brethren were disadvantaged wherever they lived, nothing would change, argued Herzl, unless all of them realized that they needed to pull together if they were going to get themselves out of the terrible situation they were in.

Without this collective "will," the entire enterprise was doomed to fail. And most importantly, it would not just be the creation of the State that would require this "will" — its enduring success would also require a sustained resolve. Anything less than that would ultimately be a flop.

It depends on the Jews themselves whether this political document remains for the present a political romance. If this generation is too dull to understand it rightly, a future, finer, more advanced generation will arise to comprehend it. The Jews who will try it, shall achieve their State; and they will deserve it.

This idea is not, as many of his detractors claimed, a secular ideal. Although presented in the political language of the day, Herzl's idea was deeply rooted in Judaism.

In the Torah portion of Emor we are told (Lev. 22:29): וְכִי תִזְבְּחוּ
זֶבַח תּוֹדָה לַה' לִרְצֹנְכֶם תִּזְבָּחוּ — "When you offer a sacrifice of
thanksgiving to God, do it at your own will."

The commentators are puzzled. Why are we not instructed to
bring a thanksgiving offering? Why is the choice left up to us?
Why must it be the result of our "own will"?

The powerful lesson behind this is that saying "thank you" and
bringing a gift that reflects your gratitude, cannot be mandated —
it must be something that comes from within, a true reflection of
"your own will." A "thank you" offering that does not reflect one's
will, simply cannot work. It is an exercise in futility, and the Torah
is essentially telling us not to bother.

If the State of Israel was going to come into being, wrote Herzl,
and crucially, if it was going to succeed, it would have to reflect
the collective will of the Jewish people, otherwise it would be an
exercise in futility. The incredible generation who brought Israel
into being was indeed made up of men and women of great
resolve. Their achievement cannot be overstated.

But the achievement of our own generation, that continues to
demonstrate the will and the resolve to ensure that Israel remains
a success story, is no less remarkable. You and me, and every Jew
who involves himself in the success of Israel, is part of that
success, and we are living proof of this Torah ideal. Our own will
is the real force that ensures the survival of the State of Israel on a
daily basis.

Because "if you will it, it is no dream!"

YOM YERUSHALAYIM

THE BEATING HEART OF JEWISH HISTORY

first published May 30, 2019

I f you do a Google search on any Jewish topic, you will almost certainly be directed to the site myjewishlearning.com. This website is one of the several media outlets that form 70 Faces Media, "the largest nonprofit, nondenominational Jewish media organization in North America", which is funded by a range of familiar Jewish philanthropic names — among others: the Samuel Bronfman Foundation, the William Davidson Foundation, and the UJA-Federation of New York.

According to the "About Us" page, myjewishlearning.com "is all about empowering Jewish discovery for anyone interested in learning more, [offering] thousands of articles, videos and other resources to help you navigate all aspects of Judaism and Jewish life."

This website is certainly one of the internet's most prominent storefronts for Judaism and the Jewish world, which makes the assertions in its article on Yom Yerushalayim startling beyond belief:

> **Unlike Yom Ha'atzmaut — which is a day to celebrate the existence and successes of the modern Jewish state [of Israel] — Yom Yerushalayim can make some politically liberal Jews outside of Israel uncomfortable, due to the continuing conflicts over the future of the city. Even some Jews who believe that the city should remain undivided and under Israel's control choose not to emphasize Yom Yerushalayim as a day of joy because of the deeply emotional, violent, and controversial state of affairs surrounding the Arab portions of Jerusalem.**

Yom Yerushalayim, or Jerusalem Day, is the annual anniversary for the reunification of Jerusalem, when Jews across the world celebrate the liberation of the eastern side of Jerusalem on June 7, 1967 — and particularly the Old City and Temple Mount — from the control of the Jordanians, who had captured the eastern part of the city during Israel's War of Independence, expelling all Jewish inhabitants from their homes, and removing the Jewish presence that had persisted there across the centuries.

On that heady day in June 1967, for the first time since the Roman era, Jews were finally in possession and control of their capital city Jerusalem, the beating heart of Jewish life since the days of King David some 3,000 years ago.

Why a website that professes to promote Jewish learning and Judaism would choose to focus on Jews whose disconnect with their Jewish heritage is so profound, that they fail to see the miraculous Jewish hegemony over Jerusalem as the fulfilment of countless prophecies, is beyond puzzling. And if the answer is that the website must offer a balanced view, the mere fact that the insidious opinions of antisemites and fringe radicals has progressed so far into the mainstream that they need to be cited in the cause of balance is extremely worrying.

I studied at a yeshiva in Jerusalem in the late 1980s. At the time it was just over 20 years since reunification, and the city was a bustling metropolis, with luscious public parks and modern suburbs situated alongside updated and upgraded older neighborhoods. The Old City of Jerusalem — which had languished terribly under Jordanian rule — was accessible and fresh, with access to the holy sites available to Jew and Gentile alike. Already then, tens of thousands of visitors came from all over the world each year, able to stay in world-class hotels and to take advantage of this ageless jewel, a city that was as invigorating as it was safe.

What a sea change from the Jerusalem of history, so aptly described by one nineteenth-century visitor, Sir Frederick Henniker, in an 1823 published account of his visit there:

> **The streets of [Jerusalem] are narrow and deserted, the houses dirty and ragged, the shops few and forsaken; and throughout the whole [city] there is not one symptom of either commerce, comfort, or happiness.**

Today, 30 years since my time in yeshiva, Jerusalem has further exceeded itself — it is a thriving city with every modern amenity, and a public transport system that outclasses many in the western world. Moreover, Judaism and Jewish life, including a vast range of Torah institutions and countless synagogues to cater for Jews of every shade and stripe, have at no point flourished over our long history as they do in Jerusalem today.

What further proof do we need of the advent of Messianic times than the rebuilding of the ruins of Jerusalem into this gleaming beacon of Jewish life? Right before our very eyes we can see the realization of biblical prophecy.

In 1718, the Italian Jewish traveler, Rabbi Immanuel Ḥai Ricci, visited Safed in northern Israel, and decided to settle there while he studied kabbalah. In 1731, he published *Hon Ashir*, an eclectic work containing both a commentary on the Mishnah and a poem set to music. Rabbi Ricci also used the book to describe his time in Safed, noting the fulfillment of the prophecy in Beḥukotai, as iterated in the Talmud (Sotah 49b) regarding the Messianic era — "and the Galilee shall be in a state of destruction" (Lev. 26:33): וְהָיְתָה אַרְצְכֶם שְׁמָמָה וְעָרֵיכֶם יִהְיוּ חָרְבָּה — "Your land shall become a desolation and your cities a ruin."

In Rabbi Ricci's words, "I saw with my own eyes how the Galilee lay in ruins — but thank God I was also happy to see … that new houses were being built every day, and in my opinion this [reconstruction] is truly a sign that the Messiah is on his way."

Just imagine if Rabbi Ricci would visit Jerusalem as it is today, to see the ruins of this ancient holy city overshadowed by countless burgeoning neighborhoods full of life and vigor, teeming with proud Jews who have returned to their ancestral homeland.

Yom Yerushalayim is not just an anniversary celebration; it is a day that reflects the anticipation of a nation over thousands of years for the ultimate redemption. And if there are people out there who find this primary Jewish directive slightly awkward in the face of unresolved political issues, perhaps they need to reflect on their true commitment to Jewish identity. Meanwhile, it is certainly the case that such people have no place in an article on Yom Yerushalayim.

POSTSCRIPT: As a result of being made aware of this article, the myjewishlearning.com editorial team updated their Yom Yerushalayim entry to neutralize the bias. In an email after they edited the article they wrote, "The [Yom Yerushalayim] article you cite was in fact more than 15 years old and your email prompted us to update it."

JERUSALEM IS OURS, AND IT'S TIME WE SAID SO

first published May 23, 2017

O ne of the first Talmudic passages taught to young Jewish students is a Mishna in tractate Bava Metzia that sets out a case in which two people find an abandoned cloak at more-or-less the same time, and both claim that it belongs to them.

> **Shnayim Oḥazin Betalit: Two [people] grab hold of a cloak. One says: "I found it!" and the other one [also] says "I found it!" [The first] one says: "It's all mine!" and the other one [also] says: "It's all mine!" [The first] one takes an oath that he owns no less than half, and the other one [also] takes an oath that he owns no less than half. And they divide it up.**

The very same Mishna goes on to deal with a similar dispute, although this time one of the parties claims the whole cloak is his, while the other one claims just half of it, perhaps conceding that both of them had picked it up at the same time. In any event, the Mishna informs us that the oaths taken by both parties are now revised as follows:

> **[The first] one takes an oath that he has no less than three-quarters, and the other one takes an oath that he has no less than a quarter. The former**

receives three-quarters, and the latter receives one quarter.

When I first studied this passage, I was just ten years old. Even then I was struck by what I perceived as an injustice that lay at the heart of this civil legislation. It seemed to me that in the latter case of the Mishna, the second party in the dispute was being penalized for his honesty. After all, he could have said he owned it all, and ended up with the half that was rightfully his.

A number of Talmudic commentaries address this question and offer a selection of wise and erudite answers. None wiser, in my view, than the simple observation that this dispute no longer has anything to do with the first half of the cloak — after all, both disputants seem to agree that the first half belongs to the one who is claiming the entire garment.

Which means that the dispute is now only about the second half of the cloak. And with that in mind, the fair solution is to treat the second half as if it is an entire cloak in dispute — and then to divide it up on the same basis as the full-size disputed cloak in the first part of the Mishna.

Using the same logic, it is clear that the so-called Peace Process between Israel and the Palestinians is more similar to the second case in this ancient text, than to the first. After all, when Moshe Dayan foolishly handed control of Temple Mount to the Muslim religious authorities in 1967, in accordance with a senseless ideological philosophy — he is on record as having said that the Israelis had "not come to conquer the sacred sites of others or to restrict their religious rights, but rather to ensure the integrity of the city and to live in it with others in fraternity" — what he was essentially saying was that Temple Mount itself was a "half of the cloak" that was not his to claim.

The long-term result of this strategic error has been an absolute disaster, with the dispute over the hallowed ground of Temple Mount and its environs reduced to the other "half of the cloak" we claimed as ours but are now forced to defend. Had we insisted then that Temple Mount was an exclusively Jewish holy shrine and had been for a full 1,500 years before Muhammed was even born, things might look very different today.

But it is not too late. After 50 years of watching Israel's politicians dance around this issue, frightened to tread on political territory that is fraught with danger, it is time for this matter to be taken out of the hands of the Israeli government alone, and for it to be taken up by Jews (and Christians) who are outraged that a site whose holiness and sanctity cannot be overstated is being stolen from us in front of our eyes.

Never before in Jewish History have Jews turned away from this duty. Even after both Temples were destroyed, the first one by the Babylonians, the second one by the Romans, Jews could already see the new Temple rebuilt in their mind's eye, and they prayed for it each day, multiple times:

שֶׁיִּבָּנֶה בֵּית הַמִּקְדָּשׁ בִּמְהֵרָה בְיָמֵינוּ — **May the Temple be rebuilt speedily in our days.**

But here's the thing — how can we expect God to take our prayers seriously if we spurn every opportunity to vigorously and vociferously articulate our claim to the location on which the Temple will be rebuilt?

And while I can understand how secular Israeli politicians and diplomats are uncomfortable putting forward positions that have religious implications — no doubt they feel they will not be taken seriously — what excuse can any religious Jew have for not publicly saying explicitly what it is we all pray for daily, namely for the day when there will be no mosques on Temple Mount, and our Temple will be rebuilt there in all its splendor?

And, by the way, my question is not just addressed to Religious Zionists — it is addressed to every shade and stripe of religious Jew, from ardent Zionists to anti-Zionist Satmar Ḥasidim, and to everyone in between. This is a belief we all share in common — and if our current claim to Eretz Yisrael is to be taken seriously, and if we want to be taken seriously as Jews, it is time for us to insistently claim the entire cloak, and not to reduce our claim to a mere half.

After fifty years of being in control of this piece of land, it is the least we can do.

INDEX

Usage notes: Many of the people listed in this book don't have a surname. In those cases we alphabetized by first name – for example: Ephraim of Bonn, Rabbi. If an item begins with "A" or "The" (or, in another language: for example, "Die" or "Der") we alphabetized by the next word in the item – for example: Jazz Singer, The, or Geschichte vom Daumenlutscher, Die.